T0194185

IT'S YOUR DUTY

"THIS AIN'T NO SHIT"

A COB'S MEMOIR: THE EARLY YEARS

CHIEF GARY A. GOESCHEL

U.S. Navy Retired

authorHOUSE®

AuthorHouse™
1663 Liberty Drive
Bloomington, IN 47403
www.authorhouse.com
Phone: 1 (800) 839-8640

© 2017 Gary A. Goeschel. All rights reserved.

No part of this book may be reproduced, stored in a retrieval system, or
transmitted by any means without the written permission of the author.

This is a work of fiction. All of the characters, names, incidents, organizations, and dialogue
in this novel are either the products of the author's imagination or are used fictitiously.

Published by AuthorHouse 07/24/2020

ISBN: 978-1-7283-4727-1 (sc)
ISBN: 978-1-7283-4726-4 (hc)
ISBN: 978-1-7283-4731-8 (e)

Library of Congress Control Number: 2020902973

Print information available on the last page.

Any people depicted in stock imagery provided by Getty Images are models,
and such images are being used for illustrative purposes only.
Certain stock imagery © Getty Images.

This book is printed on acid-free paper.

Because of the dynamic nature of the Internet, any web addresses or links contained in
this book may have changed since publication and may no longer be valid. The views
expressed in this work are solely those of the author and do not necessarily reflect the views
of the publisher, and the publisher hereby disclaims any responsibility for them.

CONTENTS

ACKNOWLEDGMENTS

I lived the sailor's life, documenting my episodes, and writing my sea stories so you the reader will embrace knowing about my experiences. My daughter Debra Goeschel had the first editing of my stories. She suffered the most miserable writing. Her helpful contribution discovered flaws allowing me to make corrections and continue writing. Without Karen King, Francis McGrath, Paul Savage, and James B Willis providing editing and encouragement, my stories would not have clarity and accuracy. Francis, James, Karen, and Paul found embarrassing errors and offered invaluable correction recommendations. Paul, also a submariner, discovered facts that were unbelievable as first written. I will always be grateful for Debra, Francis, Karen, James, and Paul's involvement, allowing me to polish the writing, resulting for the reader an enjoyable, readable, and believable collection of Sea Stories and Tall Tales.

I must include my Uncle Calvin Goeschel and Aunt Lorna Goeschel for intervening with my family dynamics. Cal and Lorna took me into their household and supported me during a period where I lacked the wisdom to prevent a bad situation and the means to finish High School. Their intervention allowed me opportunities that without high school would not exist. I will be forever grateful for their stepping in, providing security, and offering guidance. Treating me as a son has been a blessing. Their support and love allowed me to start my career's plotted direction that culminated with a rewarding life.

For all who crossed my Navy's charted course, I would like to thank all the outstanding naval leaders and shipmates who provided inspiration, guidance, direction, help, and counseling. Without their involvement, I could never have lived the career I loved. The material to author this book would not be available—my life story would be different.

Surpassing all, for her love, insight, inspiration, and encouragement, I am sincerely thankful to my wife, Janet M. Goeschel. She managed the Homefront, allowing me to play sailor. At sea, I did not worry about my family; Janet took good care of the children and all the household issues faced without my help. Her capable ability to take care of the family allowed me to devote my energy and attention to my duties. Also, drafting this book, to find errors, I read the stories to her. Janet was quick to hear the mistakes, expressing, "You should rewrite that sentence," or "That paragraph doesn't make sense." Janet is the love of my life.

SEA STORIES

Sea Stories are sailors' entertaining accounts that amuse, excite, or sadden. Sea Stories recounts a sailors' history, what sailors have seen and experiences they endured, facing dangers, experiencing adventures, and stirring emotions. Some stories describe the sailors' loves won, passions lost, devotions wasted, or affections never gained. Other tales depict the sailor's gratification enjoyed, the loathing detested, and the dangers faced. Senior sailors use Sea Stories to motivate subordinates to do one's duty, getting and keeping the subordinates' attention to teach lessons about any subject concerning an issue that requires further discussion.

No matter the rank or rate, sailors tell Sea Stories in places with an audience to listen. When circumstances allow, the storyteller's yarns are told during idle times, waiting to take the next watch, lingering in chow lines, awaiting shipboard events, expecting drills, anticipating battle stations, unwinding between taxing incidents, relaxing ashore in bars, socializing in clubs, or loafing in barracks.

After a storyteller repeats his yarn many times, the narrative may develop into tall tales. For entertainment's sake, the chronicler may overstate the facts, add inventions, and make exaggerations making the story's truthfulness questionable. Sea Stories require a quantity of truth, however. The storyteller bases his tale on a happening he experienced or heard about while living the life of a sailor.

For unknown reasons to convince an audience that a story is valid, the storyteller begins or ends his sea story with, "This ain't no shit!"

THIS AIN'T NO SHIT

In my lifetime, I accomplished many things, but before I could, I needed to learn HOW. In that quest, I endured lessons that were unpleasant, painful, laborious, embarrassing, but all became rewarding. This memoir, a collection of sea stories, conveys my initial naval education.

CHIEF GARY A. GOESCHEL
FTGC (SS) UNITED STATES NAVY RETIRED

The stories within It's Your Duty, show how the Navy turns inexperienced and undisciplined youngsters—like I was into motivated, dependable, skilled warriors and admirable sailors. These stories are about my first two years in the Navy, starting young, having a miss-focused attitude, and not fully accepting authority. The narratives reveal my transformation, progressing into a motivated, dependable, competent sailor, qualifying in submarines, learning leadership skills, and revering my leaders. The tales depict my development, portraying events confronted, presenting my experiences, ordeals, difficulties, unpleasant occurrences, humorous incidents, fascinating escapades, and ventures while learning obligations. The accounts show my thoughts on the challenges I faced and the reflections about the associations with the men whom along with I served. Many of my Navy leaders fought in submarines during WWII. Their devotion to responsibility and guidance turned a miss-guided youngster into a submarine sailor. Embedded within these stories are their lessons— It's your duty—Do your duty. To get my attention, these remarkable leaders employed unpleasant and embarrassing instructions. The trials I handled furnished the knowledge and values acquired that matured to treasure living the sailor's life at sea with voyages full of adventure while contributing to our country's defense and forging me into the man I have become.

Whereas many of my high school classmates attended college, I advanced my education in a different path by living ventures and experiencing adventures, broadening knowledge outside the classroom. The learning I gained was not a traditional lesson taught in a school. In the classroom's place, I studied others, observed leaders, discovered their effective methods, and inquired why they blundered. Wisdom and learning development included a price distinctive from tuition. The costs for my teaching, were embarrassments for my mistakes, doing work the hard way, and then learning by repeating the job yet again correctly and with efficiency. With practice, I developed skills and learned from making and correcting mistakes. Great ventures furthered my training. Atlantic, Mediterranean, and Westpac, deployments provided unique journeys that allowed visiting strange exotic lands and historical sites in distant places encountering distinctive cultures so unlike home.

The Navy exploits encountered started with a minor involvement in the Cuban Missile Crisis. Then, I experienced an adventurous Antarctic exploration followed by a Vietnam submarine mission. The USS Billfish (SSN 676), a fast attack submarine, played crucial roles during the Cold War was my last sea-duty. To support ship operations, I acquired essential responsibilities, developed seafaring competency, and accomplished tasks I never considered possible.

Most of my Navy career was underway at sea. In my naval calling, I was fortunate that I have served on four submarines and three surface ships. Each vessel provided pleasurable and sometimes painful happenings, riveting risks, and gratifying rewards. Frequently we faced uncertainty with menacing threats, and numerous events transpired into extreme danger, but at the time, I'm inexperienced and didn't realize the hazard until afterward. In ships and submarines, I lived in close quarters, working with the best men on the planet, accepting a shipmate's characteristics, appreciating his good habits, and tolerating the unpleasant. When I put to sea, I sailed in harm's way, encountering hazards, including the sea's fierce storms, flooding, a fire, an explosion, line partings, and a near collision. Because other dangers happened later in my career, I will include these perils for a future book.

On ships and submarines, I sliced through vast seas and plowed through storms. On the *Spikefish*, we sailed through a tempest off Cape Hatteras. The *Arlington*, a much larger vessel, rode out a far more enormous gale in the North Atlantic. The gale-force power ripped off two of my forward fire-control radar antennas mounted on twin three-inch guns in gun tubs set over 45-feet above the waterline. This storm also tore our 40-foot utility boat off the ship's starboard aft boat mounting. The worst weather I faced was in the Southern Ocean, during Deep Freeze–65[1] when the *Glacier* survived a most terrible storm crossing the Antarctic Convergence. Unofficially she's allegedly caught in a trough between gigantic waves hitting her broadside. The

---

[1] Deep Freeze–65 is the name of the Navy's Antarctica exploration operations. For the USS Glacier this was the 10th consecutive year supporting the Antarctica operations.

Glacier achieved 70-degree rolls—if the ship reached 75-degree rolls, the gun mounts, the exhaust stack, and the loft con[2] on a mast tower would have torn off the ship—if that happened, you wouldn't be reading this. The Antarctic Convergence is the stormiest region on the Planet with the fiercest storms as its typical calm weather. The storm produced a state of agitation with the ship's violent pitching rolling deck with increased awareness of great danger. The storm's violence and power made me revere a higher authority.

The boundless seas' tranquility humbled me. Regularly the sea delivered gentle refreshing breezes comforting me. In the Southern Ocean, I admired the Southern Cross and marveled at the sight of St. Elmo's fire. A vast lit night sky over an enormous black sea in the Pacific put me in awe. At sea, in the Atlantic's far North, Northern Lights' magical displays of moving art brightened the nights. Often, the seas offered contentment of colorful sunsets and glorious sunrises, displaying brilliant colors painted on cosmic horizons. These views predict the weather. "Red sky at night, a sailor's delight. Red sky in the morning, sailors take warning."

With shipmates in the Atlantic, Westpac, and Mediterranean ports—every get-together was exceptional, ashore on liberty, while sharing our sea-stories friends bonded. Both day or night, we met, during pleasant occasions, unwinding our stress, enjoying a drink or two, and sometimes more, spinning yarns, revealing our experiences, imparting humor or sorrow. With camaraderie taking place in bars or clubs, the likes that proper church members would condemn, we told our stories. In these establishments, I experienced the orgasmic rush of a good-looking barmaid, thinking she loved only me, finding out later she didn't—she loved everyone. In other places, I learned about

---

[2] The loft conn is a conning station on masts tower high above the bridge, allowing the conning officer and lookouts to see further while breaking ice.

life and women. From women, I discovered that living is worthy and enjoyable, yet unkind and brutal at times. Afterward, recalling these gatherings provide me abundant contentment for the sailor's life I led.

Comparable to my shipmates, our parents, families, friends, or lovers wouldn't know a young sailors' full story. In letters home, the sailor won't report embarrassing, unacceptable drunken conditions. Because sailors don't explain how they enjoyed cleaning sanitary tanks, or discuss the mean talks they endured, the consequences their leaders provided to keep him on course—the result received for not meeting standards. The Brown Speckled Sparrow Club[3], a club to which no one wanted membership, a sailor wouldn't boast, telling how he joined it. Sailors kept private how they might have died facing dangers when flooding could have sunk their boat. Sailors won't describe the hazards faced, confronting rough seas without help for recovery if washed overboard. Sailors don't write home describing how Divine intervention helped in their survival of many perils. But I realize without Divine intervention's aid, I couldn't be around to author my book of Sea Stories and Tall Tales, *It's Your Duty*. Up to now, I kept the details on my naval events to myself.

So, let me tell you about my adventures. But first, I must brief you regarding the Navy and its sailors, so you will appreciate why I'm so proud of my Navy service.

Today, the Navy's ships and submarines are essential for our nation's defense. Throughout the U.S. Navy's history, a commendable Navy served our country admirably and will continue serving in the future. The Navy's value and successful performance were tried and

---

[3] Brown Speckled Sparrow Club, when someone blows a sanitary tank's contents inboard all over himself, he unwillingly becomes a club member. I will explain this fully later.

tested in past wars. In World War II, the Navy's ships and submarines displayed their importance.

For example, in World War II, the U.S. Navy's Pacific war strategy was to control the seas and the skies over it. The Navy's task—attack Japan's warships and merchant ships. Besides fighting Japan's Navy, the U.S. Navy used carrier task forces and surface ships to give logistic support for amphibious operations, island capture, and forwarding bases. Therefore, U.S. submarines undertook roles of vital importance in the Pacific battle.

In the Pacific battle, American submarines sunk 201 Japanese warships, including one battleship, four large carriers, four small carriers, three heavy cruisers, eight light cruisers, forty-three destroyers, and twenty-three large submarines for a total of 540,192 tons of fighting ships. More importantly, U.S. submarines sunk 4,779,902 tons of Japanese merchant ships. Altogether, submarines sent 55 percent of all Japanese ships sunk to **Davy Jones's locker**.

Submarine achievements did not transpire without consequences. Before World War II, nine submarines sank with a significant loss of life. The submarine cost without fighting has been high. **During World War II, the submarine force had the highest loss rate of the U.S. Armed Forces—a severe price.** The submarine force lost fifty-two submarines from combat's beating, leaving 3,500 crewmembers on eternal patrol. From these sunken submarines, few crewmembers lived through the experience and survived the war. After World War II, during the Cold War, the Navy lost two submarines with their crews.

Before the war's start, the U.S. Navy adhered to Alfred Thayer Mahan fleet strategy doctrines. Mahan's strategy used a battleship fleet as an overwhelming concentrated force to destroy an opposing fleet. Mahan's approach did not consider aircraft and submarines as battleship deterrent weapons. Aircraft and submarines made the battleship obsolete. After the Japanese Pearl Harbor attack—the U.S. Navy realized a dilemma; the battleships are out of action. The U.S. Navy had no overwhelming force. The battleship losses caused the U.S. Navy to recognize the superiority of aviation and submarines. And then the American fleet quickly converted from slow battleship fleet to a faster carrier fleet strengthened with submarines.

At war's start, the U.S. Navy needed a proficient submarine force. But prewar naval submarine tactics and customs resulted in undesirable submarine leadership and tactics. Early in the World War II Pacific battle, the U.S. Navy Submarine engagement was ineffective. Few naval leaders learned the German submarine lessons during WWI and were again using subs in the WWII Atlantic Ocean battle. U.S. submarine commands conducted the first war patrols with excessive caution. Few submarine commanding officers made regrettable errors. For several commands, torpedoes' flawed performance degraded their expected accomplishment. Torpedoes' failures resulted in causing the unfortunate officer to appear inept at conducting war. At the war's beginning, neither submarine officers nor torpedos were ready for combat, and these issues resulted in an inadequate submarine performance. In time, the submarine leaders learned how to use a submarine to defeat the enemy in battle. Aggressive, capable officers replaced the ineffective officers who conducted war patrols with excessive vigilance. The submarine force perfected submarine tactics and solved the weapon issue. The submarine Navy learned from mistakes and continued improvements throughout the war and afterward. Throughout my career, I watched new effective methods accomplishing daily activities—the Navy always looked for enhancements.

During World War II, sailors fought in submarines called Fleet Boats. These seafarers created submarine methods that differ from the surface Navy. Sub sailors altered the daily routines. On subs, a sailor's everyday routines are informal, but when one is on duty, the strictest rules apply, when standing a watch there's no fooling around.

The WWII sailors who fought are all heroes. Unique to this group are the sub sailors. At war, the submarines' seafarers displayed incredible valor facing danger, fighting enemies, and meeting war's horrors. War experiences embedded beliefs in their views and affected their performances. These warriors live by the highest standards, having astonishing strengths, exceptional values, fantastic principles, notable beliefs, and surprising fortes. War experienced shipmates likewise have shortcomings, weird quirks, puzzling idiosyncrasies, and outlandish vices. Shipmates' abilities, coupled with their imperfections, made them fascinating leaders for me to study. The U.S. Navy sailors are more interesting than imagined maritime characters I found in the written text. War experienced shipmates are akin to the personalities found in stories that aroused my interest. For me, my shipmates connect to legends liking to the swashbuckling sailors displayed in movies and books. These incredible seafarers could contribute to seafaring folklore. But my shipmates are distinguishable from the characters found in fictional tales—they are real combat-experienced heroes.

Many of these war experienced fighters were my shipmates, instructors, and leaders, and they taught leadership skills with proven ability—they inspired. These naval war veterans oversaw my development, kept me on course, and added a visualization of the submariners' essence. These Navy warriors encouraged, guided, motivated, and trained me well. These leaders influenced my thought, shaped my values, directed my sense of duty; well, they gave meaning to my service.

My early naval instructors and shipmates who fought in WWII boasted how the United States submarine was one of the most devastating weapons used in the Pacific battle, and how the American submarine service had achieved such an impressive record. They taught the submarines' wartime history showing how the submarine service as a World War II weapon played an essential role in the final defeat of Japan. As the war continued, U.S. submarines prevented men and materials from moving on or off the Japanese home islands and resupplying their island fortress. The submarine service played significant roles in the island-hopping strategy, which allowed MacArthur's return to the Philippines, and submarines were also rescuers of downed pilots. Most importantly, to the war's end and the U.S. victory, the U.S. submarine devastated Japan's naval ability to wage war. Japan's war effort became unsustainable after the U.S. subs destroyed Japan's merchant fleet. After the destruction of Japan's merchant marine, Japan lacked fuel for her Navy and materials to replace war losses. The battle of Okinawa was an example of Japan's fuel shortage when Japan sent the battleship, *Yamato*, to her doom in a suicidal attempt with only enough fuel to get to the fight but not enough to return.

The Navy's history and working with war heroes influenced my thinking and affected every undertaking throughout my naval career. With motivating mentors, I worked, played, and faced threats. Every leader displayed personal examples doing their day-to-day duties, taking on responsibilities, and influencing my sense of duty. The best sailors in the Navy impelled the young crew, such as me, to serve and preserve our country by doing one's duty. These mentors taught, "Do your duty." With such remarkable leaders, it's no wonder I gained their principles because I couldn't help learning from them.

While I served with these remarkable sailors, I gained details for my sea tales. Now, to honor the great sailors and the outstanding leaders who taught and guided me, I included them in my accounts to start the folklore. *It's Your Duty* explains how, in my early years, remarkable Navy leaders kept me on course, directed my progress, and instilled motivation. The stories tell how seniors calibrated my unacceptable behavior by applying unique discipline when I didn't meet standards. The tales informed how senior sailors encouraged me with purpose and forged into me—Always do your duties. The stories that follow will show some of these attributes.

I've been out of the Navy longer than I was in it. After twenty years of service, I retired as a Chief Petty Officer from the U.S. Navy. Then, as a systems engineer, I continued serving the Navy, providing systems engineering, delivering advanced technology during the new construction of submarine and ship projects. Throughout my career, I produced successes, using proven naval leadership methods. As I recall, my seafaring achievements provide enjoyment and pride. Today, I can share meaningful experiences with my shipmates, friends, family, and you. As sailors' tales, they present my adventures, the mistakes made along the way, and the torment my blunders produced. These narratives share a common theme, do your duty.

The stories explain my development, learning skills, earning advancements, and what I encountered while learning to contribute to the defense of this country. Those instructions to gain my attention, I'll declare, were unpleasant, painful, challenging, and embarrassing ordeals. But once I understood the teachings, the training became a rewarding education. Without accounting for specific missions, my descriptions show what I have observed, the encounters I lived, the responsibilities I held, the dangers I faced, and the awesome adventurous events I experienced. Also, my tails reveal the actions, behaviors, and activities of others who shared my ventures. Tales show my impressions and aroused emotions when confronting hazards or undergoing discipline, and embrace the **young enlisted sailor's view**, a description lacking in most naval accounts. For a whole image, I relate good times, the skillful day-to-day approach to duties, and the successes that filled me with great pride. For a complete picture, I account for the flaws, embarrassments, and mistakes I made along the way. The tales also give lessons from the mentors who guided, taught, molded, and motivated me. Navy leaders shaped my personal and leadership development that allowed numerous accomplishments.

I stand proud of serving the U.S. Navy, supporting the Navy's vital role as a dominant force, and contributing to national security in preserving our freedom. This successful experience gave me the confidence to accept new challenging tasks. My Navy career, packed with exciting events that provided abundant pleasure, yielded rewards beyond envisioned and gave me priceless satisfaction. Now, how those incidents influenced my life in and out of the naval service amazes me. I'm astonished that I survived the dangers confronted, and astounded that I endured the hardships faced.

I'm a sailor who lived through adventurous events, experienced perilous encounters, faced dangerous incidents, and received many painful and enriching lessons. After living voyages full of adventure, now I'm ready to tell you about my experiences and their outcomes with accounts of exploits to convey. Sea-stories from my first two years in the navy show a young sailor's life at sea on a submarine.

May you get pleasure reading the tales and gain the insight and direction I painfully acquired so you can adapt these to your circumstances. When you read *It's Your Duty*, you'll discover enjoyment in the read. The book contains leadership guidance that's adaptable to your work and family. The outcome, my stories have a shared theme, "It's Your Duty—do your duty." This ain't no shit.

SPIKEFISH SEA STORIES

When I was the Billfish's COB, I told the following Spikefish Sea Stories.

FLOODING IN THE CONN

One night on patrol, I'm the Diving Officer. The watch was a taxing and grueling routine, poking holes in the ocean, experiencing heavy seas, and conducting periscope depth operations. Many unfriendly contacts made the watch stressful in staying undetected. At PD, the heavy seas made depth-keeping a challenge. After completing a hectic watch, I left control and headed to the Goat Locker, seeking tension relief and a breather from our wearisome routine. In the Goat Locker, I filled my mug with robust, hot, and black-tar looking coffee—just the way I like it. I sat at the table occupied with my fellow Chiefs. The Chiefs were deciding whether to watch a flick or start a poker game. I didn't join their decision-making exchange. If we did something enjoyable, I didn't care what we did. As I considered their unfruitful bickering, I decided to have some fun. Instead of viewing a flick or starting a poker game, the Chiefs needed a challenge.

Can't help myself grinning when I ask, "What is the scariest experience you've had in the Navy?" I gaze at each of the Chiefs, giving an obvious dare. Then I challenged, "I bet I had more terrifying experiences than any of you, landlubbers."

The Chiefs' discussion stopped. In the Goat Locker, a curious silence sustained. The challenge worked; the Chiefs are engrossed in thought—a rare phenomenon. The Chiefs are thinking. They make little noise when thinking. It's unusual for Chiefs to devote much time in profound philosophical thought, making serious thought infrequent, challenging, and tedious. Before acting, Chiefs would instead respond than ponder. Only when it's necessary, Chiefs, think about what they must due. For Chief's brains, thinking is arduous.

I recalled my own experiences facing death, when Divine help protected me, saving my ass, and keeping me alive. I've lived through many life-threatening and fear-provoking events that often make me wonder why I'm alive now. I speculated what the Chiefs terrifying experiences would convey. Did they confront similar threats as I?

Sach, the oldest Chief among us, took the bait. Sach glared at me as he responded with a loud deep-bass mumbling tone, "Shit-fire! Landlubbers?! You got brass balls to call us landlubbers—we're deep-water sailors. You candy ass young pup, I bet before you turned into a submariner, the Shallow Water Club rejected you because you weren't tall enough—couldn't qualify—you're not six feet tall and couldn't walk ashore with your head out of the water if you fell overboard!" He paused, looking at us, checking our attention, and proceeded. "Scary experiences, I had my share of terrifying times—damn scary."

Sach is beaming like a kid with a secret to tell, exposed his tale. "If you boot camps will pay attention and keep it down, I'll tell you about a damn scary experience—scared me good, it did. If you boot camps had an experience as I had, I don't think you would have held up—would have terrified you too much. You would've had heart attacks and died of fright right on the spot—you would've!"

Sach was old Navy—before the UCMJ—starting his career during the time of Rocks and Shoals, the time when Chiefs and Petty Officers upheld discipline with iron fists. The scuttlebutt—never proven—held that Sach blackened eyes on occasion. His "A" gang respected him, feared him, and loved him anyhow. He would give the shirt off his back to help a shipmate. Sach acted as if he wouldn't take shit from anyone, but anybody who had been around him long enough found Sach a good shipmate, a likable individual, and a friendly person. Sach is an outstanding, inspiring chief, and more so, a loyal friend.

Sach had a vulnerability found only in the Goat Locker—I can spin him up to a seething fury any chance I felt like it. For fun, during the past two weeks, I felt like it—a lot. Gullible to my antics, Sach was an easy target. Just to spin him up, I smiled as I interrupted Sach, ignored his input, and prevented him from speaking. Then, I presented my serious face, getting eye contact with the Chiefs, and continued my story.

"This ain't no shit," starts my sea story that showed why submariners get Sub-pay, why submarines are just damn dangerous, and why the best submariners might consider their future upon hearing my tale. A threat's description that if they encountered it would have made skimmers and landlubbers shit their pants in a panic.

I wouldn't tell you this if it wasn't valid. A guardian angel must look after me. I recall at least five times where Divine Help kept me alive or out of peril. My first frightening experiences nearly sank the boat, drowning the NAV, the XO, the Helmsmen—and I was the Helmsmen—and then the rest of the crew. To the best of my recollection, this happened—This ain't no shit.

Heavenly help kept me alive in the face of danger. The first time happened when I was a young kid, a designated boot seaman just out of FT A school and subschool. After subschool, the Navy assigned me to my first sub, the USS *Spikefish (AGSS 404)*. The *Spikefish* held the world record for most dives—over 10,000 dives, she did. The *Spikefish* was a World War II veteran fleet boat, a non-snorkel diesel submarine with six torpedo tubes forward and four tubes aft, home-ported at Key West, Florida—a great place to start a Navy career. Not knowing the *Spikefish* was obsolete, I considered we were invincible. It was enjoyable being young and foolish, two weeks qualified as helmsman and planesman, standing a watch that put me in peril, unaware of how menacing things get until after it happened.

One pleasant day at sea, submerged, I started my watch under normal conditions, but before the watch was over, my watch almost ended in a disaster. The Spikefish had significant flooding that might have sunk the boat, giving us a quick stop at Davy Jones's locker. Flooding was an experience I will not forget.

After completing a planesman two-hour watch for watch rotation, I relieved the helmsman, Seamen Miller, in the CONN. Miller briefed me on what we were doing, "We will surface soon to do some housekeeping." After I took control of the helm, Miller went below.

I stopped my tale enlightening them, "Because some of you never rode diesel boats, you need a little history. For landlubbers, jarheads, air-dales, ground-pounders, surface-skimmers, shallow water sailors, and Nukes, on Fleet Boats, the Conning Tower is part of the submarine's sail. The Conning Tower is a people tank, a small watertight compartment above the main hull. This space holds the Helm, NAV Plot, Radar, Torpedo Data Computer, and supporting equipment."

Then I continued my story. In the CONN was the OOD, LTJG Always Alert, and the NAV, LT Hanson. The OOD tells the NAV, "We will surface soon."

I overhear discussions about surfacing and what housekeeping we would do on the surface. Because we won't be on the surface long, the CO wanted the boat's housekeeping completed soon after we're surfaced. The OOD directed the Dive to get ready to pump bilges, blow sanitaries, start a battery charge, air charge, and dump the trash. The OOD explained to the NAV, "The CO wants to gain radio communications as soon as we surface. Furthermore, for this surfacing, he wants to reduce the high-pressure air used during a normal surface. We will be surfacing differently from normal procedures. Use speed, get an up bubble and use air to get to the surface, almost like an airless surfacing. Once the decks are awash, the dive will secure the blow and then use the low-pressure blower to finish blowing the ballast tanks dry. I briefed the Dive; he knows what to do."

The OOD ordered, "Dive prepare to surface. I will let you know when the forward decks are awash, then you secure the blow and start the low-pressure blower to finish blowing the ballast tanks dry. Once on the surface, we will pump bilges, blow sanitaries, start the battery and air charges, and dump the trash."

The Dive answered. "Prepare to surface aye-aye. When you report the forward decks are awash, I'll secure the blow and start the low-pressure blower to finish blowing the ballast tanks dry. On the surface, we'll pump bilges, blow sanitaries, start a battery and air charge, and dump the trash."

So, I wouldn't screw up; I mulled over about what I must do.

Then the OOD ordered, "Come left, steer course Zero Thuh-REE Zero[4] all ahead Two Thirds."

"Come left, steer course Zero Thuh-REE Zero, all ahead Two Thirds, Aye-aye sir," I replied while selecting ahead 2/3 on the Engine Order Telegraph. The Engine Order Telegraph pointer reached 2/3, telling me that Maneuvering responded. "Answers all-ahead Two Thirds, coming left to Zero Thuh-REE Zero," I called out.

The OOD responded, "Very well."

The NAV chimed in with, "After we finish this turn, we will surface, and once on the surface, I'll get a fix."

The XO came up, making the CONN crowded, asking, "NAV, where are we?"

---

[4] See Appendix E, Standard Submarine Phraseology

With the khaki ass brass around me, I made sure I kept on course. The sound of shuffling charts caught my interest but can't see what was going on because I was concentrating on making the course change. "Passing Zero FO-wer Zero ten degrees from the ordered course, sir," I bellowed.

The OOD stated, "Very well. After we're steady, we will surface."

"Aye-aye, sir," I replied. I liked Mr. Always Alert because he always informed us watch-standers what was happening, which made the watch go smoother with less hassle—you know what I mean.

After getting on course, I shout, "Steady on course, Ze-ro Thuh-REE Ze-ro, sir."

The OOD right behind me, "Very well, Dive, surface the Ship."

From below, the Dive, "surface the ship, aye-aye."

To explain, I stopped my narrative a moment. A boat's surfacing always excites me—so many things happen at the same moment. I scan the Chiefs checking that I still have their attention, then continuing my story. First, the 1MC barks, **Surface, Surface, Surface!** Followed by three blasts of the Diving Alarm: **Oh—gha, Oh—gha, Oh—gha.**

The Dive commands, "Blow bow buoyancy. Blow Negative to its mark." I can hear the air rushing into the tanks. As the boat's up-bubble increased towards 10-degree, the Dive ordered, "blow the forward group." With the roar of air entering the forward ballast tanks, the boat responds with over ten-degrees up-angle giving an elevator ride to the surface. "Blow the aft group," commanded the Dive.

As the boat's up-bubble increased beyond 10-degree, making standing at the helm a difficult, but a fun, thrilling trip. Steeper than expected, the pitch angle rose. Something's awry. The Dive bellowed, "Blow the aft group! **Blow the Aft group! Damn it!**"

The seagulls saw a dramatic sight when the boat surfaced. Like a whale jumping out of the ocean, the Spikefish looked. The sub's sizeable up-angle coming out of the water and tons of water washing off her hull had to be something to see. The OOD yells to Control, "Decks awash."

You must realize, after reaching the surface, the boat's pitch angle should drop, with the bow moving down. But this time, the up-angle maintained its up pitch-angle. The boat didn't level. I gripped tight to the helm to keep from falling when the sound of roaring air rushed into the aft tanks—something's not right, someone's in trouble—little did I know it's me.

With air rushing into the aft tanks, the Dive ordered, "Secure the Blow. Start low-pressure blow on all main ballast tanks."

I was having trouble standing at the helm, with the boat's sizeable up angle. As soon as the Sail was out of the water, the OOD cracked the upper Conning Tower hatch. In-rushing air sprayed sea mist, giving me a short refreshing shower that stops as the OOD opens the hatch, taking longer to open than usual because of the up-angle. When the hatch opened, the OOD managed to get topside at the Bridge.

The Boat wasn't level, and something's still wrong. We didn't know it, but the Spikefish with her up pitch-angle was sliding backward, sinking stern first with the Bridge hatch open. When seawater rushed through the Bridge Hatch, like a waterfall—with me as the rock the water plunged on, I realized, we're in trouble—**sinking!**

With rushing water descending from the open Conning Tower Hatch, many happenings occurred at once. The NAV rushed past me, struggling up a steep slope against a rushing stream. He climbed into the deluge of water downpouring from the opened hatch. He strived to close the hatch, but the downpour's force prevented him from reaching it.

The 1MC barked, **"Flooding in Control!"** Then the Collision Alarm **sounded**. The alarms added intensity to our condition.

The Hatch to the Control Room slammed shut with a loud, menacing hollow **thud**. The hatch thud brought back stories heard in sub school and boot camp about saving a ship by shutting a hatch to a flooding compartment and leaving expendable crewmates to perish. I'm expendable, and I'm in the flooding compartment! I can't ponder the threat—no time—too busy. Knowing, I must stay on course as long as possible—harder to do with sea-water flooding over me. The XO charged into the rushing water to aid the NAV. Strong ocean forces pushed the NAV downwards while the XO pushed the NAV into the waterpower flow, but the XO failed.

The lights went out in the CONN. Emergency lighting cast an eerie red glow, creating for a moment, a sense of dread.

In seconds, we were thigh-deep in water. As I'm sensing cold water rising towards my crotch, reasoning we won't make it if they can't get that hatch shut, so to hell with keeping course—they need help! With water up to my waist, I rushed to the ladder and pushed khaki-ass. Struggling, I got a stronger hold and pushed harder till I considered my aching arms might break from the strain.

With a loud thud, the upper hatch closed, stopping the in-flowing water. As I sensed the boat leveling, the hatch noise dogging stopped, telling me the hatch is watertight. I backed away from the ladder, grabbed the helm wheel, and detected movement. It was the XO followed by the NAV moving bobbing away from the Bridge access ladder.

The boat still held a five-degree up angle, and chilly water was up to my chest. A good bubble of air over our heads allowed us to continue breathing; we're lucky. The CONN's illuminating battle lanterns continued to bathe us with a disturbing, red glow—my sense of dread returned, we're not yet safe.

Yet I had a course to keep, but the helm wheel didn't control the rudder. I shouted the warning, "Lost normal steering, shifting steering to emergency!" After shifting to emergency steering, I verified the rudder, followed the emergency rudder indicator, and the helm-gyro repeater worked. Then shouted, "Steering shifted to emergency. Using emergency steering." To get us back on course, I started positioning the rudder.

The XO's calm voice-directed, "Conserve air, keep movements to a minimum, no talking unless urgent." With that order, my confidence returned. Then, by using small rudder changes, I got the boat back on course. Because the boat had unpredictable rolling around a seven-degree list, the Spikefish must have been close to Periscope Depth, making standing and course keeping difficult.

The 1MC barks, **"Surface—Surface—Surface."**

The boat, resurfacing, came up with a modest up angle and leveled off with a starboard list. The rolling made standing uncomfortable. Sounds of Conn's drain valve opening followed by sounds of water whooshes told that Conn's draining started. Unfamiliar noises below, I supposed it's pumping water from the bilges.

Coldwater up to my waist, chilled me, yet I received comfort in the crew trying to get us out of Conn trying to save us. The conning tower water drained, seemed like an eternity as the water level dropped from my chest to waist, to knees, and my ankles. As the conning tower water decreased, the boat's rolling reduced. Relieved, I believed the crisis is passing, and the crew's not forsaking us. The crew would not let us down—I knew it.

Crew members had to shut the control room hatch to save the boat. An open control room hatch might have caused a loss of all hands if we couldn't shut the bridge hatch in time. Those below couldn't know if we could shut the bridge hatch in time. In doing their duty, they spared us all. I bore no malice against them; they did their duty and saved the boat. When the bridge hatch opened, a pleasant refreshing air washed over me. After the control room hatch opened, in control, I saw happy, relieved faces looking back at me, but I'm beyond pleased to see the crew more than they were to see me.

Mr. Always Alert was all right, although he had his uniform well-greased for our troubles. As the boat was submerging, he helped shut the hatch against the inrushing sea; he could have drowned. The OOD saved himself by climbing to the shears, climbing to the periscope, and wrapping his arms and legs around it, hugging that scope until we resurfaced. A greased periscope barrel superbly greased Mr. Always Alert's khaki uniform—besides his soaking, his khaki uniform was his only loss.

While describing that drenched greased khaki uniform, I couldn't help chuckling as I continued the story. This event gave us two weeks of liberty while the ETs, ICs, and FTs cleaned and dried the saltwater from the Conning Tower equipment. If the bridge hatch and the conning tower hatch remained open, we could have lost the boat and all hands. With the conning tower hatch shut and the bridge hatch opened, we in the Conning Tower might not have made it. No matter, we survived.

Then I inquire, "So, was avoiding disaster the result of training, allowing the crew to respond during this emergency, or did Divine Help intervene? I suspect both were in play."

I ask, "Can you boot camp sailors top that?"

I stared at the Chiefs, challenging them to surpass my tale. But before allowing them to respond, I tell them, "I have a few more stories to tell, but you must wait until I finish calibrating Seaman New-guy for nearly getting us killed during the weapon load just before we got underway."

Then I left the Goat Locker, leaving the Chiefs to appraise their own frightening experiences while Sach bewildered looked on in dumbfounded disbelief. As I leave the Goat Locker, felling pleased because my watch stress is over. I chuckled inwardly, my challenge worked.

MOTIVATION

Leaders use sea stories to give a lesson, modify unacceptable behavior, and motivate subordinates. The following is that kind of sea story.

Early in my naval career, on my first submarine, the *USS Wahoo (SS 565)*, I experienced Navy life and leadership methods firsthand; I observed how leaders inspired men to follow regulations and orders. During that time, the COB provided an ingenious way to motivate and direct young sailors like me.

From other parts of the country, we came, yet we shared experiences, in our high schools, we played football and wrestled. In the Navy, we passed through FT A School and Subschool together. While assigned to the Wahoo's seamen gang, Billy Bob, Charlie, and I started hanging out together, becoming friends. It didn't take long before the COB called us the Dynamic-trio.

When on liberty, wearing civilian clothes, we dressed to appear collegiate, striving to impress girls by acting how we thought college students would be seen and perform. Yet we didn't understand how college students performed. The Dynamic-trio imitated scholars, which we weren't. We were inexperienced in any social gathering with women. The young ladies we were trying to sway, who saw our show likely we're not stirred by our act, because we didn't thrill them. Yet, the Dynamic-trio had overconfidence in our abilities, holding an arrogance in thinking as though we knew everything. However, our immaturity in lacking experience and tact when dealing with others was evident. Our success with the young women wanting to be with us more than one date was lacking. The Dynamic-trio had lots to learn but were not wise enough to understand that reality.

Billy Bob was the youngest member of the Dynamic-trio and the shortest with a weight lifter's muscular build. Curly dark brown-black hair covered his round head. His face looked composed of Irish, Spanish, and Asian, giving him a handsome look that girls admired. Yet his flat tanned round baby face gave him a younger appearance as if he was going on fourteen, which kept girls our age from joining us. Many times, we teased him, stating, "Your Mommy must have smacked your face with a cast-iron frying pan when you were little." That didn't bother him—nothing bothered Billy Bob. I preferred working with Billy Bob because he always pulled his weight and did extra helping others. However, Billy Bob was clueless regarding everything else—from girls to the Navy.

At twenty-one, Charlie was the Dynamic-trio's oldest member. Charlie couldn't stand teasing; we could get him in a huff anytime we wanted. Charlie had the qualities we wanted because he attracted girls like bees to honey. Charlie might have been a movie star; most girls we met considered him handsome. The girls couldn't resist his grin either—many fell in love with Charlie. On liberty, while girl hunting, Billy Bob and I liked to tag along with him because Charlie's girls had girlfriends. Also, the few times the Shore Patrol delivered us back to the ship; they never wrote the Dynamic-trio up for any infractions. Charlie helped us out, keeping us out of trouble. Charlie would put on a grin that disarmed the COB, Shore Patrol, or anyone angry with him.

Now, getting my story back on course. During *Wahoo's* Hawaii's Maui island liberty run. With the *Wahoo* anchored at Lahaina Bay, the sailors going ashore needed a liberty boat to ferry them back and forth to a pier near a beach. This event set us up for innovative leadership experience because the Dynamic-trio didn't make quarters and missed a field-day.

The first day at Lahaina, I had the duty, my liberty started the following day. Once ashore, I found Billy Bob and Charlie in a bar. They told me, "there's little to do because we already explored the place yesterday." Their assessment was not encouraging.

To check the neighborhood out myself, I left them and walked from one edge of town to the other, and then returned. The investigation trip took one hour, checking out tourist shops that lined the landside of the street. Shops are selling crap in which I had no interest or stuff, which was too pricey. The road paralleled a gorgeous tropical beach on the street's landside, bordering high hills connecting to a mountain creating a perfect romantic tropical paradise. A shaded, cool spot with an enticing bench overlooked one of the world's most scenic and romantic places I had ever seen. The bench lured me to sit and dream, where I enjoyed the view of a beach that invited skinny-dipping with an envisioned good-looking young woman—I was fantasizing. Then a couple walked by me, laughing, arousing me from my vision. As I watch them pass, holding hands, giggling as lovers do, I realized I have one big problem there's no sweetheart to share this heaven. In this idyllic beach, the lovely girls are hooked up with a man. In this romantic place, girls aren't accessible, not even one gal for me. My friends' analysis was correct; we're in a one Road Town with little to do.

Back at the bar, moping, we considered our options, fishing but no equipment, swimming, but we didn't bring swimwear or alternative hiking, but we didn't think of it. In this utopia, adult fun wasn't possible. The Dynamic-trio couldn't even hook-up with Westpac Widows in this paradise—none here.

After finishing a round of rum-and-cokes, I bought another round. Then three local fishermen brought in a Wahoo they caught. The fishermen acted proud and happy, holding the fish, displaying it at the bar, and allowing everyone to study the fish. The Wahoo was a fierce ocean predator, with its length over six feet. I was extremely impressed as I examined this fish.

The first named submarine *Wahoo (SS-238)* experienced combat in WWII. She bore the name of this fish. The *Wahoo* was one of the most effective subs in sinking Japanese ships in the war. Unfortunately, the Japs sunk the *Tang, Trigger, Wahoo, Trout, Gudgeon,* and *Harder* in WWII. Honoring Admiral Dick O'Kane's old boat, the *Tang (SS-306)*, the Navy named the first boat in the class of postwar submarines the Tang. Tang class subs named submarines after WWII subs that contributed to the submarine's success in the war, including the *Tang, Trigger, Wahoo, Trout, Gudgeon,* and *Harder.* The *USS Wahoo (SS-565)* took her name after the *Wahoo (SS-238)*, a WWII submarine. While studying the Wahoo fish, I considered the submarines' dangers faced, the responsibility of duties, and the importance of missions.

Later, the bar staff brought out a platter of prepared Wahoo. As hungry sharks in a feeding frenzy feast on a baby whale, the bar's patrons and crew devoured the fish. A Wahoo was tasty fish, we appreciated the cuisine, and we're more grateful for the meal when we learned that it was free on the house. We took a liking to the bar's gang and made new friends. They likewise enjoyed our company. Without other things to do, we stayed in that bar, socializing and telling sea stories with the staff and other customers that arrived and left, sharing rounds of drinks, one followed by another.

By coincidence, the Dynamic-trio became like college students on spring break, away from a parent's watchful eye at a party town—we became drunk. We lacked skill in drinking, not knowing how to keep a zero float by drinking slowly over time to prevent drunkenness. At the bar's closing, we left inebriated. I don't know how we ended on the pier and missed the last liberty boat. Because of missing the boat, we didn't attend the morning muster and averted the pre-underway field-day. But later, we experienced the COB's wrath receiving much ghastlier work than the missed field-day—the extraordinary work was repulsive.

The following morning after missing the boat, I woke up with the sun's hot rays making me suffer like a slice of bread burning in a toaster. On the pier, I laid suffering. Hot and sick, I'm having the worst hangover of my life. Stomach queasiness, churning in nausea, sensing I'll puke whether wanting to or not. After I rolled over with my head over the pier edge, I puked up my guts until no more came out, puking until my stomach was empty. As I puked, I watched vomit splash on the sea below, disturbing the smooth blue-green sea with a vile mess. I suffered awfully. With an empty stomach, I then chucked up dry heaves and then spit, trying to get the terrible flavor out of my mouth—spitting didn't work. With a dry mouth, I tasted something identical to chewing on dry turds or something worse, even something more disgustful. The taste sickened me.

With my stomach empty, I regained composure, and I heard noises on the pier. Slowly, I rolled back around and faced a pack of tourists from a tour bus stopped to give sightseers a look at our submarine anchored in the harbor. Even with blurred vision, I saw mothers pushing their daughters behind them. On display, we laid on a dusty pier as if we're a danger, carrying infectious diseases, or worse. We presented to their girls our wickedness—sinful drunkenness. The mothers had to protect their daughters from us, drunken sailors.

After sleeping on the pier covered with brick-red dirt and dust, my uniform is coated with the brick-red soil, making me a spectacle. With my sick and embarrassed sensation, I couldn't hide or control rolling over and puking a dry heave. After vomiting, my ill feeling improved, but I was sweating, my uniform stuck to my wet skin. I spotted my shipmates. Billy Bob was a mess sleeping across the pier, and he missed the water when he puked last night. Billy Bob made a revolting sight asleep in a vomit's puddle. Wet vomit mixed with red-brown earth covered him—a disgusting display. Charlie was even worse. He pissed himself. Piss mixed with the pier's red-brown dust added to last night's vomit made a vision of messy red-brown shit oozing out of a diaper that covered his once white uniform. Charlie opened his eyes. With his bloodshot and uncomprehending eyes, he peered in bewilderment at the tourist crowd who gawked back in mute shock. Disgusted tourists took pictures, catching the Dynamic-trio in revolting splendor.

After getting up, I staggered to Billy Bob and booted him awake, mumbling, "Billy Bob, Charlie, let's get out of here." Once we're standing, we group up together with as much military dignity we could muster and then marched off the pier through the tourists. The crowd separated, letting us pass. The tourists pulled away from the Dynamic-trio as though we're too despicable to touch as if we had a dreadful disease. The tourists acted afraid of us, moving away from us, behaving like they'll catch our infection by contacting us.

The tour bus idled at the pier's end and stopped our escape. As we gawked at the bus, blocking our retreat, we grasped our error—we're heading the wrong way. The Dynamic-trio realized our foolishness. The liberty boat is at the pier's other end. With what little military formality we could muster under the distasteful circumstances, the Dynamic-trio half-heartedly marched back through that welcoming crowd of tourists—again. The tourists convinced we were loathsome displayed appalled expressions and withdrew further away from us. The Dynamic-trio enjoyed an extremely humiliating experience, being such noble Navy representatives on that day.

A liberty boat at the pier's end was waiting for us. A boatswain and a machinist mate watched us making fools of ourselves as we walked through the tourists. The boatswain ordered, "Get aboard and be quick about it; you guys are lucky I'm still here. You're the last ashore from your sub's liberty party. Your COB told me to get you, shitheads. I nearly left, but I saw the commotion on the pier, letting me know you're here. You shitheads are in trouble. Your COB is pissed." The boatswain glared at us in disgust, as we stumbled into the boat, he resumes, "You had better get your dumb asses squared away. If you've got to puke, puke leeward, I won't allow you to leave this boat until you clean it. So, don't mess it up." The boatswain and the machinist follow the Dynamic-trio aboard the boat. As soon as the boat crew untied the boat from the pier, we set out towards the *Wahoo*.

As the utility boat drew alongside, the XO and the COB glared downward at the Dynamic-trio. With outrage, the XO yells, "You three are disgusting. If a report chit follows you aboard, I'll make sure you're busted with brig-time." As we're climbing aboard, the XO continues, "You're lucky. I'm not writing you up this time, because the COB told me he'd motivate you. If this ever happens again, you won't get the COB's protection. Know what? I feel sorry for you. I don't know what the COB will do, but I understand you will never forget it because it will be worse than brig-time."

"Go below. Get your dumb asses cleaned up! You have ten minutes to get topside to prepare for getting underway!" the COB ordered. Worried, we scamper over each other, getting away from the XO and COB.

Later, back in Pearl Harbor, the COB took an interest in the Dynamic-trio and invited us to his party. "Meet me in the Aft-head next Monday morning at 08:00." The COB ordered.

As ordered, we arrive at the party before the COB. While entering the head, I'm wondering why the COB wanted to meet us in such an exquisite setting in the Aft head. Might we do a field-day, but I'm mistaken. It wasn't the head we cleaned. In the head, I saw the COB wasn't there but noticed an odd, curious heap of inauspicious equipment lying in a corner. I couldn't help studying that material, surmising the gear must have something to do with the reasons we're here. To determine its use, shit, I had no idea. In silence with questioning glances, sensing apprehension, Billy Bob, Charlie, and I glared at the equipment, scrutinizing that stuff. Then, I guessed its purpose, perceiving we would use it doing something I wouldn't like— my assessment was correct.

As I was envisioning its purpose, the COB in pressed khakis, shined shoes, whitewall haircut entered the head. His brass belt buckle shined as a gold mirror. So damn military the COB appeared, rattled me. The COB guessed our thoughts. With a happy grin, snickering, he declared, "Soon, you'll find out that stuff's purpose. I had A-Division get this gear—just for you." He followed with he-he chuckles, while his muscles bulged for a purposeful effect.

As I stared at the gear for a long moment, my gut sensed trouble. Too cheerful, the COB was, and that gear looked intimidating.

The COB grinning like a kid who just found a dollar before he enters a candy store resumes, "Before we start, I have something to tell you. It concerns your next project. Sit down and make yourselves comfortable. We shouldn't take long." I was nauseous while we selected places to sit on the toilet floor like kindergartners sitting on their classroom floor, looking up at their teacher, but for us, we're looking at the COB, making me upset.

The COB leaned on a sink, seemed to locate a satisfying position. We watched him take his time getting into position. Once comfortable enough, the COB picked up his coffee mug and took a drink—never seen him without the coffee mug, he resembled my dad without the potbelly. He looked comparable to a movie star with rugged good looks that appeal to women. The COB appeared arrogant and confident—he's in charge, and he knows it. A moment of dead silence after he quit moving, then he glared right at us—right into our minds as he knew what we were sensing. With my attention held, caught in his focus, I had shivers down my spine.

Then, the COB tells his story. "This ain't no shit. Approximately one hundred years ago, like you boot-camps, I was a nonqual puke—stationed on my first boat, a fleet boat, the *USS Spikefish, AGSS-404.* Keep this to yourselves, this dates me—the Spikefish didn't have a snorkel—she saw combat in World War II, way before my time. Anyhow, one of my first duties aboard was the Shit-House Mouse."

Billy Bob and Charlie gaped at the COB with blank faces. I didn't grasp what a Shithouse Mouse was.

The COB noticed our expressions and clarified, "You know, the Head-Cleaner."

Billy Bob's and Charlie's blank looks didn't change.

The COB looked flustered, expounded, "You landlubbers, the Shithouse Mouse, cleans the heads. In the Navy, you call the Head-Cleaner the Shithouse Mouse!" Recovering his cheerful composure, he said. "The job wasn't so terrible after I overcome the image of head cleaning out of my head—and the stink. The odor was the nastiest part. Besides, the Shithouse Mouse had the best liberty. I go on liberty every night in port as the Shithouse Mouse. Well, one day, I was setting up to clean the shitters, when a group of A-Gangers arrived interrupting my work, lugging a gear bag filled with stuff resembling the equipment sitting in this head." The COB points to the stuff in the corner.

I glanced at the corner, experiencing a menacing chill looking at that stuff. What is the gear for, but I wasn't ready to seek its purpose? Billy Bob and Charlie, with concerned expressions, stared at the equipment.

The COB's story continued, "them Turd-Chasers irritated me at first. With bilge-rats in my way, I can't get the head cleaned."

Billy Bob, the dumb shit, not realizing that he might get us in trouble, questioned, "COB, what's a Turd-Chaser?"

Billy Bob was clueless about everything, from girls to the Navy, not grasping the trouble we're in, or what might happen. I didn't either, but I had no plan to make conditions worse.

Not wanting his story interrupted, the COB's gruff voice replied.

Turd-Chasers are snipes from engineering, you know, Auxiliary-men, bilge-rats, and flange-heads. Gosh, damn! Didn't you-boots learn anything in Boot Camp or Subschool? Auxiliary-men make up A-Gang, A-Division personnel, A-Gangers are the bilge-rats, they fix hydraulics, high-pressure air, and sanitary systems. A-Gangers work on toilets, shitters, urinals, and such, well, that's how they got the name, Turd-Chasers. Their friends can call A-Gangers, Turd-Chasers, everyone else risks having the shit kicked out of them by calling A-Gangers Turd-Chasers unless they are tough enough. Most who called them Turd-Chasers behind their backs, they wouldn't risk it. You know what I mean. Well, I was tough enough; I called A-Gangers Turd-Chasers in front of them. They didn't enjoy it much, but I didn't care, picking on A-Gangers, anyhow. It's a typical Diesel Boat fun. I harassed Turd-Chasers every chance I could get, and they badgered me at every opportunity.

A-Gangers were shrewd when harassing me. Turd-Chasers had me hunting the whole boat for a goshdamn bucket of steam and another time for something more substantial, a can of Relative Bearing Grease. I thought I couldn't locate the boat's longest line. And I took the longest time learning to blow sanitary two through the mess deck's deep sink. This bullshit was A-Gang Chief's requirement for my qualification. That Turd-Chaser had me hunting for important stuff like, keeping me busy, and wasting my time. Pain in the ass he was. I assumed I'd never qualify because of him.

Gentlemen, your qualifying is easy compared to mine. The new Navy is turning into a candy-ass organization full of wimps you can't trust until they prove themselves. In battle or casualty, you can't wait until someone confirms himself. In my day, the qualified crew tested the new sailor before he discovered himself in an emergency. Now we have to nursemaid every young pup like you shitheads—can't hurt your feelings—you might cry and quit. Babying nonquals is bullshit if you ask me. If I had my way, qualifying would be different. We must prepare ourselves for war, and that includes identifying the ones we can count on and sending ashore the ones we can't trust.

"What's the longest line on the boat?" asks Billy Bob, grinning at the COB.

I couldn't figure out if Billy Bob was pulling the COB's chain, or if Billy Bob was just a dumb shit; no matter, he's making it worse for us.

Startled, then showing a peeved expression, the COB glared at Billy Bob and grumpily responded.

> That's your next qual question to discover that answer. I expect you to identify it before your next liberty. Pollywogs like you will make a career aboard without liberty before they find out that answer. Now, to the issue—listen!

Then, the COB continued telling his story.

> One of them flange-heads declared, "we'll clean Sanitary Tank 2 as soon as Santilla, our new striker, shows up." Then, they set out their gear.
>
> Santilla reported aboard the *Spikefish* a month before me and completed his mess cooking and head cleaning assignments. Santilla was in his first week working in A-Gang. Santilla was quiet, never said much. The COB considered him a hot runner—you realize it's the guy who can get a job done—not comparable to you guys. Can't count on you to wipe your asses—but you will get there—I'll see to it! Now then, back to you boot-camps.
>
> As I recall from my quals, the toilets in this head dumped into Sanitary Tank 2. Then the image struck me; sanitary tank-cleaning must be the most disgusting job to undertake. Before the day's end, I discovered cleaning a sanitary tank is the most disgusting job anyone might do, I understood Chiefs' abilities.

The enthusiasm the Turd-Chasers had while setting up for the Sanitary Tank 2 cleaning gave me the opinion, they didn't enjoy the prospect for that job. The Turd-Chasers are waiting for Santilla to show up before starting the sanitary tank-cleaning, intending to give Santilla an initiation by making him clean that sanitary tank. They're just mean enough to give the nastiest job to the most junior unknowing sailor in their division, what a bunch of shitheads.

As he entered the head, Santilla saw the work preparation for the tank cleaning. For tricks played on him, Santilla was gullible and fell to a pranks' victim—every time. But on this occasion, Santilla figured out what he was in for—no tricks today. Santilla didn't look very thrilled, disgust in his eyes gave him away.

"I found the tank-cleaning suit," Sissler announced, carrying in a canvas bag more massive than a sea bag. He opens the sack and pulled out an old rain suit. The rain suit is an old dirty yellow rubber parka with a hood and bibbed rubber pants with wide suspenders attached to the pants. Sissler directed, "Santilla put on this suit, and be quick about it. We don't have all day to clean that tank."

Yes, it's Sissler, the same A-gang Chief that's on this boat. Sissler was a Second Class on the *Spikefish*, he was 100 years younger, and a thousand pounds thinner. Black curly hair covered his head.

Without speaking, Santilla stripped to his skivvies. Santilla looked embarrassed in his skivvies and the other Turd-Chasers watching him. Sissler passed him sections of the suit. Santilla strained to get into the rubber pants that were too small, making them a tight fit. But the parka was too big. Watching Santilla put on the suit made me feel sorry for him.

Then, Sissler hauled out a dark olive-green gas mask with scratched eye lenses and a pair of high black rubber boots. When Sissler pulled out two large rolls of green tape that caught my eye, I couldn't help wondering its purpose, inquiring, "What is that tape used for?"

"That's EB Green an all-purpose tape. Submariners use EB Green to fix everything—even patch holes in the pressure hull. EB Green is a useful tape. Bet you didn't learn that. We'll use it to tape-up the tank-cleaning suit seams."

Wally, the other flange-head, holding back a chuckle, included, "Santilla, tape-up your seams tight. A sanitary tank cleaning isn't so bad if your tank-cleaning suit has no leaks—shit in your socks is uncomfortable."

Santilla looked like he detested the job he was getting ready to begin. As he put on his special suit, he said nothing.

After Santilla had on his skintight pants with the parka covering the top of the pants, Sissler holding back laughter teased Santilla that he looked funny. Sissler uttered, "You look like a balloon caught on a stick—funny looking."

Joining their fun, snickering, I included, "With that balloon, you're wearing, at least you won't drown in that tank. It'll keep your head afloat. It'll hold your head above—shit!"

Sissler snapped at me, "Hey shit for brains, knock it off! If I wanted any shit out of you, I would squeeze your head. Shut up!"

Well, I ignored Sissler, thinking he was turning into a prick. That day, I couldn't keep my mouth shut. Santilla acted vulnerable to teasing. For fun, to get to him more, I pestered him further. As Santilla was putting on a black dirty rubber boot that was too big, I inquired, "How can you do that job? Are you going into that tank?"

Santilla ignored me by not explaining, and he didn't look happy about his pending job working in the sanitary tank. Santilla's facial expression showed disgust.

As Santilla put on the other boot, to harass him more, I remarked, "I would hate doing that job. You'll get shit all over yourself." Santilla uttered nothing. He glared at me with eyes growing in anger. I rubbed it in further; "You don't realize what diseases are in that shit-tank. You know, Murphy has the Clap, and Murphy shit today." Santilla's face color changed to a sickly white, yet he expressed nothing. But his angry eyes said it, as they turned to a loathed display of dread. I enjoyed his discomfort by getting to Santilla.

As Santilla was taping up the seams of his rubber outfit, the other Turd-Chasers opened the access hatch to Sanitary Tank 2. When they got the access hatch opened a crack, the head filled with a nasty stench. The stink was raunchy; so awful, I couldn't describe the horrible stink. The disgusting odor allowed teasing further, so I asked, "How can you guys do that job? Turd chasing must be the worst job in the Navy."

No one answered, but the Turd-Chasers glared at me with eyes showing anger as they continued with their sanitary tank-cleaning task. Santilla looked sick. I thought he might vomit any minute.

Believing I'm putting one over on the Turd-Chasers, I'm getting to them, but I wasn't ready for what transpired.

The head had two stalls. Well, unknown, the-Gang Chief, was in one stall hearing every word I spoke. Except for me, the crew liked the Chief the best. I had never seen him furious at anyone. Often, he offered inspiring advice to everybody except me. For me, he handed out a ration of shit. I didn't like the shithead. Later, I discovered he was one of the best Chiefs in the Navy. Eventually, we became the best of friends, but not on this day.

The source of the Chief's pending rage was me—a rage he unleashed soon after. As fury's target, I experienced his wrath.

While struggling to ignore me, the Turd-Chasers opened the access hatch. Now the most fragrant stinking stench filled the head. I constrained gagging while Santilla put on his Gas Mask. Before Santilla started into that sanitary tank, continuing my harassment, I made another remark with carefree abandonment. "Nobody, not even God, could get me into that tank."

No sooner had I uttered those words, I'm in the air. Holy shit! The Chief had me. The Chief picked me up as if I'm weightless, holding my arms to my sides; I couldn't escape. Comparable to holding a squirming baby, he carried me to the tank's hatch and threw me into the tank as quickly as throwing a wet cleaning cloth into a bucket—I'm the wet rag. Landing at the bottom of that tank, I slipped and fell face-first right into thick shit and piss a foot or two in-depth—I wasn't in a condition to gauge the crap's thickness—if you know what I mean.

While getting up, I slipped back into crap. With my hands and knees in poop, I puked up my breakfast. With extreme revulsion, I got up, wiped my face with my sleeve—a mistake that made me vomit repeatedly. When I stood up, my head hit the tank top. I sensed my head going into a layer of poop—a sickening sensation—I puked. I couldn't stand up without my head striking crap on the tank's top. With a low crouch, looking up, eyes pleading, I stared up at the Chief. He peered downwards at me with fire in his eyes. With no help to come, I puked bile.

The Chief yelled, "Now that you're in the shit-tank, you can clean it!"

How could I wash that tank? The stench was nauseating, disgusting, and just awful. I puked again, hearing Turd-Chasers laughing. In the tank, I'm humiliated as I thought I beat them with my wit, but they had the last laugh.

Knee-deep in shit, oozing around me, gave me a sensation. Not unlike the impression when changing a baby's diaper, a messy diaper with stinking shit leaching out of the diaper smearing the baby and crib, but I'm in the muck. Well, Sanitary Tank 2 resembled that, but worse, much, much worse! A layer of black, brown shit lay on top of the tank's overhead. The dripping shit landing in my hair made me afraid to look up because when I did, drops of dark-brown-black slimy excrement dropped in my eyes or mouth. A dense coat of muck two inches deep lay on the tank's sides and a bed of shit a foot deep covered the tank's bottom. The crap had the offensive consistency of dark chocolate pudding mixed with grease. On the muck's surface, solid globs of dark-brown, yellow-brown, and black-brown globs of new shit floated. Most of the globs looked mushy. Wet toilet paper and urine merged with this pudding. The disgustingly offensive stink was nauseating—what a revolting experience—what a sickening sight, making me puke again.

The Chief threw me a scraper and a hose of running water, yelling, "Scrape at the top and wash off the loose stuff as you go! That will keep shit out of your hair. Now, move your ass. Get that tank so clean; we can eat lunch in there, today!"

When the Chief finished speaking, I puked again, a dry heave because my stomach had nothing left in it. Yelling out, "I'm not doing this—no way!" Then, I tried climbing out of that tank. When I reached for the hatch opening, the Chief hit it hard with something, causing a loud bang identical to a shotgun firing, scaring the hell out of me. Immediately, I jumped back, dropped, slipped again, and fell back into the oozing excrement.

This treatment, I didn't deserve, but what could I do? The Chief wouldn't let me out of the Sanitary Tank, making me sick and humiliated. I wanted to die, thinking, I died, and I'm in hell. The stench made me again ill, heaving dry heaves, but nothing came up. I started dry heaving. After constant puking with nothing coming up, I nearly cried.

The Chief had no pity for me, yelling, "Knock it off! You're a candy-ass wimp who can't handle a dirty little job. Get off your ass and quit feeling sorry for yourself. Get that tank cleaned and have it done before noon today! If you think, crying in that tank will get you out, you're mistaken, it won't happen. I don't care if you're in that tank for your whole naval career, but you won't get out until the tank's clean—get your dumb-ass moving!"

I didn't enjoy the thought of this job, let alone doing it. I'm feeling sorry for myself, suspecting the Chief never had to clean a sanitary tank, but he's making me do it—what an ass.

After realizing I'm not getting out of the tank until it's cleaned, I must overcome revulsion and clean it. No matter, I gaged from the shitty mess over every part of me. With the hose water, I give myself a cold wash, rinsing myself off as much as possible. It must have taken me ten minutes before I touched the tank's overhead with the scraper. Then another thirty before I pushed the tool into the solid soft black, brown mass. I was nauseous the whole time. Then, I cleaned—scraping, scrubbing, and rinsing the tank—I'm a slow cleaner at first. Dam, I didn't merit this torment.

A thundering shout, "Get the lead out! You don't have all day. Shit! When I was your age, I'd clean a tank starting early in the morning and finish so we would eat breakfast in it. I expect we will eat lunch in there today—now move your lazy candy-ass!"

Reluctantly, I scraped and washed that tank a tad faster. When I sprayed the crap with water, it became wet enough to turn into a thick, slow-moving stinking liquid. Water mixed with crap formed a dense liquefied mass. Wet shit oozed and dripped down the tank's side as shit washed away. When I sprayed and scraped, shit globs scraped right off or seeped off the surface that held it. Liquid shit flowed over my hands, flowed along my arms, and dripped off my elbows. I scraped and sprayed water at the solid masses sticking to the overhead and sides. Liquified shit dripped off the overhead into the pool of sewage and on me. I was standing deep in shit.

When shit as a runny muddy shitty liquid reached above my knees, the Chief yelled out, "Start the Drain Pump!" The liquid emptied until it covered my ankles, then the Chief yelled, "Stop the Drain Pump!"

As I continued cleaning, I sensed shitty water up to my knees, telling me the tank is filling up again. On it went washing, scraping and pumping, then more washing, scrubbing and rinsing, and more pumping. As I moved, I suffered less and cleaned and scrubbed faster.

One of them, Turd-Chasers, Wally, declared, "He likes that job."

Hell no! I disliked the disgusting job. No matter, for me getting out was cleaning the tank. I made my stay in the tank as short as possible. You know what I mean.

With cleaning ongoing, I didn't notice smelling the stench. Yet, in the tank with shit covering me, I thought the job would never end. After my tank-cleaning finished, but before the Chief let me out of the tank, he made me clean myself up, showering, and washing in that stinking sanitary tank.

Someone tossed me a box of laundry soap and a brush. With soap and water, I washed the crap off myself. In the tank, I stripped, scrubbed all my clothes, showered myself, and then rewashed my clothes. I washed my hair using laundry soap, showered, and rinsed off ten times and then repeated washing my clothes one more time. When I was clean enough, the Chief allowed me to climb out of that tank. After getting out, I went to the shower and took a long one—a hot Hollywood shower. As I scrubbed myself thoroughly, I scrubbed myself beyond pink, scouring until I was sore, washing hands and feet, then cleaning fingernails and toenails. Then, I washed everything over again. Later, I laundered my clothes three more times before I would wear them.

Charlie interrupted the COB, stating, "I bet you learned to keep your mouth shut on that day, after an experience as that."

For a moment, the COB angrily glared at Charlie, then he looked at us, grinning as he answered.

> Not in your life. Shit, after wallowing around in shit all day, nothing bothered me. I became more obnoxious than ever. What's worse than cleaning a sanitary tank? I took a long time to learn tact, understanding, and feelings for others. Even longer to understand when to keep my mouth shut and express my contribution only when necessary. What I learned that day was the utmost respect for that A-Gang Chief and his A-Gangers, and I never gave a job to someone I haven't done at least once myself.

The COB finished his story, the head became silent, resembling a graveyard on a dark foggy night. I glanced at the COB; he had a shit-eating grin, expressing that he got our attention. Then I gazed at Bob and Charlie; they were as white as a sheet staring at the equipment, examining the strange pile of unfriendly stuff. I figured out we would use that gear. I'm nauseated.

With a stern glare, the COB added.

> In typical Navy fashion, even sanitary tanks must get cleaned, but they don't clean themselves, do they? Someone must get into a sanitary tank to clean it—a dirty job—a disgusting task. I've known it firsthand, how foul and disgusting cleaning a sanitary tank can be, but someone must do it. You guys, for example, when you get into that tank, you start from the top. While you're cleaning that tank, I want you to be

thinking about getting drunk, embarrassing the Navy,
and making quarters on time.

On that day, the COB pointed the Dynamic-trio in the right naval direction. Without violating one Navy regulation, the COB got our attention right off and showed his authority. The COB didn't hit us or use any other violent punishment that one expects. The Dynamic-trio didn't get our pay cut or get busted in rate. The COB was most effective. After this incident, we never gave a Chief or anyone else in authority a hard time or caused them a reason for punishing us again. Uniquely effectual, COB's method sure was.

The sanitary tank-cleaning experience didn't make us into heroes, and the incident didn't turn us into great leaders. Dynamic-trio's sanitary tank-cleaning was not as disgusting as the COB's occurrence. He provided us with protective gear. But, the experience helped us to become better sailors. Forever after, we paid attention when a leader was addressing us. For the lesson, we learned it the hard way, when the COB requests our presence, we had better not be late. After this experience, the Dynamic-trio responded to orders fasts. Sanitary tank-cleaning was a significant event in our lives, one we never forgot. The tank-cleaning changed our attitudes and allowed other incentives, making us more productive. Sanitary tank-cleaning was just one of the COB's inventive ways of motivating young sailors to conduct themselves without embarrassing the Navy and respond to orders. For the Dynamic-trio, it worked.

THE BROWN SPECKLED SPARROW CLUB

Remember when I said I would tell you about the Brown Speckled Sparrow Club. You don't. Well, I must enlighten you about the club. I bet all you landlubbers, low life surface skimmers, chit-signers, politicians, shore-duty pukes, ground-pounders, air-dales, shallow-water sailors, and jarheads don't even realize what the Brown Speckled Sparrow Club is. Do you? I thought so. I guess I'll have to start with a short description. I bet you didn't know that many submariners are members of this exclusive club. Once you're a member, you're always a club member. You cannot be kicked out of this club—ever, even if you don't pay your dues, because there aren't any. There are officers, chiefs, and many of the lower ranks in this club—seamen to admirals have membership in this club.

Because I'm lucky, I never had the honor of becoming a member, yet I came close a couple of times. You know, I'm glad I never did. Members don't join this club willingly—they get volunteered sort of—and they do their volunteering. The club's initiation is downright awful—should be a law against it, but if there was a law against it—it couldn't be enforced. Bet I got you confused by now. Therefore, to help you out, I'll tell you about a few sailors and how they joined the Brown Speckled Sparrow Club. You'll figure out the special qualifications for club membership—this ain't no shit.

Cookie was the first member I saw joining the Brown Speckled Sparrow Club. I never knew his real name; our crew assigned him the title, Cookie, representing admiration and appreciation for his cooking ability. Well, Cookie one of the nicest of guys. He's always makes something good for the crew—dam good cook, and he's an even better baker. He would stay up late, making sticky-buns for breakfast and made some extra for the mid-watch. Those were the best sticky buns in the Navy. Shit fire! A cup of strong black hot coffee and a sticky-bun hot-out of the oven covered with butter frosting and full of cinnamon and raisins, one of the best tasting treats a submarine sailor could have. The aroma of those sticky-buns was incredible—it penetrated throughout the boat. You could smell the sweet dessert baking while on watch, or it would greet you waking up. With that combination before you started your-watch or to welcome you coming off-watch—well, gosh dam, they were enjoyable. You could be talked into shipping over or extending your cruise for two northern runs back-to-back, solely for another sticky-bun—they were that good.

Anyway, Cookie had one of the most dramatic and possibly the funniest club initiations. Here is how it happened. One night on patrol, Cookie's watch was the night cook, responsible for the mid rats and baking everything from bread, cakes, pies, buns, and whatever else for treats for the crew. He also prepared for breakfast. That eventful night Cookie was by himself in the galley preparing for Mid-Rats and Breakfast, cooking on the galley range a pot of soup, baking bread in the oven, and making early stages of various dishes for breakfast. When Cookie gets a call to nature, happening so fast, it caused a problem. Cookie needed to take a dump and can't control it. With poor planning on his part, the galley is empty. He sent his mess cooks off to get something—never said what. In anxiety, Cookie secured the range and ran aft to the head.

Simultaneously, in the aft torpedo-room, the room-watch, Torpedo-man First-Class Blackheart, just finished lining up to blow the sanitary-tank—the one that the aft shitter dumps into. Blackheart had posted the blowing shitter signs, each a large sheet metal sign with chains attached on each side, with hooks on the end of the chains that allow connecting the sign across each shitter door, preventing opening any door without removing the sign in front of it. The sign has big red letters, "BLOWING SANITARY." While Blackheart starts pressurizing sanitary three, he wants to get about a hundred pounds over sea pressure to blow the sanitary-tank as fast as possible, and then in rushes Cookie.

"I got 'a-go, I got to go—bad!" Cries Cookie.

"You can't. We're blowing sanitary." Replies Blackheart.

"But I can't hold it." Cookie whines. "I need to go now! I'll flush the toilet later after your done—promise."

Well, Blackheart would scare the hell out of anyone not knowing him—he looked fearful, with a commanding voice sounding scary in normal conversation. He was a first-class torpedo-man who was in the Navy for over twenty-five years serving in submarines in WWII. The aging process was not kind to him, making Blackheart appearing scary looking and much older than his age, but having a kind heart, he would go out of his way, helping anyone in need. Blackheart could not refuse anyone, especially Cookie. "All right, but you remember, I'm blowing this sanitary, and the tank is under pressure. Remember! Don't flush until I give you the go-ahead; I have to vent the sanitary tank first." Commands Blackheart, next, he continued pressurizing the sanitary tank.

"Thanks, you're saving my life." Cookie says with relief.

Cookie grabs the chain, unhooks one side, drops the sign, and opens the head door, rushes in, and slams the door shut after him. We heard loud strange, unpleasant noises from the occupied head. Rumor has it that the head was a natural sound amplifier. The noises, well, they were not the most pleasant things to listen too—its nature talking—you know what I mean.

As these obnoxious noises stop, Blackheart finishes opening the sanitary tank's backup sea valve, but before he can start opening the sea valve, a loud tremendous roar blasts from the head. Cookie didn't remember the warning—he flushed the toilet with the sanitary tank under pressure; Cookie immediately joined the Brown Speckled Sparrow Club. The torpedo room fills up with an offensive nauseous stink.

From the head are sounds like spitting and gagging, followed by sputtering, "Spitting. Oh shit! Gagging. Dam! Shit! Sputtering. Dam it to hell! Shit! Ugh shit! Ugh yuck!" that was Cookie's acceptance speech for being welcomed into the Brown Speckled Sparrow Club,

The head door opens. Outcomes Cookie. He's a remarkable sight, so hideous. I don't ever want to see such a spectacle again. From his waist up, the residue from the contents of the toilet he filled covered him, adding to this mess was some sanitary tank's fillings—a mixture of shit, toilet paper, and urine was splattered all over him from head to belt mostly on his face and chest. The shitty paint job gave him the appearance of brown speckles all over him. Being covered with splattered shit is how the club got its name from Brown Speckled Sparrows.

What was astonishing in Cookie's situation was a big slimly dark brown Turd, better than an inch in diameter, sat on his baldhead laying in a straight line from the top of his head down across his bare forehead. The turd laid between his eyebrows and stopped on the bridge of his nose. He was trying to look at it with the strangest and funniest expression I had ever seen. His eyes were going crossed while his face held a horrific, painful look that he realized what was on his head. His expression showed that he didn't want it there, but he didn't grasp how to get it off—afraid to touch it, too disgusting.

Blackheart saw Cookie's dilemma guided him back to the shitter stall and told him to bend forward over the shitter. When Cookie bent over, we heard a loud plop when the turd fell into the toilet. Blackheart called control and informed that they must wake a replacement for Cookie to continue fixing the food and preparing for breakfast. He then ordered Cookie to clean himself up and then attack the head. Blackheart re-checked the sanitary line-up and finished blowing the sanitary tank.

You could have beaten me up with a feather—couldn't help myself. I was laughing so hard. Actually, except for Cookie, everyone else in the torpedo room was out of commission, laughing uncontrollably because of Cookie's condition. Yes, it was sad, it was horrible, it was disgusting, and we shouldn't have laughed, but dam, it was too funny—too much humor for submariners to hold back.

On another memorable occasion on the *USS Billfish (SSN 676)*, there was a double joining of the Brown Speckled Sparrow Club when the COB and Nermey joined the Brown Speckled Sparrow Club within minutes of each other. On that event, I was in the Goat locker playing cribbage with Chief Richie to pass some time before going on watch. The Aux-forward-watch is conducting the regular nightly routine, performing housekeeping, shooting the TDU, blowing sanitary tanks, and doing other routine stuff. The Aux-forward came in and started lining up to blow sanitary-tank-one. The same sanitary-tank that the Goat Locker Head's toilets, showers, and sinks along with the Crew's head's toilets, sinks, and showers drained for storage until the tank becomes full, requiring emptying often—to keep the crew happy. The officer's head also dumps into this tank.

For you non-quals, you may need a little understanding about what happens, on surface ships, toilet waste dumps directly to the sea. In a home or apartment toilet, waste flushes down the toilet to a septic tank or a sewer. But on submarines, toilet waste collects in a sanitary tank and saved until it is safe to get rid of it without compromising the submarine's stealth. After the tank gets filled, blowing the waste to the sea empties the tank.

Here is a brief qual lesson on the sanitary system. On submarines, a sanitary system makes this work while submerged or surfaced. For a normal line-up, sanitary-tank tanks vent inboard through a charcoal filter, allowing gravity to flow waste into the sanitary tank. Associated sinks and showers gray-water drain to the same sanitary-tank as the toilets. Toilets sitting above a sanitary-tank, connect directly through a ball valve to the sanitary-tank. By opening a toilet ball valve allows flushing the shitter, making a direct gravity path to dump waste into the sanitary-tank. A Hull and Backup Valve connects the sanitary tank to the sea. When shut, the valves isolate the sanitary-tanks from the sea. Throughout daily use, the tank gets filled. At least once a day, a watchstander empties the tank's contents by blowing the waste to the sea.

To blow the tank to sea requires changing the sanitary system's normal line up. First, the sanitary-tank must be lined-up to blow the tank. Isolating the tank from the people tank requires shutting all sources that drain into the tank. A watchstander shuts each sink and shower isolation drains, also he shuts the tank's vent valve. Most importantly, the watchstander shuts each toilet ball valve that performs toilet to tank-isolation. Second, after watchstanders complete the tank isolation line-up, he then opens the tanks air pressurization-valve, to get the tank pressure above sea pressure. As soon as the tank's pressure is higher than sea pressure, the watch opens the tank's hull and backup valves. By opening these vales, allows the tank pressure to blow the tank's contents to sea. After the tank is empty, the pressurization-valve and the hull and back-up valves get shut. Opening the tank's vent valve causes the tank's air pressure to pass through a charcoal filter, venting into the boat's interior. Then the watch opens all the drain isolation valves, making the system useable. That's how it should happen.

But, with a pressurized a sanitary-tank, when an individual opens a toilet-ball valve, a dynamic event happens. The sanitary-tank's contents take the path of least resistance through the toilet-ball valve inboard. Then, as soon as the toilet-ball valve is open, the toilet-ball valve operator gets splattered with crap because the operator is directly over the toilet when the valve opens. Being over the toilet makes the valve operator a target for the sanitary tank's contents. For the valve operator, crap hitting him is most unpleasant.

I think, even the low lives, surface skimmers, and pollywogs can figure out that the Sanitary tank's contents are something that you would not want to play with or even touch—just nasty—like the stinky mushy load filling diapers that require changing.

Well, back to the story, while we were finishing a hand, a loud inrush of air discharges from the crew's head, followed by a most unpleasant stench, letting us know someone joined the Brown Speckled Sparrow Club. Shortly after, in comes the COB, Wally, laughing uncontrollably, looking at me sputtering, "Nermey, blew shit all over himself, what a dumb shit—he's an FT, it must be an FT requirement to be a dumb shit."

I figured that he was trying to get my goat, so I didn't respond to his insulting foolishness.

Still laughing, Wally goes into the head, removes the blowing sanitary sign on the shitter door, and enters it, laughing while closing the door after him. Shortly after entering the shitter, another louder blast of inrushing air. Wally immediately joined the Brown Speckled Sparrow Club. The entire contents from the toilet, and the crap that missed Nermey, splattered Wally. A higher tank pressure than what Nermey experienced blasted the sanitary tank's contents forcibly hit Wally.

From the head came weird sounds like spitting and gagging pursued by a robust unpleasant stench that filled the Goat Locker and followed by Wally's acceptance speech for being welcomed into the Brown Speckled Sparrow Club sputtering, "Ugh! Yuck! Shit! Dam! Shit! Dam it to hell! Shit! Ugh, dam shit! Ugh! Yuck!" Followed with a selection of obstinacies that would have embarrassed a Key West barmaid.

From the head comes a shocking sight. Excrement covered Wally's face, and uniform like the residue of brown mud found as if he was brawling in a pigpen. Repeatedly spitting, Wally was trying to get crap out from his mouth. His eyes blinking in agony showed his distress.

At first, we thought he's hurt but quickly realized he wasn't, but he was utterly humiliated, spitting excrement out of his mouth, trying to hide from our glaze, then rushing to a sink, gagging, and frantically washing his face and the rest of himself off.

After checking him out, I realized that he wasn't seriously hurt, then controlled humor of the event took over, causing us to chuckle at the COB's expense while he was doing his newly assigned duty of cleaning the head. Finally, cleaning conditions allowed leaving the head for a clean uniform. With a humiliating expression, his blood-shot eyes caught my gaze. I responded with a grin, "I see that your IQ increased to the level of an FT." He glared back in quick anger, knowing that I got to him.

As you can guess from what I have just told you, for the members who joined, the Brown Speckled Sparrow Club is a polite name for the dumb-shit club, because you just cannot become a member unless you make a dumb-shit mistake. After all, for a brief instant, each Brown Speckled Sparrow Club member experiences a massive brain fart that directly caused a sudden most unpleasant happening. As new members of the club, for a moment, they were dumb-shits. For club members, the initiation did not stop just because of excrement, piss, and used toilet paper sprayed all over you. New club members had to clean themselves up and afterward clean up the head they messed up—an incredibly humbling experience. Besides, they became the brunt of ridicule to remind them of their stupidity until the next new member took over those pleasant duties. Far too often, this doesn't take too long for the next new member to join the Brown Speckled Sparrow Club.

STARTING OUT

During a pleasant early spring morning, the day when unknown forces made me want to tell my stories. I stopped to admire the Submarine Memorial, in Groton, Connecticut. Gentle warm breezes were blowing, causing the memorial's flags to wave in splendor, creating an impressive display. The Goldstar Bridge towers over this memorial and makes the monument majestic, fitting for its representation. Caretakers, submarine sailors, many who fought in World War II and others preserve the memorial. They display it with affection, reverence, and remembrance for those brave sailors who have waged war and perished in the fifty-two submarines lost during WWII.

The memorial is the sail from the USS Flasher (SS 256), during World War II, the Flasher earned three Presidential Unit Citations and six battle stars. The Flasher was a Gato Class diesel submarine from the first mass-production of U.S. submarines during WWII. Plaques identify the subs lost in the war's battle and flags surround the monument. Within the sail is the sub's conning tower. Later in the war, their sisters, the Balao, and Tench classes diesel submarines joined the fight. Submariners call these diesel submarines, "Fleet Boats."

The United States Navy's World War II submarine fleet destroyed most of the Japanese merchant marine and much of the Japanese Imperial Navy. When I joined the Navy, men who fought in World War II on Fleet Boats filled the submarine crews. I consider all these old-time warriors as heroes.

At this Memorial, I cannot help thinking about World War II submarines and their crews. The Navy's use of submarines was a vital force in winning the war's Pacific battle. The submarine sailors who fought during World War II produced the US submarine service traditions that submariners still faithfully adhere to.

Another Memorial visitor was a younger man near my height, thin yet muscular, clean-cut. Black hair cut military short capped his head. In civilian clothes, wearing polished black shoes, he held a straight posture looking militaristic. Watching him, I felt older, aware of being overweight and out of shape. My full head of white wavy hair with breezes maintaining a style of random disarray is making me self-conscious. Why does this kid bother me? Could he have been me fifty years ago?

As we strolled around the monument, reading plaques, studying the sail, we're aware of each other. When our paths crossed, I flexed my muscles, tightened my stomach muscles to show an unknown strength, tried to impress, tried to appear younger, but looking younger didn't work.

The youngster at first looked annoyed; I'm disrupting his solitude. With curiosity, I speculated what he's thinking. Watch that old fart; I bet he's a farmer who has never seen a lake, let alone an ocean, shit, that old man doesn't know the difference between a boat and a ship.

I'm irritated and annoyed because the youngster interrupted my solitude, disturbed my reverence towards the monument. Thinking, why is that young pup here? He must be in Subschool, a boot most likely, a candidate for the brown speckled sparrow club.

When I couldn't see him, I sensed his presence. I sought to avoid him—it wasn't happening. Yearning for solitude, we're a crowd, strolling around the monument, deep into our thoughts. Not wanting to leave, I wished the youngster to go. But that didn't occur, we struggled to stay apart, but the kid was quicker than me. We met and acted politely but were uncomfortable maneuvering around each other. Each meeting interrupted my meditations. I watched his respectful admiration as he examined the sail's details, softening my feelings. What in the hell am I doing? Whom am I trying to impress? I'm feeling foolish, being uneasy in his presence.

The Memorial has an atmosphere that induces a remembrance for submariners. When meditating at this memorial, submariners may recall long-forgotten memories. Submariners remember their actions: noble, sad, horrifying, and rewarding. Submariners' recollections reappear like they're reliving the experience.

Unexplained, the monument's atmosphere awoke my memories. Recollections returned as vivid as if I was reliving the experience. I recalled going into the Navy, Boot Camp, my first Navy School, soon after Subschool, and my first boat. Then I understood, I must tell this kid my experiences. As if the monument ordered me to launch his naval course because somehow it saw this young man's destiny would be a submariner.

Time passed the silence ended when I inquired, "Are you in Subschool?"

A prompt reply, "Yes, Sir, just started, only in my first week." His eyes widened with a grimace telling me he regretted letting me see he's a boot.

"What caused you to go into subs?"

"Don't know, I suppose for adventure and doing something special. Anyway, I always liked submarine movies, like *HUNT FOR RED OCTOBER* and *THE BOAT*. I guess I watched every submarine movie ever produced."

"For starters, sub movies aren't exact. The moves don't show how sailors work and play on subs. Movies portray submarine crews' thoughts and actions that are nothing like how submariners think, perform duties and find amusement. *THE BOAT* most likely is the most realistic, but most movies never show actual submarine life."

As if he selected a wrong career, he looked worried when he asked, "Well, what are subs like?"

As I point at the plaques displaying the names of boats lost in the war, "Look at these plaques. A place in my heart holds admiration for the sailors on eternal patrol—all are heroes. Submarine crews realized their next mission puts them in harm's way. The crews were aware of the subs missing or overdue from a patrol. They realized their friends on these submarines are on eternal patrol, knowing they will never meet them again. On their next patrol, the submarine crews understood they would meet the same hazards, yet they departed on their next missions, anyhow. Submarine crews did their duties facing war dangers—understanding on eternal patrol they may sail."

As I studied him, I stared at him eye-to-eye and decided he's sincere. His eyes showed me he wanted to learn. "If you have the time, I'll tell you the Navy and the submarine's reality."

"All I have is time, today, I'm broke, and payday isn't until next week."

"There's a diner up the hill," I commented as I point up the road towards the hill overlooking the monument. "Let's walk to the diner, and I'll buy you a coffee. To inform you about submarines may take a while." Walking to the diner, I started my story. "That's a landmark;

I had many a breakfast and coffee when I was your age around fifty years ago. The diner looked old and changed little. Often, I stopped for breakfast after a night on the town or getting dinner before we started. That diner offers good coffee and food in abundance. A bar sits next to it; what's strange, after all this time, I never entered that bar. My Dad, during a visit, checked out the place. The men's room shocked him. He told me, 'The head looked old with peeling paint. It was dirty. And it stank with a stench smelling like an old outhouse.' He's convinced it was an outhouse. An old sailor's bar, that Bar is one."

As we enter the diner, I spot an empty booth next to the bar's side entrance. "Let's sit at that end booth." After we're sitting, the young man focused on listening to my every word, his eyes following my every single movement. Inspired with a purpose, I have a captive audience. The young sailor and I ordered coffee. Then our eyes locked, eye-to-eye, I have the youngster's interest and full attention.

"I'll tell you how actual submarine life is. Submarine life isn't for the fragile wimp. When you're a non-qual—you will meet unpleasant times that will tax your resolve. A submarine crew will test you in ways you have never considered possible, getting your attention, causing you frustration, driving you to quit, while motivating you to continue. A crew knows you're just out of subschool, untested, a threat to yourself and your boat, that you have lots to learn in minimal time. Crews recognize you don't have the knowledge to handle an emergency. And, if you do something wrong, it could contribute to something terrible— such as getting them killed. With the purpose, submarine crews include harassment as part of the qualification method of deciding if you fit into a submarine lifestyle. Harassment is that aspect, and in today's navy, a few uninformed seniors regard harassment as bullying—but qualification harassment isn't bullying. The qualification tradition tests you for submarine knowledge and suitability for subs. The method depends upon you to receive qualification harassment with dignity, but you must learn from the crews' guidance.

"On my first sub, I was comparable as you'll be at your first boat. Except I didn't have someone tell me about submarine life. My lack of submarine knowledge made me unprepared for submarine qualifying. For submarine qualification, you need to understand the boat's equipment, and know-how to operate the systems. Besides qualifying, you need to improve your skills and develop leadership. Study your leaders and gain for yourself the leadership skills your seniors follow. The seniors provided leadership methods that worked, and the same leadership methods work today. If you don't adapt and learn, you will go through a troublesome time—then you will either advance with struggle or fail.

"Don't make it grueling for yourself as I did when starting on subs. When I reported aboard the *Spikefish*, I brought with me an arrogance. By beginning with an abrasive haughtiness, I caused friction and strained the patience of the qualified crew. My brashness required recalibration to make me fit in with the crew. Often, petty officers and Chiefs squared away my dumb ass when I needed it—at first, I needed it a lot. To this day, I don't understand why I gained a know-it-all attitude. The COB set my course back on track; he was ingenious in stopping my insolence. As if it happened yesterday, I'll remember it forever, because my COB's methods were mind-altering. The COB made my life an excruciating experience when he captured my attention.

"For you, I must start from the beginning. Before I joined the Navy, I had a strong attraction to the sea. I didn't grasp why I had this craving, being a landlubber, living inland away from any sea exposure. What enticed me to the sea, I wondered? As a child, I knew my dad served in the Navy during World War II. After studying at my father's collection of war pictures and reading his issued *Bluejacket's Manual*, could that have given me interest? Might my enjoyment by reading sea stories and watching sea exploit movies planted my fascination with the sea?

"Possibly in a past life, I sailed the seas as a crewmember of a sailing ship. Aboard this ship, we navigated the sea-lanes of exploration, investigated exotic places, and experienced voyages full of adventures. The journeys provided contentment and excitement. We're going through the majesty of the open ocean when a strong wind drives the ship to record speed when the ship cruised under sail in perfect weather. Then, sailing through storms where howling winds and violent waves try to destroy, we experienced the dangers from angry seas. For me, all voyages were exhilarating.

"With passion, I read stories of tall-ships and fighting-ships. I studied the Clippers in the tea trade sailing to foreign locations. While building ship models from plastic kits as the famous Flying Cloud, I imagined the adventures, sailing around the Horn, and cruising across the Pacific. I envisioned two Clippers side-by-side racing under full sail. These tall ships are trying to break speed records. On the winner, I'm a crew member sailing on an exciting voyage. A youthful fascination could have directed me and set my course to the sea, leading me to the Navy. A passion for the sea made my Navy career start before I finished high school. No matter, my course is set, perhaps from purpose. More likely, Divine guidance allured me to the sea and provided an interest in everything to do with the oceans.

"No matter, a force higher than I drove me to the Navy and the sea, it resulted in a Navy career. On ships and submarines, I faced challenging seas and explored exotic places sensing enjoyment and facing danger. I experienced challenges with voyages full of rewarding adventures—but not without obstacles.

"I cherish the sailors, the seafarers, who served with me, who taught me, and who provided guidance and friendship. My duty performance gives me immense satisfaction for accomplishments far more than I could imagine when starting in the Navy—looking back, what I encountered during my Navy career amazes me.

"In high school, I took college preparation courses, but my academic performance lacked an achievement. By barely passing most classes, I showed limited scholastic ability. Too much time daydreaming about girls interfered with my attention to studies. Misused attention degraded my academic achievement. I misdirected skills, caused unproductive efforts, and failed to meet responsibilities. Lacking self-motivation, I produced obstacles essential to maturity development and academic success. When I left high school, I lacked the skills, wisdom, and inclination to overcome immaturity, and I had no plans or expectations for my future. I realized I could improve, but I don't understand how. Misdirected energy affected further college education—at first preventing it. Not grasping the value of education, my want of aim leads me to a Navy recruiter appointment versus filling out college applications.

"The Navy was a blessing, allowing me to work with the best men on the planet, enabling me to learn from them and develop into the man I became. I received more than the Navy promised—more than an adventure. I gained leadership skills along with the pride from accomplishments well done.

"My U.S. Navy career started at the Federal Building in Detroit, on June 30, 1961, as I stood with a large group of kids. Most of them completed high school that year, each of us in civilian clothes, lined in ranks, looking nothing resembling a military unit. Someone ordered us to attention, ordered us to raise our right hands, and an unknown officer gave us the oath of allegiance—swearing us into the U.S. Navy.

I stood standing straight and still as I could. I was nervous and proud of what I was doing, more pleased when I promised to defend the country and the Constitution from all enemies. Afterward, someone picked the largest new sailor there, his size is the only known qualification, 'You're in charge of this group. Deliver them to Great Lakes.' In this direction, a bus took us to a train station, where we boarded a train that brought us to Chicago, Illinois. From that moment on, my adventures, exploits, achievements, and antics allow me now to show happenings that provoked strong emotions, anger, fear, resentment, love, excitement, joy, and ecstasy. Looking back, I realize the Navy fulfilled their pledge—I lived through adventures, exploits, and escapades, yielding accounts, stories, and insights to tell you now.

"But first, let me inform you about the hierarchy of duty aboard Navy ships. The commanding officer, the CO, is a line officer in the actual command of a submarine or a surface vessel. COs have full responsibility for the ship and everyone aboard. The crew addresses the commanding officer as Captain, and they refer to the Commanding Officer as the CO, Skipper, or the Old Man. No one aboard would ever call the CO the Old Man when addressing him. The CO is senior to every staff officer assigned to his command. In my career, I observed submarine commanding officers exhibiting excellent skill and common sense.

"The COs achieved the best performance from their crews because they understood crew strengths, weaknesses, and needs, and using this knowledge, the COs took care of the crew's needs, strengthened the weak spots, and produced superior crew performance. The commanding officers understood when to enforce policies and rules, and when to tolerate undesirable minor behavior for letting off steam. This intellect provided a safety valve and reduced the stress of a mission deployment. In meeting assigned missions, the COs did their duty, sailing into harm's way to meet mission requirements.

"The Executive Officer, the XO, is next in rank to the CO and is senior to every other staff officer. The XO will assume CO duties if the CO becomes incapable of executing them. The Executive Officer answers to the commanding officer, but the crew receives the XO's orders as coming from the captain.

"On the Billfish, one of my XOs displayed terrific leadership ability. The XO could make junior officers, chiefs, and the junior enlisted crew follow his orders and achieve success by using a calm, spoken direction, without yelling or degrading subordinates. Magical was his ability. I always wondered how a leader, such as the XO, gained his leadership style and skill. After watching my XO, I wanted to acquire his leadership ability. To lead using his methods, I took an effort to follow his example, to control my actions, and to think before reacting when dealing with subordinates and others.

"On submarines, under the XOs are the officers that stand watches, including the Department Heads. Each department head leads their department and takes responsibility for everything concerning their department and its divisions. The departments [5] include the Navigation or Operations Officer. The Navigator, the NAV is the senior watch officer and is third in line after the CO and XO. The other Department heads are Weapons Officer, the Engineering Officer, and the Supply Officer. On submarines, each department head may have other duties.

"Under the department heads are divisions led by a junior officer or a chief as the division officer. For example, the Weapons Division Officer, the WEPS, may have over one division, the Torpedo, the FOX, the FT, the Sonar, and the Deck. On subs, the First Lieutenant has the deck division officer's responsibilities. The First Lieutenant is

---

[5] Not all departments and divisions are listed.

responsible for topside maintenance, weapon rigging, and loading and off-loading weapons. On the Billfish, I, too, held the position as the First Lieutenant. The weapon division officers answer to the WEPS in every matter regarding their division. Most officers on submarines and smaller crewed vessels besides having a Department or a Division Officer's responsibility are accountable for other collateral duties.

"Submarine officers are exceptional leaders who motivate, guide and listen to juniors. When it's reasonable, they use and give credit to a junior's contribution to solve an issue or produce task efficiency. Submarine officers make themselves accessible for juniors' needs from personal to qualification. When resolving problems, they displayed skill and ability. In keeping with the best naval traditions, officers supported the command, performed duties upholding the highest naval standards. The officers typically achieved outstanding results and took ownership of their successes and failures. I observed excellent performance from officers with whom served, verifying their exceptional leadership.

"Unique to submarines is the chief of the boat, called the COB, who accepts the senior enlisted rate on submarines with no direct equivalent in other services' E7, E8, or E9 ratings. The COB has exceptional authority with unique responsibilities that are not always defined but for all involved needed. The chief of the boat will carry out some situations respectfully, discreetly, and tactfully where the CO or his officers might find difficulty, like solving berthing issues for non-crew riders or getting a drunken crewmember out of jail without creating an embarrassment to the Boat or Navy.

"The COB is a direct link to the CO for crew issues, supporting the command he provides counsel, information, and recommendations and will use his influence on policy changes. For the enlisted and a few officers, the COB's word is the law. The COB guides junior officers frequently and provides direction as needed. A COB runs the boat, organizes the daily routine, takes care of day-to-day issues, originates the enlisted watch bill, supervises the crew's daily activities, and oversees the goat locker—the chiefs living in the chief's quarters. He resolves minor enlisted disciplinary problems without the report chit, used too often in the surface navy. The COB acts as a lawyer when needed to keep a crew member out of jail. While training the enlisted, he becomes an instructor that ensures qualification progress. The COB's involvement will free up the CO and his wardroom's time and effort so they may increase their focus on learning to fight the boat, respond to emergencies with most effectiveness, and attend to their other duties. When undefined predicaments occur, the COB resolves them.

"The COBs with whom I served were outstanding professional and competent leaders who dealt with various authority levels within and outside the command. They motivated the crew to support the command's commitments, always encouraging the crew through tough times while carrying out their duties. COBs were instinctive when providing crew guidance. With an admiration of their performance and abilities, I resolved to be a comparable leader, like my COBs, and inspire others as they had done.

"During WWII and beyond, the CO appointed his COB. In today's Navy, the COB position is a fixed submarine billet. On submarines, the COBs' standing became so useful the surface navy set up a similar title as the Command Chief—E7, E8, and E9 billets. Senior enlisted from the other services do comparable duties as a COB. These leaders apply the same leadership skills; their subordinates respect them the same—their contributions are valuable, but the distinction—the COB takes more undefined authority.

"During my last sea-duty, I was the COB on the USS Billfish (SSN 676), a nuclear-powered fast attack submarine—a high honor for an enlisted submariner, and a noble distinction serving as a submarine's COB. As a COB, I reported to the CO. When dealing with the chiefs, I upheld the opinion that if I must tell you what to do, then you are not doing your duty; only in a few incidences did I intervene in a chief's activities. The chiefs were outstanding self-motivating leaders.

"The U.S. Navy gives Navy Chiefs more responsibility than any other equivalent enlisted rating, E-7, E-8, and E-9 in the world's military, and that includes the U.S. military. In the Navy's history using Chief Petty Officers, the Navy Chiefs seize tasks and took responsibility before an assignment became required. When the officers saw what the chiefs were doing, they welcomed the help.

Over time, the chiefs took on more responsibility, performing tasks with excellent results, reducing the officer's burden, and freeing up his time. The officer discovered successful chiefs running their divisions or departments made the officer look good, helping the officer's advancement. Navy chiefs earned the reputation as being the expert in their rate, dependable in executing their duty, and supporting the command and the Navy. The chiefs take ownership of their responsibilities, oversee, train, and mentor their people. Chiefs make sure essential supplies, equipment, and tools are available, allowing their gang to carry out duties without interruption. Navy Chiefs produce superb performance and demand exceptional work from those they have direct responsibility.

"The Navy's enlisted petty officers are noteworthy. Petty officers will work tirelessly, making equipment or other assignments ready to support the ship's mission. Petty officers are accountable, taking ownership of their equipment and spaces. While doing their duties, they show pride, perseverance, and patience. On submarines, they take the extra effort teaching, guiding, and helping the non-qualified sailors who must learn complex systems found on submarines. Navy petty officers are quick to give a shipmate a hand. Without seniors compelling them, the petty officers are the driving force completing tasks—they get the job done. And more significantly, Navy petty officers make work a pleasure.

"At every level, a submarine crew is remarkable. With all the outstanding leadership guiding the new sailors, they develop skills, become motivated to do their best, and learn to do their duty. The new guys become valuable, useful shipmates.

"For sailors to encounter both submarine and surface ship experience is rare. Even though serving most time on subs, I saw firsthand the submarine's unique methods and traditions that differ from the surface Navy. Most surface ships have a larger crew size than found on submarines. The interaction between officers, chiefs, and junior enlisted is formal compared with the regular crew dealings found on submarines and the smaller crew sized ships.

"Surface Navy Officers, Chiefs, and petty officers are competent. The surface ship leaders expect everyone to do their duty. The senior officers, junior officers, Chiefs, and petty officers support the command and their seniors. With one exception, I never saw a junior giving pushback to his senior for an order of which he did not agree. This event is for another book. Nor did I ever witness any reprimand a senior officer gave to his junior. With good leadership, reprimands transpired privately. The crew respected and even revered the officers and Chiefs. Day-to-day conduct proved their ability, making most officers and Chiefs great role models.

"On two of the surface ships I served, I injected the submarine way of doing activities into the surface craft routines, but the commands and crew didn't embrace my views. When I implemented my ideas, they gave me trouble. The ones who didn't listen to my input used the established ineffective methods and found impediments that impaired their performance, making them look flawed to their seniors. That experience I'll tell you about later. The surface ship leaders, both officers and enlisted, taught me leadership skills I could apply in most settings. Then, I learned to figure out how to fit these skills into the submarines' informal atmosphere. I'm fortunate that my career includes surface ship experience—it was the same as getting a second major while working towards my focused degree. The surface ship experience was priceless.

"Now, let me tell you about submarine missions. Post-war through Cold-war and beyond submarine missions are vital, silent assignments that keep the nation secure. Crews can't divulge their mission's details—security prevents this. And because we lacked the need to know, crews didn't gain complete mission details. Without a mission insight, crews still did their duty. Submarine crews understood the entire mission's importance afterward when senior officers passed out medals and letters of commendation—someone higher up, Captain or Admiral, always knew mission importance.

"At mission start, after leaving port on patrol, the submarine set wartime conditions. The sub rigged for silent running and sailed in harm's way. Each mission had dull periods during fast transits drilling holes in the ocean. Then an order, 'All-stop.' The boat at zero speed for lengthy periods made the boat a bubble in the sea. On submarines, maintaining this condition for long periods causes tedium. Occasionally, vicious turbulence gave submarine crews severe discomfort. Or we had our routine interrupted with unsettling alarm, with heart-pounding drama, and gut-wrenching excitement when reacting to an undetermined threat. Submarines faced constant dangers from the unfriendly ocean, sea pressure at great depths, ship's equipment failure, and enemy discovery—any risk might cause mission failure and death. Westpac and Northern-Run missions added severe danger. Once, an adversary shot a torpedo toward us, and let us recognize we are not in a safe place.

"On submarine missions, the perils faced are telling, making operations exciting. The crew understood the missions' dangers and importance, so everyone did their duty, operating their boat. Submarine crews faced perils with traditional courage and professionalism, and their collective actions resulted in successful missions. Successful missions build pride from tasks well done and impart a sense of honor and ability. For example, on a Cold War mission near a foe's shores, the crew's boldness, 'The enemy should surrender now because we have their ships and subs hemmed in—our boat is ready to take on the entire opponent's Navy.' More boast than reality, but we had confidence for success, including the expectation to return home. For sailors, your duty was to your country, family, and shipmates. Everyone aboard knew our boat missions were to protect the nation. The most significant contribution we achieved was to serve in the US Navy on submarines knowing our country was safer on our watch.

"On one mission, an example, of a CO showing great ability, occurred as I watched my CO's action after Sonar reported—giving the alarm, '**Torpedo in the water**....' Torpedo in the water alerted everyone in Control. The torpedo filled the depths with noise. Sonar reports to Control, 'torpedo.... zero bearing rate.' For us, a threatening situation—a moment of concern. The zero bearing rate means the torpedo is attacking our boat. In Control, we realized that if the torpedo hit us, no one will survive. The Captain took Conn and ordered a course and speed change, 'Flank Speed... Maneuvering Conn cavitate.' Everyone's performance in Control and Sonar showed a sense of determination to do their jobs—alertness never better, attention given to every detail, and no unnecessary chatter—no panic. After evasive maneuvering, the torpedo bearing rate changed. The boat is outrunning the torpedo, then the order, '**All-Stop**!' As the boat slowed, the Captain instructed Sonar to listen for signs of detection. Then, we discovered we weren't the torpedo's target and weren't detected—the foes were conducting other affairs.

"With the satisfaction by outrunning the torpedo, I felt relief, then a moment of, **Holy shit!** When the Captain ordered a course change and increased speed back towards the torpedo-firing submarine. **Honor replaced the alarm** by taking the boat back into harm's way. That day, the commanding officer resembled the aggressive COs in WWII, who attacked the enemy versus running away from them. Everyone in Control understood if the submarine firing the attacking torpedo realized we were there, the foe would attack us, and our ability to come home might be remote—a real threat. The CO's ability controlled the condition and brought the boat back into a suitable position. The Captain's actions showed the aggressive nature desired for submarine commanding officers and the skill to succeed. The CO created crew confidence, pride in doing our duty, and inspired professionalism.

"The boat investigated the other activities and studied the subs firing their torpedoes, trying to discover what they were doing and why they were doing it. During this event, the crew's performance was outstanding. The Tracking party, Sonar, Maneuvering, and Ship Control Parties demonstrated how well the Commanding Officer had trained them. A confident and determined crew performed their duties without panic or nervousness. Observing the crew in action, I considered that it was comparable to watching a well-oiled mechanical clock, each part working in perfect precision. The boat met mission requirements and brought back something worthwhile. The successful mission gave the crew pride displayed on their faces at the mission's end. It's an honor to **distinguish outstanding leaders as our CO, and a privilege to be a member of his crew.**"

The young sailor's attentive expression revealed that I have a captive audience. So far, I told you a little about myself and not about submarine life, but you needed that submarine information. Now you're ready to learn about submarine life and how it will affect you. As I told my sea stories, revealing my saga to this young sailor, well, it took days. As done many times before, I continued recounting the following sea stories with, "This ain't no shit."

BOOT CAMP

Recruit Training Command, Great Lakes, Illinois
June 1961 to October 1961

The Navy Hymn[6]

1. E-ter-nal Father! Strong to save, Whose arm doth blind the rest-less wave, Who bid'st the might-y o-cean deep Its own ap-point-ed lim-its keep; O hear us when we cry to Thee For those in per-il on the sea.

2. O Sav-iour, Whose al-might-y word The winds and waves sub-mis-sive heard Who walk-edst on the foam-ing deep, And calm a-mid the storm didst sleep; O hear us when we cry to Thee For those in per-il on the sea.

---

[6] 370, Eternal Father! Strong to Save, William Whiting 1860, 1869, The Parish School Hymnal, no Publisher or date of publishing listed. Most likely my grandparents used the hymnal during service at Nativity English Lutheran Church, Cor. Philip and Frankfort Aves., Detroit, Michigan. Many other versions exist, see official Navy' web site. The version that I heard sung in Boot Camp is unknown to me.

3. O ho-ly Spir-it, Who didst brood Up-on the wa-ters dark and rude, Who bid'st their an-gry tu-mult cease, And give, for wild con-fus-ion, peace; O hear us when we cry to Thee For those in per-il on the sea.

4. O Trin-i-ty of Love and Power! Our breth-ren shield in dan-ger's hour; From rock and tem-pest, fire and foe, Pro-tect them where-so-e'er they go; And ev-er let there rise to Thee Glad Hymns of praise from land and sea. A-MEN

Seaman Apprentice Gary A. Goeschel
His Boot Camp picture

BOOT CAMP

After high school, I realized I must improve and do something worthy of my life, with a purpose that's relevant and better than what's available in Michigan. To accomplish advancement, I must add value to my life. Yet, I didn't understand how to gain a positive direction to develop into something noble. So far, I'm unaware of my potential, yet my destiny seemed predetermined. With no way to control my aim's call, alongside my unawareness of planned goals, occurring as if a higher power prepared my fate for me, I sensed I might be part of making history. It appeared my future was laid out for me in the Navy because Devine intervention planned my life. Then, as a Seaman Recruit without a course direction, Navy Boot Camp started my voyage, which turned into a naval career.

When I entered the Navy, I had much to learn. A recruit doesn't start as a Chief or a submarine's COB because he's not qualified for these positions—a sailor must learn the profession, the leadership skills, and then earn the titles. After I left Boot Camp as a Seaman Apprentice, it took time to gain the knowledge. As a beginning seaman with inexperience, I held incredible responsibility. Akin to most sailors, I started young, worked twenty-four hours a day, seven-days-a-week, while having an awesome responsibility for such inexperience and pitiful wages. The knowledge gained in these early years developed my professional skills and leadership methods that made my achievements possible. The Navy's history and working with war heroes influenced my thinking and affected my every undertaking throughout my naval career. Over time, I became skilled at the Chief's position, and with more time, acquired the wisdom to be effective as a COB.

Boot Camp experience didn't provide anything significant beyond bare basic training. I had no earth-shattering, life-threatening, or meaningful revelatory experiences. Boot Camp was what I expected, no more—no less. Boot Camp training provided what sailors needed to be useful in the fleet and to keep sailors alive when threatened. When I look back, I realize my Boot Camp transformation continued throughout my career—I never stopped learning.

Boot Camp started the change of an immature, self-absorbed young man into a responsible, productive leader I became. Boot Camp taught sailors the basics of military life and skills which have a direct use for a young sailor. Boots learned the Navy's lingo, bathrooms are heads, beds are bunks, floors are decks, stairs are ladders, walls are bulkheads, and underwear is skivvies. Boots learned that moving about a ship is regulated. Aboard ships, to prevent traffic blockages during an emergency, sailors go forward on the starboard side and travel up the starboard side ladders. Sailors move aft on the port side and travel down on the port side ladders. This movement allows reaching battle and damage control stations without delays—no traffic jams.

The Navy jargon was also different. Juniors directly referred to a ship's Commanding Officer as "Captain," informally as the CO, the Old Man, or skipper. Seniors cautioned enlisted never directly calls the CO, "Old Man." In like manner, sailors denoted the Executive Officer as XO, the engineer as ENG, the Navigator as the NAV, and the corpsman or doctor as DOC. Boot Camp taught the change of command, military etiquette, proper wearing of the uniform, basic seamanship, firefighting, and damage control. Boots learned nonessential nonsense that becomes an inside joke—if it moves, you salute it if it doesn't you paint it. But most of all, we learned to follow orders.

A lot of yelling started my first day at Boot Camp. Petty officers yelled at us to start everything we did. Added to the noise of reveille's bugle call over loudspeakers was the wakeup yell, "**drop your cocks and grab your socks!**" Followed by Petty officers yelling to get us to hurry up so we can wait to get breakfast, lunch, and dinner. Before we did anything else, seniors yelled at us to make us hurry up to wait to stand in line to get our uniforms to get our first haircut. Every Boot received the same style. The barbers cut our hair so short the fuzz on a tennis-ball was longer. In a rush, we waited again standing in line for our short-arm inspection. After Doctors and Corpsman inspected every opening on our bodies, we lost all modesty.

One joy of Boot Camp was being yelled at while waiting in line to get our first series of vaccination shots. I received many. One vaccination shots caused my arm to swell up to the size of my thigh, scaring the hell out of me. The sickness made me nervous and uncertain of my condition, speculating on the worst. Then a doctor explained I contracted cowpox on my arm. The doctor told me that cowpox was a temporary setback, and it wouldn't hurt me because cowpox was treatable. Treatment would only take three days, and just to make sure he would cure me, the doc kept me in sickbay for a week. The group I started with went on without me. Reassigned to Company 289, a boot company just formed, I recognized none of the other boot sailors in Company 289, adding another challenge.

For me, a high school football player and wrestler, the physical demands of Boot Camp were effortless. I left Boot Camp in worse physical condition than when I arrived. Also, I left Boot Camp with ten fewer teeth than when I started. Inadequate dental care growing up damaged my teeth beyond repair. On my Boot Camp's third day, in one hour, a dentist pulled them all out in one sitting. Afterward, I took one week with two wads of gauze stuffed into my mouth, to control the subsequent bleeding. In that week, I frustrated every Chief and Petty Officer trying to calibrate me or get a response from me. When I responded to queries, I provided muffled noises. Then I pointed to my mouth and exposed the bloody wad. The senior's response gave me the impression they were confused about what to do. How to deal with a youngster with a mouthful of blood wasn't in their boot training. After a senior's first question, then getting my response, they didn't bother me further. The bloody wad didn't bother me any, and I enjoyed missing a week's worth of yelling back at instructors, trying to answer silly questions, while they struggled to make a sailor out of me.

One boot event got me thinking. As I look back, a minor occurrence turned into a turning point in my life. This event seemed more like a Divine intervention using a magical moment. Thinking about it guided me to question my values. The occurrence shook up my firm beliefs and then established new principles. For reasons unknown then, the incident touched and improved me.

On the day of this event, every boot company stood in the drill hall—one of the most massive buildings I had ever seen. Don't ask why we waited there; I don't know. I experienced what I saw and perceived. Each boot company, in ranks, lined up in military precision. Guessed we stood there for an award ceremony, but it might be other reasons. There were speakers, but I don't remember who they were, or the topics they spoke; I couldn't understand what they said. I remember feeling uncomfortable from standing in ranks for an extended period. My mind wandered.

Then, the band played with a lone sailor singing the Navy Hymn to the two-thousand sailors in the drill hall. The first note awakened me and caught my attention. For me, the lone sailor sings as if I'm the only one listening. The song inspired. I never heard anyone sing the Navy Hymn so beautifully. The sailor sung lyrics of worship—a prayer—my prayer. The hymn touched me. Hymn verses, sustained by inspired music, made me realize, for the first time, that in serving my country, I may have to put my life in danger and go in harm's way. The Navy Hymn heard at that moment awakened my first awareness of what being in the U. S. Navy meant: defending the country against all its enemies, both present and future.

With the hymn, I prayed, praying for the safety of all sailors at sea in harm's way. With the song, I prayed that I would never let down my country. The hymn's consoling sounds of music were carrying my prayers.

Then I focused on the singer, whose voice like an angel touched me. Across the Drill Hall, he stood too far for me to make out his features. I can see he's a black sailor. At that moment, I realized that at a later time, I might have to rely on him, or other black sailors, or sailors of a different race to keep my country free, keep me safe, as they would have to depend on me. As they count on me to keep them alive, I must trust them to do the same. I watched the other sailors in my company, not knowing much about them. Sailors in ranks are swaying with the music showing reverence, listening to the Navy Hymn, they weren't aware of my inspection or their movement. I observed sailors in other companies. Sailors who stood Black, Asian, Hispanic and White, listened to the Navy Hymn, just like me. I thought these are all my shipmates.

Throughout my schooling, I only knew one black person who played on the high school football team with me. He was a good team player, but I understood nothing else about him. As a self-absorbed teen, I only grasped a little about the racial riots in Detroit. The news reported people were rioting and burning homes. The press reported rioters shooting at firefighters trying to save burning homes. My father was a fireman, and he's angry because rioters were shooting emergency responders. My dad didn't understand why. As a fireman, he's dedicated to protecting those houses and the people who lived in them. Dad would save all lives, no matter who they were. As a family, we listened and watched the news reporting on the riots. We can't grasp the rioting's violence. The family remained uninformed about the rioters. We couldn't comprehend what the protesters were trying to achieve. For me, the rioting seemed wrong and counterproductive in fixing anything.

While standing in the drill hall, I thought about what I understood about black people or any other race, and I realized much remained missing. Everyone in the drill hall swore an oath to defend this country, making them my shipmates. As the hymn continued, I grasped to wear the uniform; you can't be prejudiced. At first, I don't understand why I had those deep thoughts as I listened to the singing of the Navy Hymn. Later, I realized that influential happening, listening to the Navy Hymn, opened my mind and heart to deep beliefs. My thoughts provided a change in my thinking that served me throughout my Navy career and beyond.

For skills excellence, Boot Companies competed against each other. For each skill category, a competition flag represented the skill. The types are academics, marksmanship, seamanship, athletics, marching, firefighting, and others. There were so many flags, I couldn't identify them all. The skills in which we didn't compete were farting and bullshitting. The Recruit Training Command awarded a competition flag to the Boot Company that excelled in an ability.

Company 289 received only one competition-flag, the Battalion "I" Flag that had a big powder blue "I" on a white background. The "I"

Flag showed we excelled over the other companies in academics. At its head at graduation, Company 289 carried only this award flag. Other companies had many flags. As the company marched in front of the commanding officer's reviewing stand during graduation review, the flags made a colorful display.

At boot camp graduation, the commanding officer presented me with a letter of commendation for receiving the highest academic average score in my boot company. The letter of commendation became my first at-a-boy[7]. The document showed my ability to excel in performance. For me, the boot camp lessons were easy to understand. The officers made a big deal about my letter of commendation, but I didn't consider it remarkable. This achievement opened doors of opportunity. But, I didn't capitalize on the accolade or realize its value. For example, the Navy's prep-school for Annapolis was available. But, I lacked the confidence to seize the opportunity. But if I had, my Navy career would have been different.

When I left Boot Camp, I had a life course in a positive direction. As I traveled home from boot camp to start a two-week leave, I reflected on my future. I sensed I would do great things. But first, I must learn how. Orders out of Boot Camp sent me to FT[8] "A" School—one of the most advanced technical schools the Navy offered. Because my high school scholastic achievements remained nothing to boast about, I wondered if I was ready for "A" School? I worried.

---

[7] "At-a-boy" is slang for praise—note, one ah-shit that is slang for a screw-up wipes out ten at-a-boys.

[8] FT is short for Fire Control Technician

FTA SCHOOL

Fire Control Technician 'A' School, Naval School
Command, Bainbridge, Maryland
October 1961—April 1962

THE TEDDY BEAR

FT 'A' School was an experience. The old, antiquated, and old-fashioned student living and class conditions met modern technology. During hot summer days, classroom air conditioning is achieved by opening windows and using large, noisy fans. In cold winter days, we opened windows to control too warm classrooms. Senior Fire Control instructors taught innovative technology in old-fashioned schoolrooms, using conventional teaching methods—lectures, paper handouts, blackboards, and white chalk. Weekly testing monitored learning progress.

The students' unsafe living environment requires being made known. FT students lived in marginal conditions; the modern world will not allow in any school environment. The barracks were fire traps. As an inexperienced seaman, I liked my new residence. The barracks were more comfortable compared to the Boot Camp barracks, so I didn't allow the dangers the barracks held bother me.

The barracks were similar in size and layout to the Boot Camp Great Lakes barracks that were wooden framed with open barn-like dorms. Boot Company 289 occupied one of the old barracks for two weeks. I joined them, residing in the old barracks. It was depressing entering the barracks. The building showed aging with signs of neglect, peeling paint, siding that required repair, and a few faucets and toilets not working. The barracks dorm wings were exposed spaces with rows of bunk beds lined up against the long walls with a window between the bunks—no privacy possible. We kept it clean. When we mopped the decks, it was like mopping a dirt floor. It was hard to tell the difference between a dirty floor or the worn vinyl deck covering. Later, we moved into a sizable new building to complete boot training. A luxury living condition compared to the old barracks.

For fire fighting training, the Navy lit one of the Boot Camp barracks on fire. From fire start, it took only minutes until the building engulfed in flames and less than that to disintegrate it into a mass of burning timbers. The seniors acted as the barracks were fire death traps. Recognized as a fire trap, in Boot Camp, and at FT school, we had many fire drills.

Still, a fire trap, however, the FT School at Bainbridge kept the barracks in a better condition than found in Great Lakes. The school command updated the buildings and kept them useful. Fresh paint made them look like new buildings. Clapboard siding painted white was the building's face. The barracks are old buildings built possibly earlier than the WWII military buildups. A long narrow two-story building had its main entrance at its center, with two dorm wings attached at each side. The center area held the quarter-deck, head, showers, and utility closets.

In the FT barrack dorms, the FTs arranged bunks and lockers to make four-man cubicles. Each occupant had a large stand-up locker and a smaller locker. The stand-up cabinets created walls to form four-man cubicles and provided a degree of privacy. Because of the proximity of living close, friendships formed as FTs worked, studied, and learned to help one another.

Not knowing any better, I embraced the experience of the FT School's daily routine. Reveille 0500, FT students wake up, rush to the head, shit, shower, and shave. Students hurry back to our cubes to dress, stow shaving gear, clothes, and books leaving nothing adrift. Before breakfast, we make up our racks—boot camp style. Assigned junior students scrub the heads, cleaning everything, the toilets, and stalls, the shower room walls, and decks. With a fast polish, they make the sinks and mirrors shine as new. Senior students rush to swab the decks, spread a coat of wax to old wood flooring. Buffers go over the floor, polishing the wax until a deep black-brown shine radiates from the deck. In stocking feet, we hasten to finish getting ready for the day's activities, stepping across the shining floor—shoes leave unacceptable marks. School leaders allowed no scars on the deck floor.

When inspection ready, everyone rushes outside the barracks to fall into ranks. The duty night instructor performs the morning barracks inspection. After his inspection, the instructor orders the FT 'A' school students lined outside each barracks to march to the chow hall. As soon as we hear the order, "Forward March," our drum corps of four to six drummers drums a marching rhythm. FT 'A' school is the only school command at Bainbridge that required their students march. We march to the mess decks for breakfast. At the front of the group, senior students eat first. Everyone chows down, eating fast. After breakfast, the FTs reassemble in ranks. With the drumming marching beat, we add sounds of cadence as loud as possible as we pass the base administration building. At 0700, we arrive at the school, a newer brick building compared to our barracks. In ranks, the instructors hold a muster, followed by the School's leading chief giving us praise, approving how we disturbed the administrators as we marched pass by their building.

The Chief's praise, "You produced too much noise for their delicate ears—good job. The same candy-ass administrators complained every morning about your commotion—keep it up." I guessed he likes how we upset them. Perhaps he believes by waking them; they will improve in performing their duties. Nevertheless, we took pride in showing the base "proper military marching." FTs displayed big smiles as we marched with pride through the base exhibiting proper military marching. At 1130, students fall in ranks and march to the chow hall for lunch, making more noise than we achieved during breakfast. At 1630, we march back to the barracks. For the evening meal, the FTs don't march to the chow hall.

Bainbridge was a training command that included the FT 'A' School, Radiomen 'A' School, the Prep School for Annapolis, and the Waves Boot Camp. The Waves Boot Camp was for new female sailors. As another base within a base, the Wave's boot camp was apart from the rest of the schools. The base command allowed no interaction with the waves. The boot waves only get one liberty day towards the end of their training. At Bainbridge, the FT students believe we're special, enjoying overnight liberty when we wished. The other schools have Cinderella Liberty during the week, demanding student liberty ends at midnight.

On the base, there was one club for students, Fiddler on the Green was its name. The club sold 3.2 beer with low alcohol content. Sailors under 21 could get this beer by the glass or pitcher. I never understood the reason for three-two-beer; drunkenness happened when sailors drink too much alcohol. Sailors became drunk no matter if they drank too much regular beer or three-two-beer. The distinction was sailors had to consume three-two-beer in higher quantities to become intoxicated. Many a night, my friends and I laughed and sung as we staggered back to our barracks. Drunks produced loud noises that woke up the sailors and Marines in the Annapolis prep-school barracks across from ours. This lead to clashes as the future officers tried to quiet us from making too much noise and interrupting their sleep. These sailors and Marines were preparing for Annapolis, so they were earnest regarding their studies and understood they needed sleep. Knowing we were getting to them when returning from the Fiddler on the Green, we liked to rattle their chains when we could—not recognizing what the prep-school students were experiencing and that they could be our bosses one day.

FT "A" School was not all study; during the Christmas holidays, the school shut down, allowing students to take leave to visit families and loved ones. Most of us took full benefit of this season, leaving Bainbridge as soon as possible before someone changed their mind and gave us other important work. I was able to take two weeks leave over the holiday.

My friends and I planned our getaway. Lacking funds, I explained that I planned to thumb it to Detroit. One of my classmates invited me to stay with him at his parent's home in Cleveland, Ohio, on my path to Michigan. The stopover will break up my trip and give me a safe, warm mooring for one night on my journey. He was getting a bus ride home and predicted that he could meet me at his home. My friend assumed that his bus trip is quicker than my hitchhiking. He suggested we'll make a night of it, and his parents will not mind my staying with him. The stopover made sense; I agreed and accepted his invitation.

Before I started on this trip, you need to know the history that leads to its result. Before I joined the Navy, my Uncle Cal gave me a high school graduation party. That night, Cal told me, "Your mom gave birth to a baby boy; you have a new brother." That was the reason she wasn't at the party. It sunk in, I now have a new infant brother, Jimmy. Now, I'm in the Navy, expecting leave over the Christmas holiday season, and looking forward to seeing my brother for the first time. With no idea of what he or my mother needed, I realized enough to get a Christmas gift for baby Jimmy.

In the Navy exchange, I spotted an assortment of teddy bears—a teddy bear was the gift to get. For the perfect gift for Jimmy, I selected the biggest teddy bear displayed. Then, I lugged it to the barracks. While packing for leave, I realized that I didn't think this decision through. The teddy bear was half the size of my full seabag—no room for it in my seabag. I didn't see how I will get my seabag, the gigantic teddy bear, and myself from Bainbridge, Maryland, to Mt. Clemens, Michigan. Only one solution worked, I carried my seabag over my shoulder holding the bag's strap with one arm and carried the teddy bear in my other arm.

My friends were in the same boat, lacking funds for commercial transportation. We planned to hitchhike to our destinations. Together we gathered with those heading in shared directions, North, South, and West. With so much baggage, I had trouble just getting off the base. It was difficult keeping up with the westward traveling group, Charley heading towards Chicago, Bob towards western Pennsylvania, Ben heading to Ohio, and I towards Michigan. We were lucky, one instructor, seeing our problem, took us to a Pennsylvania Turnpike entrance. On the Turnpike, hitchhiking was illegal. He dropped us off where we had a long walk to the pike entrance.

I sensed a problem, throngs of troops stood in clusters at the pike's entry. Uniforms represented each military establishment Marines, Army, Air Force, Coast Guard, and Navy. Military travelers with seabags or other luggage lined up along the Turnpike entrance. Troops made a line of young military contenders a half-mile long. All are looking for a quick ride. With so many hitchhiking, I wondered how long it would take me to get a ride, as we made the line longer when we joined them. As we approached a spot along the road, looking at the competition for the rides, I thought I might never get home for Christmas, guessing that just getting a ride will take too long.

Then a Christmas miracle happened. As soon as I stopped, standing along the curb, wishing I made a sign showing my destination. I faced oncoming traffic heading towards the Pennsylvania Turnpike. Towards the entrance, over one hundred other sailors in uniform strung out in a long line. The sailors needed and waited for a ride to start their journey. More sailors arrive after me. Towards the end of the line, I stood thinking, this is the worst location for a quick pick up, with worry, imagining this will be a long night. An approaching car slows, driving past dozens of hopeful sailors and stopped next to me. Welcome words, "Need a ride? Get in." Followed with a question, "Where are you headed?"

"Cleveland."

"I can't take you there, but I'll get as close as I can, and it will have better prospects for connections to your destination." The driver responded. In the car, we drive off. I'm lucky and astonished by being picked up so quickly. As we drive past the military travelers who were waiting before me, I felt sorry for them. Spoiling my holiday enjoyment, I felt guilty as if I cut in line. But I had no control over who picked me up. Then the driver drills me with questions regarding the teddy bear. During the ride, I explain why I'm carrying a Teddy Bear. My driver takes me along the Turnpike, passing two exits. On the third exit, he drives around and drops me off at the pike's western direction entrance, expressing, "You should be able to continue your journey from here without trouble."

After I got my stuff out of his car, I thank him, "Thanks for the ride, it helps, Merry Christmas."

"Don't thank me, I'm thanking you for your service, you will be the one defending this country, good luck, and Merry Christmas." Then he drove away.

At this stop, I find myself with an even bigger crowd. Each military establishment represented more Navy, Marines, Army, Air Force, and even Coast Guard. Uncountable different military men made an impressive sight. I'm thinking, getting a ride here today may be impossible, and it won't happen soon. As soon as I had this thought before I could put down my seabag, a car pulls up next to me. Two ladies were in the car, the passenger rolling down her window asks, "Where are you going, sailor?"

"I'm heading for Detroit, but going to Cleveland first."

"We're not going that far, but we'll get you close. That should help you. Hop in."

"Thanks, I reply as I stuff my seabag and the teddy bear into the backseat. Felt like I cut in line again.

The welcome words "Hop in" again followed with teddy bear questions. This conversation repeated three times with the last driver taking me from the Pike's exit to my friend's home.

I arrived at my friend's home four hours before him. He took the bus, but I thumbed it, making my travel success a marvel. In his absence, his parents provided a warm welcome, treating me with hospitality as if I was part of their family, an excellent hot meal, and a wonderful welcome to someone they have met for the first time. His parent's friendliness and hospitality implanted in my mind a fondness for the people of Ohio that continues today, I always enjoy going through Ohio. On many of my trips through that state, I interacted with friendly people. Later that night, my friend arrived. We had little time to celebrate. A warm bed to sleep replaced partying. The following morning, his parents took me to the turnpike entrance, where I restarted my journey. As soon as my seabag, teddy bear, and I are out of the car, someone drove up and invited me for my next ride. I had seconds to say thanks to his parents.

In Michigan, I met baby Jimmy for the first time. The Teddy Bear was bigger than him and scared him at first. Later the Teddy Bear and Jimmy became best of friends. The holiday with the family was a welcomed pleasure. I was amazed at how quickly I made the trip. To the discomfort of my friends, I couldn't stop bragging about my quick trip home.

Afterward, I figured out why my travel was faster than a bus ride— it was the Teddy Bear, but was it? The Teddy Bear gave me the benefit of traveling fast. But I had a quick trip when I returned to Bainbridge— without the Teddy Bear. The rides were available. My friends expressed that they had short waits before someone picked them up, heading home, or coming back—a good experience for them.

Years later, I haven't forgotten about the Teddy Bear trip. Every time I remember how everyone treated me so kindly gets me thinking. I cannot explain why, but when thinking about this trip, I awaken feelings about the Vietnam war. The Teddy Bear trip took place before the Vietnam War. There is no apparent connection between my Christmas trip and the war. The link that makes me remember my feelings about the war was the contrast of how I was treated early in my career compared to how the public treated our military during the Vietnam conflict. The public actions and demonstrations against the military upset me when it happened. I felt so strongly about doing your duty by serving your country. My shipmates and I weren't prepared or trained on how to respond when public elements turn against you when you're doing your duty. I rode a submarine during the Vietnam War. My brother and cousins fought in Vietnam. They came home scarred from battle, seeing things one should not see and doing violence one usually would never do—the war's hell. My family was blessed; other families' loved ones were missing in action, didn't come back alive, or came home broken.

POLISHING EVERY SPITTOON

After retiring from the Navy, I worked for Lockheed Martin in Manassas, Virginia. While working for Lockheed Martin, an opportunity allowed my wife and me to meet up with my last Navy boss, Floyd Crisp[9], and his wife, Cine. Floyd was one of the most impressive and intelligent officers I know. Floyd had a common-sense of judgment and wisdom, dealing with people issues. Cine is just a delightful woman who makes you consider you're more than welcome. She always projected the sincere impression that she enjoys your company. Both made conversation pleasant, our debates respectful, and topics discussed fascinating.

We met at a local eatery. Restaurant reviews reported that it served large quantities of excellent food. The restaurant sports atmosphere made it an enjoyable place. The restaurant displayed giant TV screens that hung like paintings in an art studio. The screens showed current sports events or sports reruns. Our evening started as a special meeting with friends. We caught up after years of separation, talking about our families, and describing our current endeavors. Conversation leads to potential future work for me with Floyd's engineering company, Group 81. Floyd started Group 81 after his Navy retirement as a Chief Warrant Officer.

The evening service started enjoyably. We had drinks, ordered appetizers, wine, and the main course. The appetizers arrived, looking

---

[9] Floyd Crisp has passed, he is no longer with us.

delicious. While eating our appetizers, the server delivered our main course, overcrowding the table, and spoiled the moment. Irritated, I express my displeasure regarding the unsatisfactory service, but Floyd responded, "This happens in restaurants a lot. It's the management's way of trying to rush customers to finish. It will work out."

"I never had this happen before. We should send it back and tell the manager." Annoyed, I replied.

Floyd responded as if he had experienced this happening many times, "Don't sweat it. It will work out, you'll see." While continuing our conversation, the rude service was a nagging irritation as a splinter in a finger; one cannot get out.

During our spirited conversation, we discovered that Floyd and I went to Fire Control Technician A-School at Bainbridge, Maryland, but Floyd was in A-School two years before me. While we worked together, we didn't discover this knowledge. For Janet's and Cine's sake, Floyd and I explained that FT A-School was our first school after boot camp. FT A-School taught advanced technology in subject blocks: basic electricity, basic electronics, synchros, servo control circuits, weapon ballistics, fire control radar, and a Gun Fire Control Computer. The computer was an electromechanical analog computer at the time the computer was high tech. The discovery of our mutual beginnings led me to tell Floyd and Cine my experience of how I ended up polishing every spittoon in the school's classrooms.

As I started my story, I mentioned that I started as a good student with an average of eighty-five percent for the first seven weeks. In the eighth week, I barely passed the weekly test, and in the ninth week, I failed my first test. This excellent performance led to a visit with the lead instructor, an older chief. The chief's reputation was taking a keen interest in every student. The chief's duty was to make sure every student gets thorough knowledge from his school experience. A real dedicated, sharp individual the instructor was.

During our first day's indoctrination, the lead instructor warned, "You must study hard in this school." The chief exclaimed, "If you fail, you'll see me. Trust me; you won't enjoy what happens." Then the lead instructor boasts, "I've heard all the student's excuses for their failures. My daughter's gerbil escaped, and we spent all night looking for it... I was sick for the past three days and couldn't study... My wife, she... My girlfriend's parents showed up unexpectedly... For FT students, what we teach will be hard for a few of you. When you're having problems, you get help. Everyone must study hard, and there will be no excuses for failure."

When I didn't meet expectations, the lead instructor displayed offense, letting me know I'm in trouble. The meeting was a typical chief motivating a junior, except the old chief, assumed he discovered all the excuses, but he didn't get what he expected—the chief wasn't ready for me.

The chief, looking stern, with angry eyes peering into mine, growled "What in the hell is going on with you? You started okay, but the last two weeks are unacceptable. Is something bothering you?"

"Nothing is bothering me."

"Then, why did you fail the last week's test?"

"I didn't study."

The chief sat back, his eyes opened wide, with a facial expression of astonishment. The lead instructor seemed unprepared for my honesty, looking flustered, losing eye contact, his eyes searched his desk, and with an annoyed face finding no help. Then, he recovered as his eyes engaged mine with a steady glare. The chief's attitude showing an angry look worried me. The chief didn't say a word as he studied me. Livid eyes examined me for less than ten minutes, but it seemed like four hours as if eyes were reading my mind. As I stared back, I felt apprehension.

With a deep voice of authority, the chief responded, "You didn't study? You must study hard to get through in this school; didn't you get that message on your first day's indoctrination?"

"Yes, I did."

"Then, why are you telling me you didn't study? Your admission is direct disobedience to a direct order. You are in deep trouble, young man."

"I didn't think about that," I replied as I worried. I'm in more trouble than I expected.

"We'll see you get your studying done. I am assigning you to night-study for the rest of this block. After the evening meal, you muster in with the duty instructor every night at 1800 and study the assigned curriculum until 2000. Do you understand me? You be there and study hard. If you need help, the night instructors are available to help you. There're no excuses for your failure."

Because the punishment wasn't as harsh as I expected, I felt relieved, "That sounds great, but Chief, I made no excuses for my failing my last test." Silly me, I had to remind the Chief that I had made no excuses while responding, and I appeared happy about it.

At once, the Chief looked even angrier. Eyes are scowling, his face bright red, he bellowed, "Stupid-study doesn't bother you at all, does it?"

"No, it's fair. Stupid-study is for me." As I grinned back, responding—another mistake on my part.

The Chief alternated between looking bewildered and frustrated as he glared at me, showing he was struggling to contain building rage. "I'll tell you what; you now have stupid-study for the rest of A School! Got it?"

"Okay, that is fine for me," I said, still grinning.

A stern voice replied, "I don't see what in hell you consider is so damn funny about this. For you, it's serious. If you don't improve your grades, if you fail one more class, I will see you shipped out to the fleet with no further training. In that case, you'll be a deck ape assigned to a deck-gang, cleaning up shit, chipping paint, and repainting—a never-ending job. The cruiser Boston is getting ready for a round-the-world cruise. Her deck gangs would love to get a shithead like you to keep her clean and beautiful. Now get your dumb-ass out of my sight before I change my mind and send you to sea."

After that meeting, I realized I didn't reason my punishment through—Stupid-study results in missing the evening movie that starts at 1900. Now the penalty bothered me. Knowing I could improve my grades after I finished this block, the rest of the school seemed appealing. I was looking forward to that instruction.

When a sailor is in a school greater than thirty-two weeks, as time goes by, he attains knowledge on how to get out of doing tasks he doesn't want. Likewise, he learns how to avoid unpleasant rules and getting caught when he bends the rules. Instructors get to know him and can recognize him in a group. Instructors will grasp if he is sincere or not, if he's fooling around, or if he is performing up to his potential. In my case, after twenty weeks in the school, the instructors knew me; several even liked me. Most instructors put in extra time and effort to help me, and they understood I had a permanent assignment to stupid-study—a condition that caught up with me.

After attending Stupid-study for a few weeks and getting my grades up, I discovered I could muster in at 1800, let the night instructors see I'm around, study for an hour, and then at 1900, sneak to the movie hall and watch the evening movie. For weeks, I snuck out until a night instructor caught me.

On Tuesday evening during week twenty-four, the night instructor made the check-up rounds after the 1900 muster. Was he more dedicated and responsible than other instructors? Perhaps, other school instructors are proficient, but most instructors were unaware that students might skip out of stupid-study. No matter, the night instructor realized I should be in the building, and he didn't see me in his second check. As he searched for me, he walked from classroom to classroom, asking all students spotted if anyone saw me, getting the same response, "Seen him earlier, he must be in the lab… in another class… in another room… or in the head." Fellow students had him searching in the entire building. Because I wasn't in the building, the night instructor couldn't find me.

The following morning before class starts, the leading Chief orders me into his office. There I greet the night instructor. He is looking angry at me. The Chief starts the inquisition.

"Where were you last night?" The leading Chief's first question.

"Stupid-study," was my reply.

"After 1900?"

Honesty kicked in, "I went to stupid-study and finished my work early because I'm having no trouble with this block, and then I left for the evening movie."

Surprised again by my direct honesty, the Chief stuttered for a moment. The Chief glared at me with the silence of pending doom. Not knowing what can happen, I was a bit concerned.

"You have eight more weeks until graduation. The Navy has invested too much time and money in your training. By kicking your dumb ass out of school now would waste the Navy's investment—your training. But, when I give an order, I expect it obeyed! Do you understand? Always follow orders! To keep me from writing you up for disobeying my orders—which means you'll get a captain's mast. A

CO's mast can bust in your rate, take your pay, or give you extra duty or brig time, all that might happen. That's the punishment you deserve, but you can volunteer for something else to remind you I damn well not allow you to disobey my orders!"

As I studied the Chief, I realized it wasn't going well for me. I didn't understand what the Chief wanted me to do. Yet, I sensed a pay loss isn't desirable. "Okay, Chief, I'll do whatever you want me to do," I answered.

"In this building, you will polish every spittoon during Stupid-study under the watchful eyes of the night instructors. A report chit, or polishing, it's your call."

"Polishing is for me; I'll polish! Thanks for the break." I realized I was in more trouble than I assumed, and the Chief was giving me a way out.

That night, I started my spittoon polishing. Polishing spittoons is a dirty, smelly, and disgusting job, but it's better than the alternative. Back then, in FT School, instructors and students still used spittoons, doing fashionable behavior. They chewed tobacco and then spit out chaw juices into never-cleaned spittoons. Uncleaned until I volunteered to clean them.

Spittoon polishing was nasty dirty work, but it wasn't the most disgusting job I did in the Navy, discovering later that sanitary tank cleaning was much worse!

To my joy, telling my story got Cine and Floyd laughing. They recognized and understand how young and foolish sailors get in and out of trouble. The FT School behavior I did was beyond anything Floyd might have considered doing, making my school experience different from his school experience. Floyd then expressed his FT "A" school experience, shocking Janet and me after Floyd started his tale.

As if it happened yesterday, I remember my first day in class. Within the first hour of class, the Chief instructor interrupted the class and directed me to follow him to his office, closing the door after we entered.

The Instructor barked out, "What the hell are you doing in this school? Niggers aren't smart enough for this school. Niggers will waste our time and end-up failing. You must quit."

The lead instructor was a racist, and he can cause me trouble in this school. With no intention of quitting, I'm facing this problem and wondering how I will complete the school. With determination, I replied, "I won't quit, and I will get through this school."

The instructor snarled, "Get back to your classroom nigger; I can't stand the sight of dumb shits like you; you will fail."

Believing as I left the office with the realization, I must do everything right, keep out of trouble, and study hard—there will be no joy attending this school.

After my first test, the racist comes in, seizes my test paper, and graded it. A disgusted look of disbelief, the Chief instructor, handed the graded test to the class instructor and ordered him, "Record the grade." I aced the test. The Chief instructor checked every test while I was in school. I finished with an average that made me second in class standing. The first in class standing beat me by two-tenths of a point. The Chief instructor was a racist, but at least he was an honest racist. At graduation, surprising me, the racist shook my hand and praised me, expressing that he had misjudged me.

After leaving A-school, the Navy assigned me to a cruiser. The day I reported aboard, someone sent me to the deck force. When the weapons officer found out I was an FT A-School graduate and second in my class, he ordered me out of the deck force gang and assigned me to Fox Division. From then on, on that cruiser, I worked alongside experienced FTs and learned my systems. I learned to watch the Officers and Chiefs, observing their leadership and how they interacted with one another and with their seniors.

I liked that weapons officer who treated me fairly. We developed a friendship that lasts to this day. I learned a lot from him.

Floyd stared at me from across the dining table, reflected, "You were lucky having youthful fun at your start. My start in the Navy and FT school is a bitter memory."

It made me angry just listening to Floyd's experience. He was one of the smartest people I know and an outstanding leader. Floyd cared for and justly treated everyone in our division, no matter their race. Floyd is a great family man, a responsible father with talented, remarkable children. Their successes prove his leadership qualities. Floyd's kids all grew up as responsible, productive people. All but one served in the military, two sons achieving higher status than a Warrant Officer. One of his sons retired as an LT Commander. Another son made Commander and possibly now holds a more senior rank. Another of Floyd's sons is a Chief Petty Officer. The Crisps, a marvelous family, I'm proud of knowing, working, and being friends with them.

During our meal, we ordered drinks, had more conversation, with more beverages and more talk, ending with coffee and dessert. Nonstop poor service accompanied the entire meal. The service was terrible, but I didn't believe that it was only from lousy service. I sensed subtle racism was in play, something I noticed more after hearing Floyd's story. No matter, the service was irritating. I'd experienced many a meal there before and in many other places in the region, yet I never encountered similar awful service.

At the end of the evening, our server delivered a bill larger than typical for this establishment, which can garner a good tip for the server. But Floyd, with a loud voice, voiced to our server, his manager, and others to hear, "I'm generous with my tips. I give twenty percent or better with good service, but tonight's horrible service deserves this." Floyd sets a penny on the table.

For him, Floyd's tip made it right. It worked out. Maybe Floyd had a plan, figuring that the server might learn to act differently, money can be his motivator. Conceivably racist behavior happened to him so often if he addressed each instance, Floyd would be in a fight each time. Constant fighting wasn't worth his effort. He learned to pick his battles.

I believe different; no one should ever be the focus for ill-treatment because of their race. Because I lacked the patience and understanding displayed by Floyd, I bore anger.

I cannot recall how many times I reflected on that evening. Because of my race, I lacked the experience living with so many hating me. I didn't learn to survive in racism's dangerous environments. On racism, over time, I concluded with no reservation that racism is immoral. My historical awareness and observation of people with whom I interacted throughout my life support my judgment. In the history of man, racism is one of the most unintelligent convictions ever fostered. Racism is a belief that has caused undeserving pain and suffering to its victims. Racism is counterproductive to any advancement of the human ideal. Racism is wrong!

SUBSCHOOL

Naval Submarine School New London, Groton, Connecticut
May-August 1962

Submarines are the most complicated ships ever built by man. Even so, submarine designs don't allow adequate space for crew comfort. For example, during a new construction end, the Navy performs acceptance inspections for the new submarines. Passing that inspection enables the Navy to accept the submarine from the manufacture. Except for the Trident submarines, most subs fail the habitability requirements, establishing them as unfit for living. With this flaw, the Navy accepts the sub. Because of a submarine's complexity and close living conditions, exceptional and knowledgeable sailors operate, repair, and take subs into battle conditions. These submariners are a special breed of individuals who live and work in tight spaces that are inadequate to live and work. Sailors must adapt to the submariner's way of doing work and follow submarine traditions that differ from the surface Navy. The Naval Submarine School is a necessary and useful beginning, making sailors submarine knowledgeable, but it's only a start—just too much to learn.

The submarine qualification process, done on a sub, completes the learning requirements. While qualifying, submarine sailors prove they fit into the submarine environment, along with gaining submarine-specific knowledge.

OUSTING THE UNFIT

During my first week, it appeared Subschool leaders acted as if their primary mission was to expel students that would not fit into a submarine environment. One beginning ordeal was the pressure test in which instructors jammed us into a pressure tank designed to hold six sailors. Instructors packed approximately twenty or more of us into the tank, ignoring the tank's capacity. Students get crammed together, chests to backs with no room for a fart between them. Once my fellow students and I were inside the tank, the tank was jam-packed—we moved barely enough to breathe. Inside the tank, I experienced what a sardine must sense being stuffed into a can of packed sardines. A loud thud told me the hatch shut. The noise of inrushing air informed me the pressure was increasing. This didn't bother me because before we got in, an instructor's brief told us what to expect. No matter, a few sailors became berserk hearing inrushing air hissing sounds. With panicked exclamations interrupting the test, "I can't stand this—help me—stop this, get me out of here...."

The swish of inrushing air stopped before any noticeable pressure built up. A new noise told me that the tank was venting. When the sounds of tank venting stopped, the tank's hatch opened. Before an instructor ordered them out, panicked sailors rushed the entrance. These seamen, in their terror, acted as shitheads—their panicked rush roughed-up the sailors closest to the hatch exit. Claustrophobic sailors' eyes are wide with fear showing they're the ones who didn't endure the confined space. After everyone was out of the tank, an instructor separated the four sailors with the embarrassing gray-white, sweaty faces. The instructors cut short the spooked sailors' submarine careers because they failed the pressure test. An instructor ordered the rest of us back into that tank without the claustrophobic four.

Once again, inside, with air rushing in and pressure building, I had a problem—I can't equalize. In torture, my ears suffered comparable to steel rods jamming into each of my eardrums—it was beyond painful, throbbing. I held my nostrils shut and blew out hard through my nose to equalize—didn't work, but the pain increased. With a sudden pop, I equalized, and the pain in my ears subsided. No longer can I sense the tank pressure rising, but I heard the incoming air pressuring the tank until it simulated a one-hundred-foot depth when the air stopped. We stayed in the tank at the 100-foot depth pressure for a half-hour. Then, I listen to the tank venting, letting me know this test is over. The venting took a while before the tank pressure equalized with the outside pressure.

Later, after we get out of that tank, a doctor inspected every ones' ears. After he examined my ears, the doctor pulled me aside and gave me a proper ass chewing.

"Why didn't you stop the test? You nearly lost your hearing. The air pressure might have punctured your eardrums, putting a strain on your eardrums—they are red and inflamed—you damaged them!"

"I have a slight cold, and I'm not letting an earache stop me from going into submarines," I replied.

"If you punctured your eardrums, which would have disqualified you from submarines. You're damn lucky that didn't happen." The doctor answered, his eyes showing both exasperation and concern.

DO YOUR DUTY

As part of Subschool instruction, student sailors went to sea on school boats for daily training trips. On these trips, we met older submariners who served in World War II. For us youngsters, they are the old-time warriors. The dolphins, a breast insignia pin, displayed above their lift shirt pocket, identified them as qualified in submarines. Under the dolphins is a Submarine Combat Patrol pin with a star for every war patrol they made. Wearing the Submarine Combat Patrol pin told everyone that they experienced combat in the war. These sailors sailed in harm's way during submarine war patrols. They are the heroes who defended our country during warfare. Crew members and instructors whispering about them with awe point them out, identifying them as if they were celebrity superstars. *"He made a war patrol that sunk two Jap tin cans... That one made two patrols that sunk a Jap submarine, freighters, and other lesser ships... or that guy over there, Jap tin cans depth charged his boat on each of his three patrols. He's lucky to be alive."* Subschool instructors and students understood they were the Navy's real, living heroes.

When I studied the warriors, I see an older-looking Chief or a First-Class Petty Officer appearing unlike most of the other Chiefs or First-class I knew. The warriors appeared older, acted wiser, and displayed immense confidence. On their war-time experiences, I speculated. Perhaps they saw the horrors of war that no one should witness. Without a doubt, they survived encounters most would never undergo. Their wartime involvements aged the warriors too fast, giving them gray, white, or balding heads, scarring them with wrinkled, leathered faces, yet bestowing them a presence that demanded respect. The old-time warriors had one common trait—their eyes always searched, studying everything looking for what's amiss.

The subschool instructors often presented us submarine history lessons, revealing, with respect and admiration, just why those old-timers were real heroes. One declared. "Just think on it," "Imagine how submariners felt waiting for the next patrol when they understood how dangerous it might be. Through the Navy grapevine, they learn submarines on patrol as the Tang or the Wahoo are gone missing, never heard from again. At that moment, you'd understand you'll never again meet your friends who are part of the lost boat's crews, realizing the worst has happened—a loss of all-hands because of enemy action. The old-time warriors experienced enemies' actions that threatened their existence on every mission. The warriors departed on war patrols, knowing their next mission will produce conditions beyond their control, understanding their next assignment will be hazardous and accepting the possibility that their boat may be the next one missing. That's why these warriors are heroes—in harm's way; they did their duty."

These lessons of how those warriors did their duty no matter the danger embedded themselves in our mindset. As Navy submariners, they put themselves into harms' way with a doubtful return and faced a threat without hesitation. Those warriors, our real war heroes, became the epitome of bravery for new sub sailors. These experienced warriors demonstrated what it meant to do one's duty.

These old-timers carried an assurance that commanded instant respect. They had a rapport with the qualified sailors giving them esteem for being in submarines. Because we were in Subschool, the warriors showed respect in treating us as exceptional sailors. They made us feel good about ourselves for volunteering for submarines—we felt part of the elite.

The old combatants acted and carried themselves different from the Chiefs and petty officers I knew in boot camp and FT A school. In the classroom or on a submarine, the warriors acted calm, easygoing, and composed, helping young sailors learn the complexities of subs and the submarine life experience. The old-time warriors pleasantly influenced students—except this one time, happening during a Subschool at-sea day trip—my first time underway on a submarine.

With a group of fellow Subschool students, I was relishing the moment, underway with a course set for sea in the most pleasant weather, expecting my new voyage—my first dive on the USS *Atule* *(SS403)*, a fleet-diesel submarine used for Subschool training. The *Atule* left the Submarine base on the surface and headed south on the Thames River toward the open ocean.

I'm in the sail on starboard lookout watch under instruction. In the shears, I'm jammed in with Seaman Brian, the lookout. Brian is nearly my age and size with a severe skin affliction, a severe case of acne. He had the task to teach me his job while he additionally performed his lookout duties. For a seaman, Brian was an excellent lookout instructor, giving me pointers on how to watch for potential dangers and to locate navigation markers. Brian pointed to navigation aids and explained their use. Then, he made me describe the next navigation aid we approached. While I'm responding to his questions, I tried to avoid contact with him, not knowing if his condition was contagious.

Brian startled me when he got his face near my left ear and whispered. "One of the important things we lookouts do is to report contacts. On the Atule, lookouts use the same standard phraseology reporting contacts as when we report over sound powered phones."

Below the shears, on the bridge, was the OOD and the CO. I could watch them, but I could only hear part of their conversations. They both appeared attentive, inspecting everything, studying the river, the currents, the wind, and the navigation aids.

Then chiefs, both wearing a Submarine Combat Patrol pin, came topside to the bridge, to enjoy the short time on the surface, and to get sunshine and fresh air. In the shears, I couldn't help seeing how these chiefs searched the river. Precisely as if the chiefs were on watch as the Officer of the Deck, or gained the Commanding Officer's duties, they studied the boat's headway, viewing and taking in every detail.

The limited-time I had to study the combatants because Brian kept interrupting my recreational moment. Between Brian's instructions, I couldn't help observing the old-warriors and wonder what they were thinking and what they lived through in their career. Both chiefs appeared to be enjoying a friendly conversation with the CO, but I couldn't catch what they said. Their interaction marveled me, seeing the respect the CO gave them, and the admiration they returned to the CO.

I observed the chiefs examining the river, the boat, and our wake. One chief's loud voice bellowed a warning. "The wake is as a snake slithering across a pond—somebody should square away the helmsman—he's not keeping a steady course."

"Mind your helm." The OOD responded to the criticism.

As I heard the order, a powerboat raced passed us. The boat is close enough for me to make out three good-looking, sexy, bikini-wearing babes waving, laughing, and teasing us. The powerboat overtook the sub and quickly passed. Binoculars locked onto the babes, inspecting each bikini until I couldn't recognize the darlings. But my imagination continued seeing bikinis and dreaming of impossible prospects.

The warriors examined our reactions as we viewed the babe-filled boat race by us. When I can't recognize it as a powerboat because it looked like a dot on the horizon, I and the other lookouts became the target of the meanest, nastiest, and most effective ass-chewing ever given. I'd place that scolding in the Navy's top ten of the best ass-chewing ever delivered.

One of the old-combatants exploded in a fury with us topside watch-standers, the targets of his rage. "What the hell are you shit-for-brains-gawking seagulls supposed to be doing? You didn't report that small boat that just passed us. None of you blockheads reported the two contacts coming in. Don't You see them? There's another one coming up your ass you don't see. Then, there's that buoy we're approaching; we'll run into because none of you shitheads have seen it and you blind-seagulls won't know it's there until we run into it." His reprimand continued with a growling voice. "Instead of doing your duty, you lowlife seagulls were ogling those split-tails! You shitheads are putting the boat in danger because you've got your head up your ass!"

The OOD ordered with an angry, loud, gruff voice. "Report all contacts! Helm, steer course Wun seven FI-yiv." [10]

Binoculars at once search the horizon. The boat makes a small course change, avoiding the green buoy off the starboard bow. After hearing the reports, I wondered if the OOD and the CO likewise examined the babes as they flew by the Atule.

Moments later, the port lookout sent his contact report to the OOD, "Submarine bearing Wun Ze-ro degrees starboard, angle on the bow starboard Wun FI-yiv, range FI-yiv thousand yards, red buoy Wun Six degrees to starboard."

The starboard lookout's report followed, and he yelled in my ear. "Ferry bearing Two Ze-ro-degree port, angle on the bow port Wun Ze-ro, range Six thousand yards, Freighter bearing port Wun Six FI-yiv, angle on the bow starboard Wun FI-yiv, range Four-thousand yards,

---

[10] See Appendix E, Standard Submarine Phraseology

green buoy Wun Ze-ro degrees to starboard." The OOD reports the contacts and his course change to the CO.

Then, one old-combatant berated us, bellowing an ear full. "Shitheads, what in the hell is the matter with you?! You should be ashamed. You're not doing your duty! If this boat had crashed into something or gone aground, causing major damage or causing someone to get hurt or worse, someone killed because you were gawking at split-tails. A court-martial can bust you in rate down to recruit, you'd get brig-time, and you would be lucky if they didn't kick you out of the Navy with a dishonorable discharge! Can your mothers and grandmothers be proud of you after they discovered you're in the brig for dereliction of duty because you were gawking at split-tails? You know damn well they wouldn't. Instead, they'd suffer sorrow, embarrassment, and mortification when telling their friends about you. They'd be ashamed of you."

"Shit, fire! If dishonorable discharge happened with brig-time, it might hound you for the rest of your miserable lives. Because you didn't do your duty, you'd find the bar trash on Bank Street will despise you, the drunks in the back allies would loathe you! The lowest scum on earth would scorn you if they realized you didn't do your duty. The Jarheads would despise you and kick your dumb asses every day you're in the brig. Marines run the brigs, and they're damn good at it. The Marines might make each of your days in the brig a living hell; they'd make you follow the red and yellow lines. Jarheads do their duty, and then they must babysit derelicts as you. For their shore duty, they get to run a brig full of shitheads. It pisses them off big time because you didn't do your duty, and they end up needing to square your dumb asses away."

In a quieter stern voice, the other combatant, "In wartime, you will be dead. An enemy would have sunk this boat because you, irresponsible, heads-up-your-asses, seagull-blockheaded playboys can't distinguish the enemy until you can recognize the ship's class. If you can recognize it, it's too damn close, got it? If you can recognize what he is, he sees you, and if the enemy can see you, he'll kill you. If the enemy saw you, you and everyone topside might be dead. Then the enemy will come in for that final kill, taking the rest of your shipmates with you!"

Then the chief spoke with a lowered soft voice, "You lookouts must detect and report all contacts before they spot you. You must spot the contacts when they are specks on the horizon or spots in the air. When you see contacts as specks so small you can't distinguish it—it might be a bird, a plane, a ship, a friend, or the enemy—you report it. Because, if it's the enemy, and he sees you first, you won't live to tell about it."

A wail of humiliation caused a moment of stunned silence topside. The old-timer resuming our reprimand spoke with a sad, soft voice. "In the war, I survived an enemy getting too close. Let me tell you, what an incoming round will do to a shipmate—your friend. You never want to see at a body torn apart. You never want to take your friend's wounded, mangled, bleeding body below in panic as the boat is submerging, trying to save itself. And, you will never forgive yourself for not seeing that contact first."

The sail hushed in the silence of embarrassment. In quietness, we reflected on what happened and judged hard criticism over our behavior. Shame loomed large as we understood the lesson—always duty before pleasure. The lookouts applied the experience, do your duty. Alertness and vigilance replaced our inattentiveness as binoculars searched for the unknown dangers.

Then, in a sound that made me glance downwards towards the bridge, the saddest voice I ever heard, "Request to go below—too many memories." I watched the chiefs. Their faces held expressions of unfathomable sorrow with eyes filled with anguish searched the horizons for one more glimpse.

With binoculars searching forward, the OOD responded without looking at the warriors, "lay below."

The CO and the lookouts were likewise searching.

The first chief going below into the hatch stopped and looked up with a slight smile and winked at his shipmate. The chief standing, waiting to follow, winked back. A grin of success replaced his expression of sorrow. Then they proceeded below.

Holy shit! The old-time warriors were acting to get everyone's attention. They used their ass-chewing to give the lesson, always do your duty. It worked. Everyone topside is doing their duty. How did they think that lesson up, I wondered? How could they be so convincing? No matter, this ass-chewing incident, gosh damn, I'll remember it forever.

USS SPIKEFISH (AGSS 404)

USS SPIKEFISH
(AGSS404)

September 1962—January 1963

Aboard the Spikefish AGSS404, at Key West, Florida, on June 9, 1963, I qualified in Submarines. These stories focus on my Spikefish experiences.

In the diner, upon entering, I meet the young sailor again, welcoming me. I noticed that we had the restaurant to ourselves. The youngster with a retired Chief who once served as a COB, well, we're building a bond of friendship. After we're settled, we ordered coffee and breakfast. The waitress is a sexy-looking gal appearing ten-years-older than my young friend. With a friendly smile, she set the coffee on our table and lingered using small talk and flirted with the youngster. Red blush on his face showed he wasn't used to getting seducing treatment, but his smile exposed he liked it. Another customer entered the diner, and the waitress stopped her flirting and waited on the new patron.

The kid's attentive wanting look tells me he's my audience for sea stories. In an eye-to-eye locked gaze, I secure his full attention.

Locked eye contact is a trick I discovered early in my career to keep a subordinate's attention. This kid is starting in sub school. I don't want to scare him away, but he wants to understand what's awaiting him. If I chose selected stories concerning my early experiences on the Spikefish, I could help him. I start with a little background.

When I first met you at the sub memorial, you wanted submarine knowledge. When you asked, what are submarines like? When I answered, I couldn't give you the complete picture. I didn't want to scare you off with too much discouraging information. Now, I can see you're committed to subs, so you're ready for submarine life details. To give you the best picture, I'll tell you what I experienced when I was your age. I'm amazed that I survived the qualification process and more astounded by the rewards I enjoyed because I progressed through the sub qual process. Living the submarine life, you must be tough. Once you learn the value of being a submariner, then you'll find submarine life rewarding.

When I joined the Navy, I signed up for a six-year enlistment to get the Polaris Missile School Training that had a pipeline of schools as a qualifier for the next school. Because there were many dropouts in Subschool, the school pipeline included Subschool, followed by a submarine tour. The Navy made sure a trainee can ride submarines before investing him in the Polaris School. The Polaris program finished with the Fire Control Polaris Missile School, and then the successful student is assigned to a boomer.

For me, after finishing FT A School and Subschool, I expected a tour on a submarine before my Polaris Missile School assignment. With classes over, everyone in my class waited for sea duty orders. The wait for orders was grueling. During the waiting period, everyone in my class performed routine Subase duties. I worked in the commissary stacking shelves. Hard work with long hours starting at 0500 and working till 1900 made me too tired for liberty. The time I waited for orders seemed like an eternity, even though it was only one week after finishing Subschool. When my orders came in, I read them with anticipation; then I felt fortunate getting them. Sea duty orders sent me to my first submarine, the *USS Spikefish (AGSS 404)* homeported in Key West Florida.

To start, as a submariner, you must cope with emergencies, poor living conditions, long hours of hard work without sleep, and added stress. You'll play and work in uncomfortable surroundings. Sometimes, you'll experience hazards and danger. Safety is a significant issue in a submarine. You'll find that working in an unsafe condition is unacceptable. Continuous training will concentrate on safety because your command requires you to follow all safety rules. The submariners' life isn't for the fragile sailor; it's for the dedicated one who knows the submarine mission contributes to keeping our country safe. The submariner understands his duty's importance.

Sub-crews use submarine traditions to select the submariner. A submarine crew knows non-quals are just out of subschool, untested, and a threat to themselves and the boat. The crew knows non-quals have lots to learn in minimal time. Submarine crews test non-quals in ways landlubbers never considered possible. The crew will get the non-quals attention, causing him frustration, driving him to quit, while motivating the non-qual to continue. Crews recognize non-quals don't know how to cope with emergencies, and if they do something wrong, the blunder might contribute to something terrible—such as getting them killed.

The young sailor's eyes grew wider at that statement, and his face showed alarm. The way he leaned forward into the table showed me I kept his interest, so I continued.

After sub school, when you report to your first boat, your command starts your qualifying. The command expects you to qualify as soon as possible. When you first arrive aboard, you'll discover that you're the non-qual. The non-qual means, you'll be the lowest life form on the boat—no one respects you—everyone fears you. When you're a non-qual—you will confront unpleasant times that will tax your resolve. You can expect harassment while qualifying. But realize that the crew's harassment is to verify your suitability to ride subs—not to destroy you.

While qualifying, you go through a taxing effort studying system after system. And then, by answering questions about these systems, you prove your submarine knowledge. Added to this, you must qualify watch stations the in-port topside security watch and the at-sea watches: lookout, helmsman, and plainsman. When you're qualified to stand these watches, you're useful. On a submarine, you adapt, you learn your boat's systems, and you learn how to use the equipment.

As a non-qual, while qualifying, you will undergo harassment episodes that provide embarrassments. To succeed, you must endure the humiliations with dignity without quitting, breaking, and causing conflicts to others. You must continue qualifying. If not, you will undergo a difficult time—then to advance, you either adapt or you fail.

The medias' day-to-day news reports define harassment as bullying. Yes, bullying is hurtful to its victims. I'll bet you're wondering how I can tell you you'll receive harassment when it's the face of bullying. Since WWII, submarine's traditions use non-qual harassment as an essential part of the submarine qualification process—this harassment isn't bullying. The qualified crew will harass the newcomer deciding if the trainee is suitable for subs or not. The non-qual pestering doesn't differ from your boot company commander yelling at you for screwing up. The treatment marines receive in their boot-camp training. And what ordeals the Navy seal-teams go through in their instruction.

Senior leaders from every U.S. military organization use agitation as a training tool. But on submarines, after your qualified, the harassment stops.

On my first sub, I didn't have someone telling me submarine's traditions. For the qualifying ordeal, I was unprepared. Don't make qualifying grueling as I did. When I qualified, I had an arrogance that required recalibration. No one could tell me anything without me taking offense. When I started my first sea duty, I wouldn't follow valuable guidance. Because I was too cocky as if I knew everything, my foolishness made my qualification a nightmare to live through.

Often, LPOs and Chiefs squared my dumb-ass away when I needed it. Too many times, they made me aware of my shortcomings. For me, my seniors provided leadership methods that were painful, embarrassing, memorable, and they worked. The same leadership methods work today. Leaders, as my COB, were ingenious, inspiring me to do well and encouraging me to continue. My COB and other leaders used inventive ways to get my attention, and they caused me to change my thinking in a constructive direction. The leaders delivered mutual guidance, 'do your duty.' I'll remember my COB's leadership methods as if they happened yesterday because his approaches were unforgettable.

As you continue in your naval venture, here's advice to take with you on your first boat. Follow the crews' guidance to learn the knowledge to qualify. Study your seniors' leadership methods—learn from them to develop your leadership skills. Because someday you'll be in a leadership position; if not, you failed.

The young sailor's attentive look told me he wants more information. Then, with the phrase that starts good naval sea stories, taking weeks to convey, I continue. "This ain't no shit."

THE KNIFE

After a humiliating incident, everyone aboard the Spikefish labeled me, Knife or The Knife. You might think a Knife title is a badass compliment, but it wasn't. I detested this title because I sensed humiliation every time someone used, Knife, or the Knife when referring to me. How I picked up the nickname was an ordeal. The Knife title is a reminder of how my COB set me straight back on course after I started drifting off—causing trouble. COB's method reshaped me. His approach was uniquely successful, but for me—awfully embarrassing, so let me tell you all about it. This ain't no shit.

After finishing Subschool, I'm expecting further schooling in the Polaris school program. Part of the Polaris program included sending students to sea to qualify and prove their suitability for submarines before entering the Polaris Missile Firecontrol School. The Navy did this because of the high failure rate for submarine duty applicants. The Polaris Missile Firecontrol School provided students with specific advanced technological instruction. When my sea duty orders arrived, I felt lucky. I received orders to my first submarine, the USS *Spikefish (AGSS 404)*, home-ported in Key West Florida. Somehow, I became arrogant, as if I knew everything. My audacity turned me into Admiral Shit-for-brains and produced lots of anguish until I wised up.

Two of my FT-A School buddies Bob and Ferguson likewise got Spikefish orders; they also went through subschool with me. I'm happy that they are going with me with two friends on the same boat that might make our tour fun. After reporting aboard, Bob, Ferguson, and I met the COB in the Mess Decks to start our check-in. The COB is one of the old-time warriors, he's a Chief, looking meaner, fiercer, and sterner than anyone I ever met. Yet, the COB meets us with a welcome beam and greets us with, "I'm glad you showed up, we're shorthanded."

When I reported aboard, I'm eager and thrilled, expecting my first at sea adventure. Believing, I should learn and work on a submarine fire control system and enjoy tropical liberty in Florida. Damn, I'm a Fire Control Technician Seaman who finished FT-A School, one of the Navy's lengthiest and demanding technical schools in the Navy. FT-A School taught fire control systems used on warships—battlewagons, tin cans, cruisers, and other combat ships. But, to my dismay, I'm mistaken in my assumptions. Instead of my desired work, my disgruntled, unwitting self, I joined the seaman gang. Shit! I didn't like it, but I couldn't change it. While working in the seaman gang, I picked up the title, "The Knife."

That first day was hectic. The COB assigned us into our duty sections and introduced us to our section leaders, officers, the yeoman, the Doc, and most of the crew, and then I promptly forgot their names. Then he brings us to Aft-Battery berthing, gave us bunk-bags, and assigned us our bunk. The COB points at an inboard bottom rack six inches off the deck at the passageway to the mess decks. "That is your bunk when you have the duty or when we are underway. You'll be hot bunking at sea. Keep your bunk clean."

Troubled, I stare at the bunk setting six inches above the deck. One end is next to the door that's between the mess decks and the crew's berthing. Thinking, how can anyone sleep in such a tight space? Shit, sharing a bunk, how in the hell are we going to get any sleep?

Bob inquired, "Where is my rack?"

"You're looking at it. You will be hot bunking. That means you'll share that bunk, sleeping in shifts, one on duty, one qualifying, while one sleeps in the rack, swapping who uses the bunk as your section rotates. When two of you want the rack, you work your situation out. I will not change your diapers for your petty issues." The COB grins at us, knowing we don't enjoy the hot bunking notion.

Bob gazed at the bunk in worried dismay.

Later, the COB took us to the barracks on the base. In the barracks, the COB provides our sheets, pillows, and blankets, then assigns us our bunks and lockers. The lockers provided enough space for stowing our belongings from our sea-bags. The barracks looked more pleasant and provided better creature comforts and privacy than any barracks I lived in since joining the Navy. After seeing the living conditions, I felt terrific. The COB informed us, "In port, use the barracks when you can. It's a better place to relax than the boat. You must keep the barracks clean."

After stowing our gear, we head back to the boat where the COB agitated the hell out of me when he directed, "I'm assigning you youngsters to the seamen gang because the seaman gang is the best place to start your submarine career. As deck apes on this sub, you must learn a great deal. In a limited time, you must learn everything topside, topside security, salvage equipment, hull preservation, line handling, and weapons handling. Topside work is important because topside is the face a submarine presents to the public, the landlubbers, skimmers, jarheads, air-dales, shallow-water sailors, no-loads, and the Brass." The COB gave us a warning when he growled with authority. "You always keep topside squared away; so, you must learn to keep topside shipshape. If you don't heed my words, you'll deal with me and trust me. You do not want that to happen!"

With anxious thoughts floating through my head, Shit! The COB can't realize what he is doing. He's wasting our advanced training, and he should have assigned us to the weapons department. The COB must not have known any better when he delegated us to the seamen gang. Disappointed, I assumed I would work on the Spikefish's submarine fire control system to gain technical skills. The deck-ape assignment wastes our training. To get the best use of our advanced training, I inquired, "COB, how do I get into the weapons department? We graduated from FT 'A' School, it's the best technical school in the Navy, teaching Navy fire control systems. An assignment to the weapons department is the best use of our advanced training."

"You're not ready for that." The COB answered.

Then, the COB handed each of us, seamen, the Navy's large pocketknife. "This knife you will use doing topside work when rigging topside for sea, preparing topside for painting. It's good for scraping paint in hard to reach corners or scratching dirt out of tight spots—a handy tool. The marlinspike you'll use for splicing line. We don't do splicing as much as done on a surface craft, but enough to cause you to learn how to line splice. When going into dry-dock, making safety lines, you'll splice lines to rig Spikefish's topside for dry-dock safety…"

As the COB was expounding on the pocketknife, I'm examining my knife, not listening. The knife had a straight blade cutting-edge and a blunt blade point. The blade folded back into the handle when not used. The knife had a marlinespike that folded back to turn into part of the handle. When opened, the marlinespike locked in place to use. The knife didn't impress me as having any value. Shit! I'm pissed. My suggestion didn't work. The COB didn't change our assignment. This pocketknife started a sequence of events that led me to my first attitude adjustment. These events caused me to change my opinions, arrogance, defiance, and insolence throughout and beyond my Naval career. At that moment, I'm unaware of the embarrassment awaiting me.

Then, the COB handed us our qual cards and told us. "You nonquals are useless and dangerous because you lack submarine knowledge. In an emergency, opening or shutting a valve at the wrong time can have grave consequences. Nonquals touch nothing until they become proficient on the system they will use, or when a qualified crew member directs them to do something. Nonquals as you have objectives; you must qualify to get your dolphins. But first, you qualify your watch stations Topside Watch, Lookout, Helmsmen, Planesmen, and then the rest of the boat. You're only useful after qualifying in these watch stations. Here's a suggestion, don't get behind in your quals. If you become dink, you won't enjoy what happens. Use the fundamental knowledge you learned from Subschool that should help if you paid attention."

The COB's eyes glared into mine as if he knows I'm the individual who will give him trouble. With a tone of intimidating purpose, he explained, "Qualifying on submarines requires learning and operating the boat's systems, and that takes effort. Once you're qualified, you can stand any watch station during a crisis. On a moment's notice, you might fire torpedoes, start a main engine, support any watch station, get the boat underway, or fight any causality, fire, flooding, or explosion. When needed, you will confront the unknown danger."

Reluctantly, I take on seaman gang duties. Assigned to the Seaman Gang was an obstacle, but not career-ending. So, I made the best of my unfortunate job. With a positive outlook, I started, working hard, and keeping ahead on my submarine qualification. I qualified my watch stations Topside Security Watch, Lookout, Helmsman, and Planesmen watch stations faster than expected, and getting ahead on my quals made me a bit cocky. I thought qualifying was easy—no sweat. At sea,

I discovered pleasure in standing lookout watches. In port, I found the topside work gratifying.

But there was one source of intense irritation I couldn't avoid. On the Spikefish, senior crewmembers always found fault with us new crewmembers, scolding us for any infractions, calling us, "nonquals, no-loads, pollywogs, shit-for-brains," and other demeaning names. Someone was on us no matter what we did or attempted. Even while doing the simplest tasks, a few old farts expressed how we didn't do the job right.

For example, at the end of a duty-day, we finished cleaning the aft head. Blackheart, my section leader, making his inspection, walks in the aft head and scolds us. "You boot-camps can't even clean shitters. Clean this head again, do it right this time, wash every surface, the toilets, the sinks, the valves, the pipes, and have it so clean you can eat chow in it, because—you might do that! I want the shitters so clean you can eat soup out of them because if you don't, the shitters will be your soup bowls today—got it!"

The qualified crew showed disapproval for our efforts and made our lives aboard miserable. We couldn't satisfy the old farts because we were the nonquals, the lowlife members of the crew. The old farts considered nonquals dangerous. Often, they expressed, "we might get someone killed if we did something stupid." Because of that, the old farts stated, "you nonquals are a threat to the Spikefish—a menace to the crew." The old farts' assertiveness was getting me pissed.

Later, during another field-day, Bob, Ferguson, and I were cleaning the head. Bob was in a shitter stall, scrubbing a toilet, and Ferguson in a shower stall was cleaning its walls. As I'm polishing the mirrors, thinking, the COB is making better sailors out of us—bull shit. Shit, I joined the Navy to do meaningful work maintaining essential fighting systems, but I'm making a career cleaning shitters. It looks like I'm wasting my time and talents doing this unnecessary work. Then, the COB comes in, checking on our progress.

From the shitter, Bob is whining, "I can't believe we have to do this dirty job, cleaning this shitter so often? I think the COB likes to get on our asses."

Ferguson adds his complaining about cleaning the shower. "I agree, it's wasting our abilities. Head cleaning is bullshit work; any unskilled mental midget deck-ape can clean showers and toilets. This work is demeaning and wasting our advanced training. Shit, I don't enjoy cleaning heads."

Bob and Ferguson didn't know the COB was in the head, inspecting our progress and heard their babbling. I thought the COB would jack them up, but he didn't. After listening to their complaints, without saying a word, the COB left.

As soon as the COB departed, I let Bob and Ferguson know they had a dilemma. I told them, "You might be in trouble because the COB heard your bellyaching while you were cleaning the toilet stall and shower." They didn't respond but looked worried.

After the field-day and inspections, the COB ordered the seaman gang to meet him in the mess decks at 1600. Worried, we sat at tables waiting for the COB, discussing why the meeting, speculating who screwed-up, what we might have done wrong, and guessed it was Bob and Ferguson shooting their mouths off.

The COB entered and poured himself a coffee and sat facing us on the Chief's table. The COB scanned each of us, making eye contact with each of us. His stern expression offered no warning about what he was thinking. The COB sipped his coffee, his eyes held contact, examining only me. After a silent pause, he spoke.

I have you here for an important reason. A few of you consider your tasks unimportant—wasting your talent doing unnecessary and demeaning work.

To set you straight, every person in this crew performs crucial functions, and you're part of this submarine crew. A submarine is a warship composed of many systems, each significant for the sub's mission and purpose. Each crew member performs vital functions to operate and fight the boat. Every job is necessary. So you don't dispute the CO's role, it's obvious. The officers each have their distinct duties. Chiefs run their divisions and are experts in their ratings. Senior petty-officers keep equipment running. Junior petty-officers support their seniors and takeover when capable. Each watch section operates the boat's systems allowing the boat to meet its missions. Every watch is essential, but several jobs are more crucial than others. On a sub, every assignment is necessary. The seamen duties you do are crucial.

Yes, rank has its privileges, but seniors earn those rights. You don't start as a CO or Chief. You must learn and gain the position. Every officer, chief, and petty-officer has experienced what you are going through. When I was a seaman, I cleaned my share of shitters, heads, decks, and berthing areas. These tasks are not useless or demeaning; they are essential. It degrades your quality of life, and your health is at risk if crewmembers didn't keep these areas liveable. Think about it; we live, work, play, and sleep in crowded spaces. Submarines are unfit to live in by any measure of standards. If you don't keep the living areas clean, uncomfortable living becomes intolerable, worst yet, the spread of disease can put a crew out of commission, which means the boat is out of commission.

When you do routine, unskilled, and menial tasks, it releases the seniors' time to complete their necessary essential duties, and extra functions, which includes teaching you, youngsters. How many times, late at night, has a senior taken you through a system walkthrough allowing you to stay up in your quals?

Even though the tasks you're assigned from cleaning heads, berthing, and keeping topside squared away are mediocre work, it doesn't mean the jobs are unimportant. Your work is essential. I cannot think of an occupation in which a civilian job gives youngsters as you so much responsibility as the Navy, and this command provides you. When you're standing helm watches, what are you steering? You're driving a big black expensive submarine. As lookouts, you're the sub's eyes and ears keeping the boat safe.

Each submariners' actions are essential. Without cooks, you wouldn't eat well. Without mess-cooks, crew members must clean up after eating, taking away valuable time. Technicians maintain equipment, but they can't keep up equipment without spare parts; the storekeeper ensures the boat carries spares. Chiefs train you to do tasks, so you become ready for increased responsibility. Every one of your duties is necessary. You know what happens when one sailor cannot do their duties. Most of the crew stand three-section duty at sea—six hours on duty with twelve hours off duty. Three-section duty allows adequate sleep and recreation time. Take away one of these watchstanders, and then the watch goes to port and starboard—twelve hours on watch and twelve hours for sleeping, qualifying, and recreation. Twelve hours on watch becomes burdensome for watch duties.

You seamen stand the helm, planesmen, and lookout watches. These watches are vital for the boat's operations. There is a reason we rotate the helm, planesmen, and lookout watches. After performing these duties for too long, the watch becomes stressful, fatiguing, and monotonous. In these cases, the watch may not detect danger; attention to task becomes compromised—a set-up for tragedy. For example, if the helmsman doesn't keep on course, a grounding or collision might happen. You are vital to prevent that from happening.

For you, young men, heed my word, keep the right outlook, learn everything you can, don't let someone get to you, don't let foolishness destroy you, do your duty, and you will be all right. Worthwhile pursuits with adventures will replace the hardship of qualifying. Remember, do your assignments, take pride in your work no matter what the task, maybe because it's essential because it's your duty.

Bob and Ferguson ate that nonsense up—they became gung-ho. After that lecture, the COB took a liking to my friends and called them the Dynamic-Duo.

IT'S YOUR DUTY

For me, the COB's pep talk offended me—I'm still pissed, a deck-ape, and can't do something right to satisfy the old farts. For me, I'm still unable to get into the weapons department. The COB didn't reveal what will happen.

Amplifying my misery, one-day topside, I overheard the COB complaining about us to the Tirante's [11] visiting COB. "My new replacements are causing problems. I can't understand these new sailors today. They are careless, inattentive, lazy, don't listen, assume they know everything, yet they don't crave to learn something new. The new seamen lack the wisdom to recognize the distinction between what is relevant and what is trivial. They can't do anything right. The boots are challenging, requiring more supervision than any group of sailors I have working for me. I don't think they learned zilch in sub school. It's hard to let experienced sailors hit the beach and get a break because the new ones are so lacking in ability and motivation. They do not know how important their jobs are—it's damn frustrating. Now we're in much-needed upkeep, repairing most of our equipment, replacing unrepairable parts, and the crew needs liberty. The married crewmembers want time with their families. The single guys want to catch up on delayed social pursuits, but I can't give it to them because of these shit-for-brains, no-load, boot camp misfits."

"I agree with you. I'm having the same trouble with my new people. The Navy must have lowered the standards making it easy for people to get into the submarine service. Or Subschool is failing us, or both." Responded the Tirante's COB with a frustrating grimace.

The COB must have seen me listening, because he yelled at me, "Get the Dynamic-Duo and get topside squared away. Get the slack out of our mooring lines, now! I want those lines tight with no slack in them. Flake out the lines on deck as I showed you how it should look

[11] *USS TIRANTE (SS420)* was another diesel boat in our squadron

last week. I shouldn't be ordering you to do this now. You know what to do! Why in the hell aren't you doing it!?"

I didn't feel happy regarding the new seamen, not measuring up to the COB's expectations. He's talking about me. I couldn't hear the rest of their discussion because I left the topside to find the Dynamic-Duo. The COB liked my friends. What he didn't know, Bob and Ferguson started the mischief, but I'm the one blamed for it—every time. The COB made the Dynamic-Duo's life easier, but the COB treated me as I'm the one causing him trouble.

The COB called the Dynamic-Duo his hot-runners, you know, all-around good sailors. Bob and Ferguson got into topside work as if they loved it.

Besides their admirable qualities, Bob and Ferguson were dumber than a spanner wrench and easy to fool as a seagull. They were naïve, trusting in everything the older sailors told them. Bob and Ferguson focused on every sea story as if God came to read it to them. The Dynamic-Duo can't see through someone's tale and filter out the exaggeration and the untruth. The Dynamic-Duo were gullible.

Bob and Ferguson believed what the seniors told them as truthful. Once sub sailors know someone is gullible, they take extra effort to set them up. The older crewmembers were best at it. They took Bob and Ferguson on a humiliation cruise—many times. For example, the Dynamic-Duo spent a day hunting for a bucket of steam. After a long time searching, they figured out you couldn't carry a bucket of steam. Their faces showed bright red embarrassment when they realized that an Old Fart set them up to do an impossible task. The same thing happened when they hunted for a can of relative bearing grease. The Dynamic-Duo were easy to fool as many politicians trusting in everything absurd said to them. Yet they did not grasp what to do with the information offered to them—excellent or worthless—exaggerated or not, real or fictitious. They never figured out the distinctions. For the old farts, setting them up for embarrassment was easy.

Thinking, they're unlike me. I wasn't gullible, and no one will pull a stunt on me, and knowing better, I wouldn't take any humiliation cruise. But I'm wrong; embarrassment waited for me. I allowed the Navy's pocketknife to become my source of trouble. Later using my new pocketknife, I discovered how valuable a tool a knife was for everyone working topside. But my pocketknife couldn't meet my imagined uses a knife should have.

Boot camp instructors emphasized how important a knife can be. If stranded on a deserted island or worse in enemy territory, your knife is your weapon, and it's the essential survival tool when building shelter, making shavings for starting a fire and crafting other devices or weapons, allowing survival before rescue.

Experienced sailors told us sea-stories that emphasized the value of a knife. One story, a sailor rescued his shipmate with his knife while their ship was tieing up to a pier. The bight of a mooring line with an ever-increasing strain on it caught a line handler's leg. The line pulled the sailor towards a chock. His shipmate cut the mooring line in-two with one swipe, just in time before his mate had his leg ripped from his body—saving his life with his knife. In a whopper, a sailor saved the life of his shipmate by cutting off his shipmate's foot just before a mooring line could have pulled his body through a bullnose. Another tall tale recounts a story where a sailor saved his life using his knife and fought off sharks before rescue. And let's not overlook, a sharp blade might be a sailor's sole ally in a fight.

The old-timers convinced me; I needed a proper sheath knife. Not just any knife; it must be the best blade. Older sailors told me what to seek in a quality knife. The blade's steel must be right. Steel too hard is brittle and might break, but soft steel won't hold a sharpened edge.

In your hand, the knife's handle must have a comfortable fit with no surfaces that caused blisters or cuts. The tang had to pass through the handle for greatest strength. The blade shape had to have the correct curve to meet shipboard needs. A straight blade can't cut through a mooring line, but you can shave with it. A curved blade could cut the line, but you couldn't shave with a curved blade. I considered every bit of the knife information I could gather.

Besides the issued pocketknife, most of the Spikefish's crew carried a knife of different shapes, such as a small hunting knife or a survival knife carried in a sheath attached to belts over a back pocket—quickly seized when required. The crew knew a knife's purpose—a tool—I didn't. A knife is a practical tool, but I couldn't recognize that idea. Until I worked in the seamen gang, I didn't realize that a sailor's knife is an essential tool he can carry. As a deck-ape, I became good at mastering useful knots, splicing lines, and I learned that a sailor uses a knife a thousand times a day for many tasks. Surprisingly to me, I enjoyed seamanship duties.

My Navy issued knife did not have the features desired found in the sea tales. I wanted a knife that can cut a mooring line in-two with one swipe, but my pocket knife couldn't cut one in two with a hundred swipes, let alone one. I tried it without success on a scrap line. The Navy's pocketknife is useless for fighting off sharks. Swords are inadequate for fighting sharks, but I knew no better. As for using a knife in a fight, the Navy outlawed dueling years ago. No matter, I didn't need a knife for fighting, but I wanted that ability—just in case. In a hand-to-hand fight, a knife provides confidence, but a knife fight is unlikely on a sub. A .45 caliber pistol is a better choice for close action. No matter, I had to get an acceptable knife, I considered the Navy issued knife as unsatisfactory for fighting off sharks, slicing mooring lines, saving lives, and useless in a fight.

I regarded the Navy's issued pocketknife lacking, making me want a proper sheath knife. I persuaded Bob and Ferguson that our issued knives are inadequate because it required more usefulness. Moreover, most of the Spikefish's crew carried knives in sheaths attached to belts. Accordingly, we wanted sheathed knives that hung on our belts like the rest of the crew, so we asked the COB, "How do we get knives similar to the sheath knives most of the crew carry?"

The COB informed us. "You seamen can carry a sheathed knife working topside if you get and pay for it." That permission led me to a severe career dilemma.

We looked for a suitable knife in every shop in Key West. Bob and Ferguson found hunting knives after two days of searching; they weren't fussy on their choice—didn't appreciate tool quality. The knives they bought were cheap-looking with plastic handles, plastic sheaths, and cheap. But for me, any knife wouldn't do, I had to have the perfect blade. But by chance, while searching, I found trouble.

On liberty, Bob, Ferguson, and I hit the beach, searching for a knife. I knew they only explored with me because they hoped we'll pick up chicks after searching. During the day on the beach, our fun was fishing, snorkeling, and swimming. Later while the shops were still open, we hunted for my knife. After an unsuccessful search for the ideal knife, we looked for girls but were fruitless in finding girls, which was the norm. Later, we hung out in a pool hall and played 8-Ball or Snooker. On some nights, we located a friendly watering hole after the stores closed. Since we're under 21[12], other nights, we'd get a bottle of booze when we could get someone to buy it for us. For us, getting alcohol was effortless but an occasional occurrence. Yet during my search, we ended up too often drinking booze while watching Key

---

[12] The drinking age in Florida is 21 years old.

West fishermen fish at night along a pier. Many a night, we returned to the barracks inebriated after a fruitless search.

I didn't realize my drinking was causing a problem until the COB ordered me to the mess decks. The COB was waiting for me at the Chief's table, with his coffee mug, a nasty looking coffee-stained mug. A clipboard sat on the table in front of him. "Get a coffee and sit. I have concerns about you."

As I poured my coffee and saw we are the only ones in the mess decks, I asked, "COB, what do you need?" I'm wondering what's this about as I sat down at the table opposite him.

"I need nothing; this concerns your behavior. You're showing up most mornings with hangovers, showing excessive drinking." His eyes latch on mine, ensuring that he receives my full attention, "What you do on the beach is your business, but when your behavior causes problems, it becomes my business. Drinking may be acceptable to do sometimes to relieve the stress from the pressures of work or other releases. But your excessive drinking every night is causing a problem. First, it impairs your ability to do your morning duties. Your drinking is altering your work. Your chores are half-assed completed or not done on time."

Then the COB glared at me with eyes piercing my mind. "First, your behavior is unacceptable! Second, your excessive drinking will lead to severe incidents taking place. Worst case, too much alcohol will cause you to hurt and upset everyone you cherish. Control your drinking. Never let booze control you. If you don't control this excessive drinking, it will ruin you."

That was a revelation. After judging what the COB disclosed, I considered the COB out of line, another instance of the old farts being on our ass without basis. What I do on the beach is my business, not his. I didn't know my drinking created problems, let alone understand its long-term detrimental effects. I'm too immature to accept the wisdom of the COB's message.

Ignoring the COB's warning, for another week, I continued drinking every night, while I searched for a suitable knife. Then, one night in the first shop I went into when starting my knife search, I spotted the granddaddy of knives in a back corner. The knife was an impressive sight, comprising a large thick seven-inch long shiny blade with a bone handle. The blade is polished comparable to a chrome glisten, its cutting-edge shined like a mirror. It's a hunting knife with a Bowie knife's shape blended with a skinner knife. The blade was comparable to a Bowie—the blade's top went straight from the handle to three-fourths of the way to the tip and curved downwards with a sharpened edge towards a sharp pointed tip. From the tip, the knife's sharpened edge curved, forming a precise sharp-edge arch same as a skinner's knife curvature. The sharpened curve continued to half the blade's length, then extended straight back to the handle as a straight razor. On the blade's sides, a blood groove embedded the knife. A brass oval blade guard separated the sharpened edge from a bone handle. The blade guard was the right size to protect my hand from sliding onto the cutting-edge. The handle was short and fatter than most knife handles I have checked out, yet the handle fits my hand. With a short handle attached to the long blade imparted the knife an unbalanced look, but it had the right balance, and its large size made it look menacing. I decided it's the ideal knife for me.

The knife was too pricey to buy, so I gave a clerk a large deposit to hold the knife. Then, I waited, taking four weeks to save enough cash to buy the knife. This frugality kept me off the beach and out of the watering holes. I quit drinking during this time; it was too costly. More importantly, it kept me from turning into a drunk. Being too foolish, I was heading in that path.

The COB felt that his lecture worked. He acted proud of himself when he praised me for squaring my ass away. "You're doing a good job, keep up the good work." But it wasn't the COB's doing. I had to save enough pay to get my knife.

When I went to pick up the knife, it was ready and waiting for me. At the store, my knife was not sharp enough. I sharpened the blade later. The single detail I disliked was the knife's shiny black leather sheath. I replaced it with a sheath I made afterward. On the boat, I had the biggest knife in the topside gang. I was proud of that knife. Showed it off to anyone who I can corner. About my knife, I told anyone who listened. "A knife may have two different cutting-edges depending on its purpose. For rough work, general camp work, chopping wood, digging fire pits, and opening cans, a durable cutting-edge is the one to use. This cutting-edge resist chipping during rough usage, but that's not the edge I prefer. For woodcarving, line cutting, meat cutting, or shaving, the knife's edge must have a thin, polished, honed cutting-edge blade—sharper than a razor—sharper than a surgeon's scalpel. I know the razor-sharp honed edge might chip in rough work, but it's the edge for fighting—it's the sharpness edge for me. I'll give my knife the sharpest edge, sharper than a razor. You'll see."

For an hour or more at night, and most of my noon hours, I sharpened my knife. To hone my blade was a chore and took longer than I expected using two Arkansas sharpening-stones, one a fine grit and the other a hard-super-fine stone. A coarse stone was available and would make sharpening faster, but I'm too proud and foolish to ask one of the old-timers to borrow their stones. I used the fine stone until my knife reached a sharp cutting-edge. Then using my super-fine hard finishing stone, I polished the blade's sharp edge to a shiny mirror ribbon finish making it razor-sharp. Yet I'm not done getting the sharpness I wanted. With a two-inch-wide leather belt and jeweler's rouge, I honed the blade's cutting-edge beyond razor sharpness.

Like the Cowboys in the old west shaved with a knife, I tried shaving with my blade—only did it once. After shaving, my reflection in the mirror looked as I lost a catfight with a Lynx with my face covered in deep scratches from razor-sharp claws. My blade cut my face up awful. I wouldn't try shaving with my knife again.

Many times, I proved that I could cut through a two-inch mooring line with one swipe. At every opportunity with an audience, I showed the knife's sharpness, cutting through sections of scrap mooring lines with one swipe of my blade, cutting thin strips from a sheet of paper, and then pointing out how well it fit my hand—just to show everybody my perfect knife.

This knife made me cocky. At first, my knife impressed almost everyone. Then showing off my knife started problems. Soon friends lost interest in my boast, but I was unaware of their discomfort. Shipmates liked to tag along with me while girl-hunting, yet they acted reluctant to work with me.

The COB took me aside and chewed me out, unleashing, "Your damn knife bragging is interrupting and delaying the seaman gang's work. This bragging about your stupid knife stops today—understand me! You're turning into a slacker and not pulling your weight. You're not getting your tasks done. We're getting an inspection soon and must get ready for our next deployment, so the topside gang has more than enough to do with an insufficient time to do it—I expect you to do your part—understand? Now, get your shit together. I'll be keeping an eye on you."

Later, thinking, shit, why did the COB chew my ass? I can't understand his disapproval of me telling everyone about my knife and how good and sharp it was. I didn't delay any work. How can my performance be degrading? So, how can I pay attention to his counseling—it's not warranted, it doesn't apply, besides I wasn't doing something illegal. Getting my shit together, shit, what does that mean? The COB is singling me out so he can give me the shitty details? The COB is hounding me because I became dink in my quals; it's just another old-fart finding fault. Shit, they are always finding fault. I'll just ignore the shit head.

Later, the COB assigned me duties I can do by myself, such as chipping and painting under the superstructure outside the forward line locker. As I worked under the superstructure, I discovered the work was challenging, with no room to move. The Key West sun heated the space to an intense temperature that made toiling inside it like working in a pizza oven. I'm convinced the COB disliked me.

The COB's treatment pissed me off—big time. To complete the day's work, he had the topside gang working late. The topside sailors complained about working late, but they had nothing to gripe about because the COB gave me the messiest and most strenuous tasks and made me work later than everyone else.

My reckless overconfidence was getting the better of me, with arrogance causing insolence. The COB doesn't understand that I'm helping him, or else he might have welcomed my help. You know what I mean. Pride in one's work is valuable. Because I know how to do knife sharping, it's my mission to teach the seamen about knives and knife sharpening. Think of the satisfaction the seamen will have after they have sharp blades.

When the COB was out of sight, I gathered three topside shipmates aft of the sail. With my knife as a prop, I explained the first step in knife sharpening. The COB caught me and ended my knife sharpening lecture. "Meet me in the goat locker in five minutes!" and stormed off before I can react.

At the goat locker door, I knocked and heard a loud, angry, "Enter!"

With care, I open the door, dreading what might happen. Thinking I might have pushed the COB too far. As I enter the goat locker, the COB looked peeved. He's furious with me. The COB's face is crimson, and his eyes blazed in anger when his loud, gruff voice scolded me. "If I have any more trouble or interference from you about your damn knife, I will rip off your head, stick it up your ass, and piss down your windpipe—got it?!"

"COB, you can't hurt me. It's against the UCMJ, besides it's a free country with free speech, and I can tell anyone about my knife anytime I want to—got it?" The COB's knife criticism was the same bullshit he's been giving me. But my defiant response was a massive mistake. Instead of telling him how I'm helping him, what I wanted to do, what came out of my mouth resulted from a massive brain fart—a case of quick anger overriding sound wisdom.

The COB became as livid as any man I have ever seen—his face changed to a vivid red, and his eyes bulged—he's fuming. Thinking, he lost control. I feared the COB might punch me. I backed away from his bellowing.

"You shit-for-brains when I order you to do something or tell you to stop doing something you damn well better follow my orders! If you don't, you will regret it for the rest of your born days! Don't ever, **EVER!** Question any order I give you—**NEVER! GOT IT?!**"

The COB took a breath and calmed down a scant, like dimming a bright light with a dimmer switch, his yelling going from bellowing to blustery bark, he continued his ass chewing. "I don't give a damn about your knife. I don't give a damn whom you tell about it! But, by God, you will only brag on your time, not mine! Do you understand me? If I hear about this one more time, you will regret you ever bought that damn knife! You'll be cleaning shit-tanks for the rest of your Navy career because you don't need a knife for cleaning shit-tanks! Now, shithead, get your dumb ass back to work! I don't want to hear another sound out of you!"

Even with the ass chewing, the COB was more hot air than substance. Besides, I didn't believe I was doing anything wrong. I convinced myself I'm helping him teach the crew in knife sharpening. Before the day was over, I had Bob, and Ferguson stopped in their topside work, discussing knives and how to hone them. The COB caught me again.

The COB snarled a whispered forewarning when he pulled me aside. "I will recalibrate and square your dumb-ass away."

Whatever that meant. I considered the COB wasn't an evil Chief, just misdirected, and had an attitude problem. Thinking to myself, we have a personality conflict, and the COB doesn't understand how I'm using my knife to teach the seamen knife skills that will help him. But I will get a humiliating cruise.

Two days later, the COB in good-natured humor ordered us, seamen, to meet him at 1600 in the forward torpedo room. I assumed my Goat Locker session with the COB changed his view, and he could now see how I was helping him. Upon entering the room, we found First-Class Petty Officer Sewell, who was the petty officer in charge of the forward torpedo room. Sewell was one of the seasoned warriors.

Sewell must have been the strongest man in the Navy if there is a walking crane, he's one. He picked up and carried a torpedo loading-skid end while it took two of us seamen with chain-falls to lift and move the other end. One day, I overheard the COB talking to the WEPS, "Sewell is one of the best torpedo men in the Navy, and he is one of the best shipmates a COB can have on a submarine. You can always count on him to do his duty. Sewell helps new sailors develop into reliable crewmembers by teaching quals, submarine life, and sets himself as the best example of a shipmate without ever yelling or boasting. Sewell applies effective leadership. Recommend him for Chief."

Couldn't see the justification for Sewell's praise. Sewell made my life miserable, giving me the hardest qualification questions, making me find the most useless information such as finding the boat's longest-line, or bring me a bucket of steam or getting a tube of relative bearing grease. After attempting to follow his directions, I felt foolish. How do you carry a bucket of steam? After two days searching the forward torpedo room, the aft torpedo room, and the pump room, I couldn't find any relative bearing grease. But I discovered relative bearing grease doesn't exist. Who could figure out the longest-line aboard the boat was the waterline? Sewell made me find useless information just to give me a rough time.

As we waited for the COB, I got right into showing off my knife after Ferguson asked me how I kept that sharp-edge on my blade. Bob appeared interested too, so I jumped right into sharpening instruction. Then, I overheard Sewell calling the Goat Locker and reporting, "everything is ready," but I didn't connect that the talk concerned me. I didn't detect they were setting me up or foresaw the severe embarrassment I will soon experience.

The COB entered the torpedo room and looked towards Sewell. "Is everything ready?"

I stopped my sharpening lesson and placed my knife into its sheath.

Sewell showed a sly smile and gave the COB an affirmative nod. "All set."

I didn't understand their exchange.

The COB looked at me and asked, "do you think your knife is the best knife on the Spikefish?"

"It's the best and sharpest knife aboard and the best damn knife in this man's Navy. I don't understand why the Navy wastes money buying junk knives. The Navy should issue knives like mine." With my age's arrogance, I responded.

"Wager, it isn't the best knife onboard. I know it isn't." The COB countered.

"Oh yeah, is that so? Well, who has the best knife aboard?" I shot back in a know-it-all manner, as a five-year-old reacts during a playground conflict. Thinking, I'm aware of how perfect my knife is. I can't believe the COB is acting like a three-year-old and not understanding such a simple fact—my blade is the best.

"Sewell has the best knife."

"Bullshit!" I challenged.

"To prove it, and show you how great his knife is, I bet I can take Sewell's knife and cut your knife blade in half, to show you how good his knife is."

"No knife on earth can do that," I stressed.

"Sewell, bring me your knife." The COB turned towards me. "Hand me yours."

I hand the COB my knife, handle first. Sewell moved to his locker, searched for his knife. After a few minutes, Sewell shouted, "Found it! I picked up this knife when I was on the seaman gang thirty years ago, and it's a good knife and an even better tool." Sewell then handed the COB his small hunting knife.

"Can I see it?" Then the COB handed me Sewell's knife.

I inspected Sewell's knife. Sewell's blade looked old, rusty, and messy. The blade is a thick five inches long with the color of dull gray steel. Rust spots are present where the handle meets the blade-guard. Black tar smudges stuck to the blade's sides. The knife's condition shows its age and how Sewell kept it. With my thumb, I checked the knife's cutting-edge, trying to detect sharpness—no sharp-edge.

Sewell's knife needed sharpening. The knife's blade is so dull it couldn't cut soft butter.

"There is no way that knife can cut my blade in half," As I handed Sewell's knife back to the COB.

"Put up or shut up. Bet you a six-pack. I can use Sewell's knife and cut your knife in-two, the COB replied."

"The bet's on! Prove it," I'm sure of my victory.

The COB held out his hand. "Let's shake on it to make the wager official."

We shook hands, then the COB took my knife in his left hand with its sharp, shiny honed edge facing up and held Sewell's knife in his right hand, the COB positions Sewell's knife's dull-edge over my knife's sharp-edge—sharp-edge under the dull-edge above—touching. With Sewell's knife, the COB applies as much force as he can, trying to cut my knife blade in two. The COB takes his time driving Sewell's rusty, dirty blade along the length of my knife's cutting-edge. On his first try, he couldn't cut my blade in-two—he tried again. The COB's face turned bright red as he worked harder, pushing Sewell's knife into mine, trying to cut my blade in two. I knew he couldn't do it. After his fifth try, the COB stopped his knife-cutting effort, and with a pleased look on his face, the COB handed me back my knife. "I hate to say it, but I guess you have the best knife. I owe you a six-pack for winning."

Content in my triumph and with conceit, I showed everyone my knife. "I knew it! It's proven—I have the best knife aboard." A moment of expressed exhilaration turned to dismay when I looked at my knife, inspecting the cutting-edge, seeing a jagged edge. My knife no longer had the smooth mirror razor-sharp-edge it had moments before the challenge. Its blade was now a poor excuse for a saw blade. Big metal gouges and chips were in my knife's cutting-edge. Along a short cutting-edge without chips or gouges, the honed edge curled back with the sharp-edge destroyed. "My blade! my blade, I worked so hard to sharpen my knife—you ruined it!" I shouted.

"I didn't ruin it. You must re-sharpen it. I told you to stop your bragging, but you didn't listen. You should have expected something." The COB drawled, suppressing unmistakable laughter.

The Torpedo room audience watched my embarrassment unfold. My friends burst out laughing. Laughing so hard, they had tears in their eyes.

As I hold back tears, I realized how foolish I was.

The aftermath of my humiliation traveled through the boat faster than the speed of light. I couldn't go anywhere aboard without making someone break-up into a fit of laughter, wanting to inspect my Honed Knife. Mortified, I suffered. It took a while to overcome my embarrassment. But what made this worse, I inherited the title, The Knife or Knife, that everyone aboard called me after this incident. I detested this title because I felt humiliated when I revisited my public embarrassment every time someone used The Knife or Knife when addressing me.

After honing for two weeks to re-sharpen my knife to match the edge before the knife contest, I kept my knife's condition to myself, never boasting about my knife again.

Much later, I overheard the COB talking to the WEPS concerning me. "He's become one of the most likable sailors aboard and the sailor I can count on to get a job done—and done right. Goeschel is a hot runner and makes work fun for the troops and does his duty—and that's what we need on subs, hot-runners. Hot runners work hard, play hard, and do their duty. Because he earned it, I'm reassigning Goeschel as the topside gang leading seamen for his last month aboard before he's transferred. He is ready for greater responsibilities when he works for a weapons department. Goeschel is ready for the challenges a weapons department offers."

The COB got my attention by providing a unique approach, giving me some suffering and sent me on a humiliation cruise that guaranteed I couldn't forget the experience, and he changed my brashness. The COB got the best out of me without writing me up or getting the higher-ups involved. When I heard his praise, it was a proud moment. My decision to volunteer for submarines—turns out it was a good one.

OWNERSHIP

Charlie, with his title, Barf-bucket, was working on a new title, red-lead because when painting the forward topside line-locker under the superstructure with red-lead, he got more paint on him and on many other places than the line-locker he was painting. Barf-bucket spilled a gallon of red-lead into the line-locker, stepped in the spilled paint, and distributed red tracks over a recently painted topside. While seeking rags to clean up his mess, Barf-bucket spread red foot-print tracks from the line locker hatch ran past the sail, across the brow to the pier, to the paint locker, showing his path to get rags. With rags in hand, Barf-bucket saw his trail of red-lead. Barf-bucket tried to clean one of the topside tracks, but all he accomplished was to make it worst; his scrubbing smeared the paint into a larger paint spot looking awful. With anxiety, he looked at the mess he made. It's a fiasco distributed too widely to clean.

The COB lost it after seeing red footprints topside. After a week of hard work, his topside seaman finished the painting the day before Barf-bucket messed it up. With a crimson face, eyes focused in anger at Barf-bucket, the COB barking to the topside's leading seamen, pointing at Barf-bucket, "Kenny, you get that shit-for-brains to paint topside by himself. I expect a fresh coat of flat black to cover up his red footprints. If he had any sense, this wouldn't have happened!"

I overheard the COB when he took Kenny aside. The COB asks, "Where were you when that shithead was painting topside red with his shoes? You're expected to instruct and oversee your topside crew. You disappointed me, big-time."

Kenny looked devastated by the COB's tongue-lashing.

An embarrassed Kenny seeking to redeem himself angrily directed and supervised Barf-bucket as he repainted topside. Barf-bucket finished repainting the topside in time to have liberty with the seamen gang for my 20th birthday celebration when we hit the beach, the night of October 21, 1962.

While Barf-bucket was repainting the topside, I encountered the COB getting his coffee in the crew's mess, and I asked him, "COB, why did you ream out Kenny? He did nothing wrong. Barf-bucket screwed up. It's not fair."

The COB with a grim expression pointed to a seat at the Chief's table and commanded, "Get a cup of coffee and sit." He sat opposite to my assigned place.

As I'm pouring my coffee, I'm thinking, unless ordered to do so, no way I would ever sit at that table. Am I in trouble for questioning the COB? I'm uneasy speculating as I sit down, trying not to spill hot coffee, watching the COB, seeking my answer.

The COB takes a leisurely sip from a stained coffee mug, staring at me, collecting his thoughts, he surprises me, going into a dialogue as if he's talking to one of his buddies, making me attentive.

You need to learn more leadership, so pay attention. What I say now will serve you the rest of your life no matter if you stay in the Navy or not.

The issue with Seaman Kenny is a glaring example of a failure in leadership. You assume I'm unfair, but I have a reason for jacking up Kenny. I'm training Kenny for further responsibility. He may not realize it now, but Kenny will be purposeful, taking accountability doing his future duties.

Kenny, as the leading seamen, has responsibility for everything topside, meaning he gains ownership of topside and takes accountability for the seamen in the deck gang. In this duty, he didn't train and supervise Barf-bucket. Kenny saw the red lead footprints on the topside and must have had a brain fart because he didn't start corrective action. Kenny didn't lead to square-up Barf-bucket's dumb ass mess-up. He didn't prevent Barf-bucket, making a paint mess topside—from the forward line-locker along the sail's port side to the brow, crossing the brow towards the paint locker at the end of the pier.

The leading seamen neglected to make Barf-bucket clean up his mess. Kenny's authority should have prevented or fixed Barf-bucket's screw-up—it was Kenny's duty to train his subordinates and correct mistakes his subordinates may make. Instead, Kenny screwed-up, instead of correcting the issue, he waited for me to confront Barf-bucket's mess. Kenny is an excellent leading seaman, but he has much to learn, like you. After today, Kenny will devote better attention to his responsibilities.

Look at it this way if an Admiral discovered topside's messed-up condition, he wouldn't discuss the issue with Barf-bucket, Kenny, or me, but he would have a private meeting with the CO. During that meeting, the CO would get his ass reamed for tolerating or allowing his submarine to have an unacceptable condition. The CO has the ultimate accountability for the *Spikefish*—the CO owns it. If the CO found topside a mess before me, well, I would answer embarrassing inquiries. 'Why did you allow this mess to take place, and how do you plan to fix it, so it never happens again?' The answer to the CO, I will fix this. It will not happen again."

As the COB with the duty as the First Lieutenant, I answer to the CO having the responsibility for the seaman gang, the topside condition, and related obligations—I own it. Similarly, Kenny answers to the First Lieutenant. I give the leading-seaman accountability for everything topside—he owns it and maintains responsibility for the seamen working for him. Kenny didn't take ownership of his duties—he didn't do his duty.

After you're in the Navy longer, you may develop into a leader. No matter the title, a leader could be a seaman, leading seaman, petty officer, or more advanced. When you become a petty officer, you may take charge of an FT Gang. As a section leader, you run your duty section. If you stay in longer and make Chief, you might oversee a division or have higher authority, but you always answer to a leader with a higher power. Leaders accept ownership of their duties, meaning leaders are answerable for the good and the bad. Leaders meet obligations and engage with whatever is amiss within their ability. If subordinate's performance goes astray, leaders have only one-way to respond to the higher authority. I'm responsible. I'll investigate it, fix it, and I'll ensure it will never happen again.

Watch your petty officers, Chiefs, and officers— learn from them. Find out how your leaders act towards a dilemma. Study and note their effective reaction to issues and examine the methods leaders use that you consider inadequate or incompetent. Challenge yourself, answer the question, what's a better approach to handle the problem.

If you take ownership of your duties, you will succeed in the Navy, and if you don't, you don't belong here. If you ascribe to keep yourself as the higher authority in meeting your responsibilities, as you own them, you will keep the brain farts and other embarrassments to a minimum. For example, if you know, something is amiss, if it within your means to fix it, you correct the wrong. You don't need me to tell you it's wrong, you don't need me to say rectify it, but you must keep me apprised of what you did. You follow command policies and orders while you are dealing with wrong.

Afterward, I was enjoying a gorgeous sunset, relaxing on the smoking deck. A refreshing breeze is comforting me as the boat glided through the seas. While looking forward to my next lookout watch, I reflected on the COB's leadership discourse with me. Why did this take place? I wasn't aware the COB gives individual leadership lessons to others. I appreciated that he took the time with me—guiding me. Never speculating having a leadership position in the Navy, then why did the COB choose me for our talk? Maybe, he saw in me something I didn't see. I marveled.

Many times when looking back, I recalled the COB's counseling. Following that wisdom, I took ownership of my duties, leading to great success, mainly when I was the leading Weapons Chief on the *Billfish*. After taking ownership of the fire control division and its equipment, I ensured system equipment worked, supporting the *Billfish* to meet her commitments where the Navy awarded her a Meritorious Unit Commendation. More so, as the COB, owning the COB's duties, contributed to the *Billfish* winning the Battle E. *Billfish's* achievement was not done only by my efforts. The crew from the CO to the most junior took ownership by performing their duties with professionalism.

THE CUBAN MISSILE CRISIS

The Cuban Missile Crisis was a significant historical event that scared the shit out of everyone knowledgeable enough to recognize how close we came to use nuclear weapons. The Cuban Missile Crisis produced my first naval adventure. Since I was not following any news developments, my life comprised submarine qualifying, partying, fishing, swimming, and pursuing women—no TV and no radio. At the time, I was clueless regarding the details of the Cuban Missile Crisis—oblivious of how close the world came to experience the horrors of a nuclear war. I was unaware of the issues, the breakdown of communications between the United States, the Soviet Union, and Cuba, the mistrust between each country, and their role in creating strained relationships. We knew nothing about a US U-2 plane that discovered and photographed workers assembling Soviet missiles in Cuba. These details remained unknown to us junior submarine crew members making us unmindful of approaching impending events. Events that historians later label as The Cuban Missile Crisis.

The *USS Spikefish* AGSS 404, my first sub, was in upkeep at Key West Florida, preparing for our next deployment, including a scheduled Cuban port of call. Veteran crewmembers made me eager for liberty in Cuba as they told sea stories describing Cuba as sailors' best liberty on the East Coast. They enlightened us newcomers about Cuba's friendly people, exquisite cuisine, fine rum, fine cigars, and plenty of eager, willing lovely women. The crewmembers' new accounts became racier than earlier juicy stories implying the ladies are delightful, encouraging our attention. Then, the Cuban Missile Crisis events stopped our planned Cuban liberty, ending future outstanding liberty prospects— the United States Navy's welcome terminated.

Disappointed that the scheduled liberty had changed to preparations for war, instead, I was fortunate, the Cuban Missile Crisis event provided me a naval adventure. Favorable for my perception, I remained unaware of the danger. I sailed through a substantial storm at sea. I nearly got the crap kicked out of me one night in Norfolk. That same night, I fell hopelessly in and out of love, then getting gloriously drunk replaced my pain of love lost. The following morning, I had an incredible hangover and became seasick for the first time, which most likely resulted from getting splendidly drunk—what an adventure!

My exploits started on October 21, 1962, on my twentieth birthday when my shipmates, Bob and Charlie, celebrated it by taking me to town. Not knowing about the approaching conflict, our youthful naivete led to partying hard. If we had known differently, we might have been diligent in preparing for war. On the beach that night, our assembly made a notable group, seeking female company—finding none, being too young for bar hopping. We cannot find suitable excitement or entertainment in Key West. The pool halls and movie theaters were the only establishments that catered to young people. Bob and Charlie chipped in for a bottle of booze, purchasing a bottle of Old Grand-Dad from a saloon that sold alcohol to underage sailors. Civilian lawmakers believed underage alcohol consumption an atrocious offense, and to protect us, they created a drinking law, "only persons 21 years or older can drink alcohol." Some Navy higher-ups agreed and expected the Shore Patrol and military commands to enforce Florida's drinking laws. No matter, we could buy alcohol anyway, but we can't drink it where we bought it, so we took our Old Grand-Dad to a fishing pier where locals fished. The chain of events that followed led to the realization that we should have remained sober.

Besides lacking experience in the Navy, when it came to meeting girls, we were novices. Like many young people, we lacked drinking practice and were deficient in selecting drinkable cocktails and the ability to drink without becoming smashed. For example, other than beer, we didn't know what to consume, recalling what movie characters drank such as gin and prune juice or bourbon and branch—finding out later that branch was water. Looking back, not knowing any better, in high school, I tried gin mixed with prune juice once. The drink tasted good, but I learned that gin mixed with prune juice was not a good mixture to drink in large quantities. The combination produced more than a hangover, causing me to devote a long time in the shitter. After dad found out about my drinking gin mixed with prune juice, he was unable to discipline me because he couldn't prevent his laughing. That night, I knew enough to avoid a gin and prune juice choice—Charlie's suggestion.

Typical on subs, senior crewmembers attached slang titles to young sailors reflecting a quality a sailor displayed. In our case, the seasoned crew called me, "The Knife," a title I unwillingly earned, inducing embarrassment every time anyone called me as, "The Knife." They gave Bob the title of Granny Knot because he couldn't tie anything properly, not even his shoelaces. Charlie's title was Barf-bucket because he became seasick promptly as the Spikefish got underway instantly after the OOD orders, "Cast off number one line." Underway, Charlie kept a barf-bucket in easy reach when he was out of his rack.

Well, back to liberty. On the beach, while watching locals fishing on a pier, we drank our fifth of Old Grand-Dad. Unfamiliar with the art of mixing drinks for boozing, we experimented, we sampled our bourbon straight. By itself, the bourbon tasted too harsh. To make it drinkable, we made concoctions by sweetening the bourbon with soda. We mixed bourbon and Coke—drinkable, and then we mixed bourbon and Seven-up after we ran out of Coke—still drinkable. The relaxing tropical ambiance and our drink inventions caused enjoyment. We downed our creations until we emptied the bourbon bottle, finishing the booze with a dilemma. Over time, our bodies absorbed the alcohol, drunk, we became. We couldn't hold our liquor. As we left the pier, rowdily singing, staggering, a little unsteady, smashed, intoxicated, you know what I mean—drunk as a skunk can be and yet able to walk— acting socially unacceptable.

The Shore Patrol knew trouble was looming. The commands canceled liberty and tasked the Shore Patrol to collect the sailors in town, but we didn't know about the Shore Patrol's orders. We did nothing wrong except drinking underage, drinking too much, and became intoxicated. Soon after leaving the pier, we stagger towards the barracks, then two Shore Patrol petty officers, in a pickup truck, picked us up and took us to the Subbase barracks. I was thankful for the ride. I guessed later; the Shore Patrol expected that we would do something unsocial, causing discredit to the Navy. As I reflect on it, the Shore Patrol might have been right. We wouldn't do this on purpose, but in our physical state likelihood mayhem would occur—I thought we were in trouble

After our drinking, I was tipsy, sleepy, and without a concern in the world. A professional would have perceived my condition as smashed. When we arrived at the barracks, I craved sleep, but I'm awake. I see my shipmates looking deplorable. Granny Knot is asleep in an intoxicated stupor was in the arms of the Shore Patrol. Barf-bucket staggered into the head. I overhear him buying Buicks and howling for O'-RORIC.

In the barracks, the Shore Patrol didn't put us on report but turned us over to our COB. They knew our COB would take care of us better than sending us to Captain's Mast. I learned later; this was correct.

The COB is in the barracks at this late hour. Why? Are we in trouble for our night's escapades, or is it possible he is here for something else? Inebriated, those thoughts came and went. It did not occur, nor did I care to find the answers, but I should have.

"We are getting ready for war!" Bellows the COB, and then commands, "Get your seabags packed, bring everything you need for extended sea patrol, get your shit to the Boat, and be quick about it. We're leaving Key West in the morning."

This war news sobered us up slightly. I considered I was abler than my shipmates were. While trying to pack our seabags, we were like the three stooges, falling asleep, waking up, and stumbling over one another. Barf-bucket took an item out of his locker, dropped it, then ran to the head calling for O'-ROARIC, returned to packing, and then resumed this cycle until he got his seabag nearly filled. Granny Knot fell asleep. One of us would wake him. He packed an item and then dropped back asleep; we repeatedly woke him. He filled his seabag bit by bit.

I tried rolling my uniforms—boot camp style, knowing if I rolled up every item as I learned in Boot Camp, my stuff will fit into my seabag. Rolled up uniforms wouldn't wrinkle as much as other ways of packing a seabag. In my condition, I couldn't do it to my satisfaction. I rolled an item up, unrolled it because the roll wasn't tight enough, and started over rolling my clothes. I might still be working packing that seabag at the pace I was doing it, but saving me, the COB provided motivation, bellowing. "Get the lead out. You shitheads don't have all night. The last one done will start mess-cooking in the morning!"

From my locker, I grabbed everything I had and tossed my stuff on my bunk. Then, I rolled each piece of clothing as tight as I could, cramming each roll of clothing into my seabag, stuffing it to overflowing, making closing the seabag hopeless. With frustration, I picked up my seabag and dropped it on the deck. That didn't work. Then, I sat on the bag's top and squashed rolls of clothes and skivvies into the seabag—that worked. Somehow, my seabag and I arrive at the boat before my shipmates.

No matter, I received no sleep that night. On the Spikefish, I place my seabag on our hot-bunking bunk I shared with Granny Knot and Barf-bucket, but before I could climb into the rack, the COB called the seamen gang topside to rig the topside for sea. As I climbed topside, coming out of the Aft Battery Hatch, I see Granny Knot and Barf-bucket showing up dragging their seabags over the brow.

With a red-face and eyes bulging in anger, the COB bellows in a rage, "You shit-heads, stow your gear below and get back topside. I want you two shit-heads topside in three minutes or else, and you don't want to know what the else is!"

I'm uncertain how they managed it, but Granny Knot and Barf-bucket came up topside in time for the COB to put the Topside Gang to work. We rigged topside for sea, securing extra mooring lines in the line lockers. We inspected under the superstructure for anything loose that rattled. What we found movable, we tightened, wedged it securely, or removed things we could move. We tied up locker access hatch's latches, preventing a hatch opening or rattling, so, during a depth-charging, they produced no sounds. The seamen worked until breakfast, and after breakfast, we continued working topside underneath the superstructure.

The way I suffered after breakfast made me realize this day won't be fun. Working topside, while under the superstructure, with that

Key West sun beating down, I thought I died and traveled to hell as if I'm working in an oven with the temperature set at 110 degrees, everything I touched was hot. Along with a terrible headache, I felt sick to my stomach, ready to vomit. I wasn't too quick doing my work that morning, doing my tasks as best as possible, and I got them done. That morning, I heard for the first time a fitting expression, "If you dance to the fiddle at night, you must pay the performer in the morning," discovering the payment expensive.

The COB worked us hard. He did not pity our condition, not appreciating our drunken arrival in the barracks the previous night. He made this day horrible for me, creating an unforgettable memory.

While I was enjoying my hangover on October 22, 1962, I was oblivious of the world's events, only knowing we were preparing for combat, making ready to sail in harm's way. That day, President John Kennedy delivered a televised speech announcing the detection of Soviet Union missiles in Cuba. The president announced a naval blockade around Cuba. He further made it understandable the United States will use military force if necessary. The President expressed that it shall be the policy of this nation to regard any nuclear missile launched from Cuba against any country in the Western Hemisphere as an attack by the Soviet Union on the United States, requiring a full retaliatory response on the Soviet Union.

President Kennedy described the administration's intention. "To halt this offensive buildup, a strict quarantine on all offensive military equipment under shipment to Cuba is being initiated. All ships of any kind bound for Cuba, from whatever nation or port, will if found to contain cargoes of offensive weapons, be turned back. This quarantine will be extended, if needed, to other types of cargo and carriers. We are not at this time, however, denying the necessities of life as the Soviets attempted to do in their Berlin blockade of 1948."

During the speech, a directive reached out to all U.S. forces worldwide, placing them on DEFCON 3. The Navy started the Cuba blockade, with the heavy cruiser USS Newport News as the named flagship.

Not getting underway right away with the Spikefish moored at the quayside, I observed one of the most unexpected naval happenings I have ever witnessed or heard about. This ain't no shit.

That morning, I'm still clueless regarding the world events, but I felt queasy and nauseous working under the scorching Key West sun. With my stomach-turning, I struggled to prevent vomiting. An unexpected humorous event broke up our discomfort as we watched Submarine Squadron 4, the US Navy's Sunshine Squadron of Key West, Florida, going to war. With our hangovers helping, the *Spikefish* was the first squadron boat ready for battle. We moved from our pier to the Quay-Wall in front of the squadron's office building. Why we didn't get underway promptly is unknown. Most likely, we relocated to get us out of everyone else's way. I assumed we're here at the Quay-Wall for an acceptable reason; it must be notable as waiting for an Admiral or assigned to a defensible position to protect the Squadron. Because, from our view, everyone topside saw the boats in our Squadron, getting ready for war, loading torpedoes, loading stores, and taking on fuel.

A squadron boat was in extended upkeep. We saw tugs push a floating crane up alongside the sub. With heroic effort from the crane's crew and divers in the water, they re-attached her removed screws. After completing that task, tugs pulled the floating crane away from the sub. We assumed this boat was now ready for sea.

The sub started her engines, four-diesels running, roaring loud, from her exhaust's large clouds of white smoke, forming a white blanket of fog. Within minutes smoke covered the basin. The smoke carried the whiff of running diesel engines. Through this haze, I noticed her. To my astonishment, that boat started forward. She should have been backing out into the harbor, but she moved in just the opposite direction. Her speed is increasing, going forward faster, traveling straight at the quay wall at the beginning of the pier where the boat moored.

Her bow slid over the quay wall as if the quay wall was not an obstacle. Instead of smashing the bow on its wall—lucky for the boat, she crushed an empty phone booth, sitting as a target standing on the quay wall next to the beginning of its pier. With incredible accuracy, the boat hit the phone booth centerline, knocking the phone booth over. The sound of glass breaking added to a loud noise of crashing scraping metal. The phone booth fell on the hood of a car parked just behind it. With extraordinary determination, the boat kept on coming, sliding over the phone booth until it stopped.

The boat's bow sat on top of the phone booth that was lying on top of the car's hood, crushing the front of that helpless, unfortunate car, a classic 1957 Chevrolet two-door bright red hardtop that did nothing to offend that boat to give it such an attack—unlucky for the vehicle.

During low tide, the boat could not slide over a high quay wall. Then hitting the wall might have damaged the boat's bow instead of destroying the car and phone booth. The high tide was a reason in this unusual happening allowing a submarine to attack a vehicle and phone booth.

The boat stopped its forward movement. A topside crew sent a brow over to the pier. From the dock to the sub, the brow leaned at a steep angle. The brow sat as a ladder on a wall resting on the side of that unfortunate submarine. Officers climbed the brow down to the pier. Officers come pouring out of the squadron's office building, then running faster to the dock, stopping creating an officer's cluster, inspecting the damage done, discussing the destruction. After completing their inspection, the boat's officers came back aboard, having a rougher time climbing up that steep brow than going down it. The squadron officers stayed on the pier, observing as if their supervision would prevent further embarrassment and damage.

On the submarine, a group of officers formed on their forward deck, looking as they were having a discussion. As I observed this unfold, I guessed that their conversation was how they would get their submarine off the crushed car, the phone booth, and the quay wall. Discussion over, the officer assembly left the forward deck, and then, more excitement.

I saw screw wash swirling from the boat's stern, trying to back off from that pier. The submarine was unsuccessful on its first try—the sub didn't move. A topside crew attached lines from the dock to their forward and aft-capstans. With the lines so tight like steel rods indicated a massive strain on them. I thought with the stress they put on the lines would part the mooring lines—the lines held. But backing and using the capstans—didn't work. Two tugs pull up alongside the sub, one forward and one aft. With the help of tugs, plus using their capstans and the sub backing, worked. The submarine slides off the car, phone booth, and pier. As the boat backed off the car, the phone booth, and dock, the sub seemed humiliated, causing a loud screeching noise sliding off the pier. As an act of defiance, the sub's bow dropped suddenly, hitting the water, creating a great splash, dousing the observers on the dock, and the forward topside gang, giving an unexpected saltwater shower. No doubt, a wet embarrassed forward topside gang tied up their unfortunate boat to the dock.

The tugs released from that luckless submarine moved across the harbor and re-tied up to the floating crane. Again, we watched tugs push the floating crane to the unfortunate sub. With a further notable effort from the crane crew and divers, they removed the boat's screws, turned them around, and then reattached the screws. The floating crane pushed off, signaling that this sub was ready for sea. This time, with caution, the sub backed out into the harbor basin. My confidence in that boat's ability to help the US Navy win any war diminished.

After we arrived in Norfolk, the boat's lookouts divulged what occurred, and what the officers on the bridge said. The lookouts observed what went on and heard everything, and were eager to tell their story, thinking it was hilarious. They told us their account of what transpired.

Somehow, while we were in upkeep, someone put the screws on backward. "It's supposed to be impossible to install screws on backward, but someone did it. Anyway, when we left the pier, the OOD ordered, "All Back 1/3." The boat started forward. The OOD, not knowing the problem, increased the back-bell ordering, "All Back 2/3," causing the boat to go ahead faster.

Likewise, not knowing the issue with the screws and seeing the sub's increased forward progress, our Skipper in warning panic ordered, "All Back Emergency!" He was determined to attack that phone booth and car. I don't think he wanted that. As fast as a submarine can go in a short distance, the boat's bow hit the pier, slid up and skidded right over it, crushing the phone booth, and ramming the phone booth onto the car to the dismay of the boat's Commanding Officer who owned the vehicle."

It didn't take our officers long to figure out what transpired, but they were too late to prevent it. After they had determined the cause of the issue, they solved how to move the boat backward. To move rearward, they had to use a forward bell. With a forward bell, they tried to back off the pier. That didn't work. They tried using their aft-capstan with the backing bell; that did not work either. Our CO called for tugs. With the tugs' aid and using their aft-capstan with a backing bell, our boat slid off the pier. No one expected the splash when the bow dropped."

The Captain's submarine crushed his car and that phone booth. I bet, the Captain and the OOD thought their naval careers had just ended with destroying the phone booth and car. Later, we would get a laugh; each time, we told the story of how that Captain must explain to his insurance company on how he smashed his car with his submarine. This story is worth repeating. This ain't no shit."

The *Spikefish* was the last boat leaving Key West. At day's end, I was a tired sailor. After a gallon of black coffee, I learned to drink coffee black that day. Since then, I drink coffee black. Later that day, I felt better from the previous night's escapades. In my condition, starting to the sea made it one of my worst days, an unpleasant event.

USS SPIKEFISH (AGSS 404)

CALM SEAS

The sea delivered gentle refreshing breezes
The breezes comforted me
Rays of light caress fluffy clouds
Clouds with colors shining through
Skies show majestic splendor
A calming beauty imparted wonder

An incredible sight
Dolphins playing in our wake
A transparent dark blue-black of the deep
Into the depth, how deep I might see
An admiration a wonderment

Glorious colors painted cosmic horizons
Dancing colors splash billowing flowing clouds
On cresting waves thin white strips of foam
Colors skip across ribbons of cresting foam
Foam carrying colors crest gracefully
Colorful ribbons dance on blue rolling waves
Majestic beauty overwhelms me

When cosmic heavens' stars ignite
Waves portray majestic sights
God's splendor lights the sky at night
Sparkling light covers a vast sky at night
I saw contentment that cleansed my soul

At sea a sense of bliss
The boundless tranquility humbled me
Astonishing radiance affected reverence
The sea's tranquility inspired me
God's existence no longer questioned

ON TO NORFOLK

At sea, I had the second watch after the maneuvering watch. After chow, I proceeded topside to stand my lookout watch. Once I'm in the shears, starting my watch, the sea delivered gentle refreshing breezes. I felt better. At sea, while on the surface, I stood lookout and helmsman watches. The lookouts searched the surface across the sea. When I was topside on watch, our watch section topside comprised the OOD, the Port, and Starboard Lookouts. Once out of the harbor, we did a trim dive. The lookouts rushed below to take our submerged watch stations comprising the Bow and Stern Planes, and Helmsman watches. The COB was the Diving Officer for our first dive. The Diving Officer set the boat's initial trim. With the trim set, the boat surfaced. Watch-standers went back to our topside watch stations with me as the Starboard Lookout.

Cool breezes comforted me compared from the hell I had in port; the surface conditions at sea were inspirational. In these tropical seas, I was awestruck, looking at a bright sunny and cloudy sky. The clouds protected us from the sun's full heat. I searched skyward, viewing a distinctive bright blue sky scattered with sparkling white billowy clouds with rays of light shining through, resembling light beams caressing flower petals, changing colors, adding beauty to the image, creating a sense of bliss. Gentle rolling swells caused the boat to do mild slow rolls. The rollers transporting cresting waves carried thin white strips of foam cresting gracefully over the tops of the swells, making ribbons of white foam dancing on tops of waves. As I looked into the depth, into a transparent dark blue-black of the deep, wondering how deep might I see.

Towards sunset, I searched the horizon, seeing a changing painted glory where the sea and sky touched, creating a colorful sunset, crafting a beauty that moved me profoundly. To this day, when God displays his glory, painting the sky and the seas with vivid colors—reds, oranges, pinks, and blues, showing majestic beauty, God puts me awestruck, in astonishment. Towards the end of my first watch, we lost the sight of land.

As a Lookout, I found the watch to be the most enjoyable and exalted of tasks mainly when the seas produce displays of colorful sunsets and glorious sunrises that show beautiful bright red, orange, and yellow changing pictures painted on a broad canvas. When the Horizon's sky is full of dancing colors splashing over billowing flowing clouds, I sense wonderment. When waves catch colors skipping across ribbons of foam, colors dancing on cresting blue rolling waves covering the sea. The scene portrays majestic images that allure me, showing ocean images with an astonishing radiance that affects my reverence. At different times, the sea delivers contentment with gentle refreshing breezes gusting over blue rolling waves, causing pleasure that cleanses my soul. When cosmic heavens' stars ignite, the sky at night with a blanket of sparkling light covering a black sea puts me in awe. The vast seas' might and tranquility inspires and humbles me.

The *Spikefish* was heading in harm's way, and I thought we were invincible. God is looking out for us. Crew training was the best; we worked together as one precision team. The officers and Chiefs always impressed me with their abilities. With full confidence, we could go to war, win any battles, and come back alive. The *Spikefish* was from a class of submarines that proved themselves in a real fighting war to be a powerful weapon. As part of the crew and knowing how good we were, I knew we performed together like a finely tuned machine. In the short time I was aboard, I named the boats in our squadron just by glancing at their superstructures. When I qualified as a lookout, I had to prove that ability. Qualification training caused us to look indirectly at an object to observe it better. Lookouts must spot the enemy before they detect us, and we must be ready for submerging in case the enemy discovers us first. In the case of detection, the lookouts must clear the bridge in seconds. In normal operations, we always tried to beat our earlier records in clearing the bridge.

The squadron was heading north, making a Wolf Pack. The Sunshine Squadron comprised twelve submarines. On two of the boats, attached to their bow, was a sonar dome filled with sonar transducers. The sonar dome made the boats strange and funny looking, but there was nothing comical about them because these boats were submarine hunters—distinctive killer class submarines. The boats' primary job was to find and sink subs. The killer class subs' sonar dome caused a drawback, slowing them down during surface cruising. There were two of these boats in our squadron, the USS Grenadier (SS525), and USS Balao (SS285).

Four Boats in our squadron were in the Guppy Class, USS Chopper (SS342), USS Quillback (SS429), USS Sea Leopard (SS483), and USS Threadfin (SS410). The Guppies are fleet-boats with modernized sonar, equipped with snorkels, sleek bows, and guppy sails. Guppies look fast when tied up alongside a pier, not having the sonar dome bow. The boats with snorkels could stay submerged longer than submarines without snorkels. Guppies can recharge their batteries at periscope depth while snorkeling.

Also, our squadron had two experimental boats, USS *Barracuda* *(SST3)* and *USS Marlin (SST2)*, much smaller than the fleet boats. These boats' fighting ability was unknown.

The four never modernized Fleet Boats, *USS Spikefish (SS404)*, *USS Tirante (SS420)*, *USS Sea Poacher (SS406)*, and *USS Atule (SS403)* completed the squadron's taskforce. The Fleet Boats were the fastest in the squadron while on the surface.

The *Spikefish* was ready, expecting a fight. Proud to be part of it, the *Spikefish* on the surface cruising, heading to Norfolk, Virginia, out-front, and leading the pack. For a young exhilarated sailor, I'm heading for war, standing port and starboard watches, rotating between lookout and helmsmen watch stations, six hours on watch, and six hours off.

The first two days at sea presented me a problem; I didn't get much sleep. When off watch, the COB had the seamen gang prepare for war, making us do many tasks. The seamen stored all the food and extra equipment we took on just before getting underway. Then we got rid of the packaging this stuff came in, cardboard boxes, wrapping paper, and bags. Also, we enjoyed the never-ending cleanup. The COB worked us extra hard. Maybe the COB still has not forgiven us for our conduct in port.

Understand, I did not sleep over 30 minutes in the past 48 hours, and the first part of that time, I was hungover. During my fourth watch with little sleep, around towards sunset, I got sleepy like a tired sober puppy. From boot-camp lessons, we knew during wartime, sleeping while on a watch might get you shot. To stay awake, I did anything I could, talking to the OOD, Lieutenant Always Alert[13], and the Port Lookout, Seamen Can't-See. Talking worked until the Lieutenant figured that I'm talking too much and not paying attention to my job

---

[13] Lieutenant Always Alert is the nick name for a fine officer whose name is forgotten

as a lookout. The OOD ordered me to shut up and pay attention to my duties.

Later, I spotted dolphins swimming alongside our boat. Through the crystal blue clear seas, I observed dolphins clearly through the transparent dark blue sea. Dolphins would swim right up to our bow, playing in our wake, giving me an incredible sight. I remembered old-timers telling me, "When dolphins escort your ship when you leave on patrol, it's a sign of good luck." I was enjoying watching the dolphins until I heard a yell.

"Where's the *Tirante*?"

Alerted, I searched the horizon, no *Tirante*—the *Tirante* submerged without me knowing it. The OOD saw it submerge and detected the Lookouts watching those dolphins were not paying attention. Always Alert jacked us up that day, convincing us he would have no one in his watch section goofing-off. With pleading and promises, we persuaded him that it would never happen again. After my ass-chewing, I stayed embarrassed because I had let my shipmates down. The OOD staying so alert and working so effectively all the time puzzled me, but I'm glad someone was doing his job. That officer I had to admire and respect. A valuable lesson in leadership I learned that day. The OD lead by example, a leader becomes knowledgeable in tasks; also, he is diligent carrying out his duties. Lieutenant Always Alert did just that. The OOD's attention to duties were examples to follow.

Lucky I was, having good leaders, the officers, chiefs, and petty officers aboard the *Spikefish*. Extremely qualified and knowledgeable, the Officers and crewmembers always displayed professionalism in handling the *Spikefish*. Every qualified crewmember could operate each piece of equipment aboard, from lighting off a diesel engine, blowing sanitaries, to shooting torpedoes. In contrast, I was having a rough time just doing my assigned tasks, and I became dink on my quals.

The *Spikefish* crew did not allow a delinquent status for anyone, making life difficult for the dink. Thinking, to qualify in submarines, I had to learn all the *Spikefish's* systems and know-how to operate all the systems' equipment. The qualified old farts expected me to learn all that, shit, the thought to learn what they wanted, was scary.

The crew took their jobs seriously. Sailors who fought in submarines during World War II made part of the crew. Shipmates like them set the submarine standards and traditions new crews followed. These sailors did not care how our uniforms looked, if our shoes shined, if we needed a haircut, or followed most military manners found on a surface craft. For watch standing, however, there was no fooling around. When standing watches, you either stood your watches right, or you might get a sharp smack to the back of your head, an eye blackened, or you might get a Sanitary Tank to clean. That unpleasant task, the nastiest job, I found out what it entailed firsthand, and I never want to do it again. If you're lucky, with other attention incentives, you might get an expert ass-chewing, because those old sailors knew how to chew-ass better than anybody. The old sailors would make you experience shame about what you did wrong in disappointing them, embarrassing the topside gang, or embarrassing your boat. After an ass chewing, you would find yourself an embarrassment to the Navy, the Country, your Mother, your Grandmother, or the bums in the back alleys of Skid Row, or any other lowlife creature that no one else can embarrass. You ended up believing you upset everyone and everything. After an ass-chewing, you suffered so much, you remembered the event evermore, never wanting a repeat, never doing what you wronged again. Those old-time warriors were effective at getting your attention. This ain't no shit.

BARF BUCKET

As we headed north, when first sensing the sea's forces, many shipmates became seasick, but I didn't become sick. Most new young sailors became ill first. A few nonquals seeking the head didn't arrive in time, vomiting in desperation, puking on the decks, on themselves, in sinks, in their racks, and unfortunately sometimes on others. Several sailors remained sick during the transit. A few of the seasoned sailors weren't immune from seasickness, either suffering seasickness when we entered stormy weather. The seasick sailors learned to carry a barf bucket while doing their duties. An enemy won't put a fight on hold because the foe's crewmembers get seasick. Sailors must keep the ship on course, make sure the engines run and perform the job for mission achievement. Sick sailors worked without their typical enthusiasm found without seasickness, but they carried out their tasks anyway.

The worst seasick event took place when Seaman Barf Bucket just made it to the head to vomit. Moments before, Petty Officer Second Class Hitfirst rushed into a stall, dropped his pants, and just made it—you know what I mean—he had to go. Hitfirst didn't lock the stall door when entering. In that stall, Hitfirst was reaching to shut and latch the door. When Barf Bucket opened the shitter stall door as vomit was coming out of his mouth uncontrollably straight onto Hitfirst. Barf Bucket gave a generous burst of vomit at Hitfirst. Hitfirst tried to get out of the vomit's path. His first reaction, he bolted up, but nowhere to go. Yellow-green-brown vomit ran down the front of Hitfirst, and with globs of shit dropping from his legs.

Hitfirst yelled, "You dumb shit!" and punched Barf Bucket right between the running lights.

Barf Bucket went down—out cold, with his seasickness cured for a moment.

Hitfirst looked at Barf Bucket lying on the deck, and his fury at once turned into regret. Hitfirst uttered, "Gosh Damn! I shouldn't have done that. That son-of-a-bitch couldn't have helped himself." Hitfirst cleaned himself off as much as possible, and then he proceeded to a basin, rinsed out a number 10 can, filled it with cold water, and threw it on Barf Bucket.

Barf Bucket came to, set up with water dripping over a pale white ashen face, looking sick. Blood dripped from his nose, his eyes swollen were turning purple. The Vomit over the front of him looked disgusting.

Hitfirst tried apologizing for punching him. "I'm sorry about that. I reacted too fast.

Barf Bucket groggily replied, "I'm sorry, I couldn't help myself for puking on you," looking as if he would cry. Instead, he puked again— entirely over his lap.

"Well, let's clean up this mess. You carry this barf bucket with you. Use it when you must, it will save your running lights." Hitfirst's soft words told him he was remorseful.

Barf Bucket strained a weak smile, mumbling, "Thanks."

Both cleaned the mess. As Barf Bucket was struggling to wash puke up, his head came near the vomit on the deck, and he used his barf bucket for the first time. After he cleaned the head's mess, Barf Bucket left the head with two of the most magnificent identical shiners I had ever seen.

Seasick sailors learned that if they made a mess, afterward, they would have to clean it up. Also, when nauseated, cleaning vomit made you sicker. In time, everyone prone to seasickness carried barf buckets.

A STORM AT SEA

An ominous gray overcast sky replaced pleasing billowing clouds
A dense menacing drab gray covered the heavens
The transparent bright blue sea now dark-blue-green
Mysterious onerous looking massive blue-gray-black rolling waves
Waves carried cresting foam
A pitching and rolling deck made work and pleasure trying
Many seasick sailors
Difficulty doing simple tasks

Chilling winds sent a warning
Gale winds catch whitecaps' churning suds turning
foaming lather into a stinging spray
Winds violently blast horizontal rain as spears of pain
Howling winds, wailing loud, shrilling moans, and
menacing shrieks roared to terrorize
Threatening, violent gale-force winds attacked
Testing us

Giant walls of water crashed with churning rolling foam
Immense waves carrying whitecaps crested over the bow and topside deck
Waves attacked with foam that tumbled down on
the forward deck in terrible turbulence
Roaring waves rumbling in violent commotion shake the hull

Mighty seas with rolling suds of froth and churning
blasting foam washed the forward deck
Massive waves crested hit the sail with the sea's deluge
Drenching lookouts

The night presented a specific danger
Blackness detecting the horizon a guess
Darkness hid the waves
Ship's movement offered a hint of onrushing waves
Running lights lit ribbons of churning froth topping waves
Eerie white strips of rolling foam vanished into the dark
A black sky and threatening sea
The heavens and sea become one
Blackness a dread

The seas repeated its brutal force
The violent storms caused me to dread
Training told me, hold on tight
One hand for duties the other for me
We couldn't control the storm's might
Nature's overwhelming force
I revere a higher power

What a thrilling experience!
Mighty seas gave a tremendous exhilarating adventure
I respected the storm's turbulent violence and power
The tempest gave the understanding might
Adventure gave confidence, removed fear, and made the excitement
I loved every minute in the storm's fury
Not everyone shared my view
The immense tempest might humble me
God's purpose not fathomed

ROUGH SEAS

During the Cuban Crisis, President Kennedy, with our Admirals, Generals, and other leaders, worried about the potential for peril—the horrors of a nuclear war. The leaders waited for a Soviet response to a showdown at sea, creating the uncertainty of a probable nuclear conflict. All uncertain what that reply would be. At the ready, the *Spikefish*, along with the Sunshine Squadron from Key West, Florida, was preparing to support the Navy to defend our country.

I'm unaware of these concerns. Yet, I find myself aboard the *Spikefish* during this crisis. Along with the Sunshine Squadron of submarines, the *Spikefish* headed north to Norfolk, heading into stormy weather, sailing towards a storm brewing at Cape Hatteras. Old-timers told me the seas off Cape Hatteras are the meanest, roughest, and most dangerous places on the East Coast for a ship during a storm. In the Squadron's path, the weather kicked up to the fiercest gale. The *Spikefish* would cross those Cape Hatteras seas at its nastiest.

The *Spikefish* left Key West in ideal beautiful weather, and a refreshing breeze made standing lookout a bliss. Blue skies teemed with pillows of fluffy white clouds produced a reassuring effect. A clear aqua blue sea transporting small low rolling swells allowed seeing dolphins sporting in our wake escorting us north from Key West. The *Spikefish* sailed along Florida's East Coast. As we cruised north, the climate sent a warning, and an ominous gray overcast sky replaced the sky's pleasing billowing clouds we enjoyed when we left. Then the heavens changed to a dense, menacing drab gray-black cover. The bright blue transparent sea turned to dark-blue-green, then to the more mysterious onerous looking blue-gray-black sea. Slow rolling waves with cresting foam became massive and fiercer. Immense waves carrying whitecaps would crest over the bow and topside deck. The bigger waves made the *Spikefish* pitch and roll with more significant deck movement, causing work and pleasure trying. Gentle, comforting breezes changed to chilling winds. Then the winds increased to a gale, carrying sea spray, stinging any exposed flesh. Stronger winds with menacing, fiercer gusts provided powerful forces trying to blow lookouts off our shears.

Many shipmates became seasick, but I didn't. Some sailors stayed sick during the transit. New young sailors became ill first. A few of the seasoned sailors weren't immune from seasickness either. Few experienced sailors suffered seasickness when we entered stormy weather. Seasick sailors learned to carry barf-buckets because they must still do their duties. In war, just because crewmembers get seasick, an enemy will not stop trying to kill them. Sailors must keep the ship on course, make sure the engines run, and do the job for mission achievement. Maybe sailors worked without the usual enthusiasm found without seasickness, but they carried out their tasks.

A savage storm reached full ferocity while the Sunshine Squadron crossed Cape Hatteras. Our Squadron leaders' incredible skill ensured our arrival was when the seas were the most dangerous. The Squadron leaders' excellent planning, skillful navigation, and precise timing made charting the Squadron's path a plotting achievement. Every time I reflect on our Cape Hatteras crossing, I'm impressed at this remarkable navigational accomplishment. During the Cape crossing, our Squadron met the full impact of a storm's extreme turbulent seas and powerful winds blasting us with brute force.

During the crossing, the *Spikefish* sailed into gale-force winds, driving heavy seas at her. The *Spikefish* received the full impact of the storm's violent weather. That Cape Hatteras's storm was my first time in rough weather, where I received a sample of the sea's incredible raw power, and it was exciting. Not becoming seasick during that tempest allowed me an enjoyable crossing. During our passage, I experienced dread and excitement. Perhaps we were becoming too cocky or too good for our usefulness in stormy weather. The sea's mighty power humbled me, letting me know the supremacy of the sea's power, letting me know God put us in our place, setting us straight.

The first time on watch in the rough weather, the Chief of the Watch gave us lookouts a warning. "Before you head topside to relieve the lookouts, you be careful up there. We're doing 40-degree rolls with 20-degrees up and down pitching. In these conditions, you keep one hand for the boat and the other hand for you." He ordered.

To stand lookout watches topside in rough sea conditions, lookouts dressed in rain gear comprising thick waterproof pants that draped over rain boots and a hooded rain parka covering the top of the pants. This gear keeps us dry when raining, but the rain gear made moving difficult. In this rough weather, it was a chore just getting topside, let alone climbing into the shears. The shears exposed the lookouts to the whim of the weather. Early in WWII, to give a distinct advantage, submarine COs added shears, a small platform with a handrail that put the Lookouts high above the bridge, providing a lengthier visible range. Newly built subs arriving in the war zone installed shears because this feature permitted lookouts to see an enemy before they detected them. The flaw in the shear design exposed the lookouts to nature's elements with no protection from a scorching sun, frigid winds, striking rain, and a storm's might.

Under storm conditions, when changing the watch, the lookouts climbed to the shears or scrambled down to the deck while the boat was rolling and pitching. When we changed watch stations, climbing to or off the shears, was our most dangerous situation. The lookouts couldn't fasten themselves to anything, making this task the most hazardous part of the watch. Lookouts not secured to the boat made us vulnerable to waves smashing into us, knocking us down. A greater danger would be the wave's power washing us overboard. If washed overboard, you're a goner and no chance for a rescue with no way to recover anyone from those rough seas.

Once in the shears, lookouts lashed themselves to handrails. Otherwise, a wave hitting lookouts might knock us down, knocking us off the shears, and wash us overboard. We couldn't attach ourselves tightly because we had to move while searching the surrounding sea.

Gale-force winds roared to terrorize me in the shears, the winds howled with loud wails, shrilling moans, and menacing shrieks. The violent action produced a fierce wind that grabbed the froth making sea spray. Storm winds violently blasted sea spray at us, hitting lookouts with a vicious force, hurting exposed flesh, hands, eyes, and faces. Gale winds tried to knock us off the shears. Relentless violent winds hit us with constant force, challenging us.

Looking forward to the incoming seas, I observed breakers' whitecaps cresting with churning froth. And I saw gale-force winds catch whitecaps' churning suds, turning lather into a horizontal rain, throwing spray at us as spears of pain.

Giant waves like massive surf formed breakers of deep blue-gray-black walls of water attacking us. As the Spikefish crashed into a sea mountain and penetrated a wave, the wave crashed over the bow and created churning, rolling foam that tumbled down on the forward deck in terrible turbulence. Like rapids in violent commotion, the current rumbled down the top-deck, carrying rolling suds of froth, washing over the forward deck towards the sail. When the torrents crashed into the sail, the violent flow attacked the lookouts.

The bigger waves formed longer, soaring walls of water. The boat would plunge into a wave. With resolve, the *Spikefish's* bow smashed into the walls of the sea, plowing in with determination. The boat tremored, diving into enormous waves. With tenacity, the *Spikefish* drove out of those massive waves, flaunting at its power. She flaunted the storm's force, seeking to stop her as she proved her ability to handle such an assault. Before full force waves reach us exposed lookouts, the bow would rise with the larger rollers, as if we were in a roller-coaster car climbing a high hillside. The *Spikefish* would ride up through the waves, slide over the waves' crest, and then glide down the backs of the rollers. The breakers top's crested and washed over the forward deck with violent swirling water and churning foam.

The *Spikefish* charged into the waves with a determined purpose; she smashed into the seawalls of power, wanting a better challenge. She crashed into the next wave's seawall, charging the coming onslaught. With sheer tenacity, the *Spikefish* smashed into enormous waves, plunging through them, bursting out of waves shuddering, displaying toughness in triumph, craving more. For me, this was an exciting adventure, giving confidence, removing fear, and making fun. The *Spikefish* did this throughout the storm, giving me a bigger thrill than any amusement ride might provide. The seas would repeat its brutal force on us—throughout the storm.

More enormous waves would crest down on the forward deck with churning blasting foam, hitting the sail with a sea's deluge, drenching lookouts. Massive waves presented a dangerous threat as they washed over the bow as the boat passed through. A wall of the sea reached the sail, producing tons of seawater smashing down on anyone topside, seeking to tear lookouts off the shears and wash their catch overboard. Even while we're holding on as tight as possible. No matter, giant waves knocked me down more than once, but being lashed to the handrail protected me. What a thrilling experience! I loved the storm yet learned to respect the tempest.

In this storm, having a watch at night presented a specific danger. Darkness prevented seeing massive waves. Blackness made the ability to detect the horizon a guess, barely able to identify the Squadron boats' running lights when we're going over cresting waves. In the blackness, our boat's running lights lit up ribbons of churning foam that topped the waves close aboard, producing eerie white lines of rolling foam vanishing into the night. Darkness hid the waves; darkness like one gets in a theater just after the lights go out before a movie starts. A black sky and an even darker sea made the heavens and sea become one. The howling gale conditions with the boat pitching and rolling made the blackness a dread; we couldn't see the waves attacking us. Only the ship's movement provided any hint of onrushing waves. Training told me, I must hold on always, prepared for the worse—one hand for ship's duties and one hand for my safety.

Bruce, a lookout under my instruction, almost fell overboard. We were the ongoing watch and were heading to the shears to relieve the lookouts. Bruce was right above me when a massive, mighty wave struck us, dropping Bruce into my arms as I was about to climb into the shears. Bruce nearly knocked me off the ladder to the shears as I caught him in my arms. While hanging on tight to the ladder rungs, holding Bruce's weight, I thought my arms would break. Bruce's weight strained my hands and was agonizing. I worried I couldn't restrain him from falling overboard.

The OOD, Mr. Always Alert, saw our dilemma and helped after the boat pulled itself out of the wave's assault. After Bruce was off me, I saw blood all over Bruce's face and assumed he's seriously hurt. Bruce proceeded as nothing was amiss and started climbing back up into those shears to stand his watch. But the OOD ordered him, "Lay below and see the Corpsman." We did not see Bruce for the rest of our watch. Later, we learned that Bruce cut his forehead requiring ten stitches, and he broke his nose.

Bruce reported aboard a week before we got underway. He was a big heavyset muscular likable guy. Bruce played high school football as an offensive tackle. From the first day that I met him, he usually displayed a stern, severe look telling you to mess with me you'll regret it. Therefore, nobody messed with Bruce by giving him the newcomer treatment. Now, Bruce looked silly with his head bandaged up, two black eyes, and a swollen nose.

Word spread throughout the boat about Bruce's condition and his narrow escape. The crew stopped by checking out Bruce. Because he was all right, they would laugh and joke about him and his strange appearance, teasing him about keeping one hand for you and one for the boat in heavy seas. In relief, we laughed, with Bruce laughing with us. We're glad he was alive, with no severe injury, and that he would recover. Bruce took a liking to me. He believed I saved his life. All I did was hold on to him and didn't consider I did anything extraordinary; he landed on me—I had to catch him.

One night, after I finished a mid-watch during the worst of the storm, leaving the shears, I felt like a sailor who has met the elements and survived. Belowdecks, stopping in the head, looking into a mirror, I saw a ghost as white as a sheet covering me. Fine white crystallized powder-like white dust coated my clothes, my skin, my hair. After I tasted the white powder, verifying it was salt. Salt had formed all over me. A layer of snow-white salt coated every part of my rain gear. The foul weather outfit was unprotected from the storm's attack. I grasped this must be how the term, "old salt," formed to describe ocean-going deep-water sailors. As I looked at my condition, I realized what I experienced. I knew I'm a member of that club—I'm proud of being an old salt.

The *Spikefish* crossed the Cape on the surface; she had to stay surfaced; diesel submarines must ride out the rough weather on the surface[14]. The *Spikefish* got through Cape Hatteras using good seamanship with help from a higher authority. The boat proved she could deal with the harsh weather even though it taxed our abilities. The storm's fury gave me a most exhilarating experience, an excellent adventure, and fulfilled a reason for joining the Navy.

The *Spikefish* sailed into the Cape's gale-force winds that drove heavy seas. A storm had mighty seas the *Spikefish* couldn't control; she endured the full impact the storm's turbulent weather. The gale gave crewmembers the experience of the sea's terrible power. Mighty seas shook the hull as roaring waves crashed into us. Violent gale-force winds attacked lookouts with threatening force—testing us. Yet, the storm gave me an exhilarating experience, a grand adventure, and fulfilled a reason for joining the Navy. In that rough weather, many sailors were seasick. Everyone aboard had difficulty doing simple tasks. Not everyone shared my view, but I loved every minute in the storm.

The Sunshine Squadron met the full impact of the Cape Hatteras storm's turbulent seas and mighty winds. That storm gave crewmembers the experience of the sea's tremendous power. With good seamanship and permission from above, the Squadron crossed Cape Hatteras. After

---

[14] In rough weather, diesel submarines without a snorkel must sail on the surface. Storms may last longer than their ability to stay submerged. Diesel submarines with a snorkel operating surfaced must remain surfaced and if they are submerged, they must remain submerged. If a large wave hits a submarine while it's surfacing or submerging, and when the center of buoyancy meets the center of gravity, this may result in an unrecoverable rollover, causing a loss of boat and crew.

passing Cape Hatteras, the seas became tolerable. Later, I'm standing lookout, watching the storm subside, chilling winds reminded me of the tempest we went through. I'm thanking God for experiencing his might and surviving the storm's violence. Then, I'm grateful for facing the adventure, while the event is being tattooed in my mind.

Some modern naval leaders might consider my first experience in this crossing an example of poor leadership. Those leaders would consider our CO did not take care of his crew during the Cape Hatteras crossing. There was no reason to be standing watches on the bridge or standing lookout in those shears under storm conditions. The OOD and the Lookouts using the periscopes might have done the job more efficiently and safer if they stood their watches in the Conning Tower. One of the primary rules of good leadership is to take care of your men. Those leaders would consider our CO did not take care of his crew during the Cape Hatteras crossing.

Not knowing this rule may be an issue; I could do nothing about it. Unaware of a safer way to stand our watches, we followed orders and got on watch. Under those conditions, lookouts watched out for themselves. "One hand for the ship, the other for you," the old-timers drilled into us. On a watch, I hardly saw the horizon when the boat sailed over-the-top of a wave, occasionally spotting another squadron boat. Were they managing as the Spikefish? I wondered. Now, I speculate, did their lookouts and officers stand their watches topside—during the storm?

A weak leadership assessment must be wrong. For the topside watchstanders, maybe the CO wasn't aware of the danger of the storm. Most likely, the CO lived through many fierce storms and was preparing us, making us ready for when the worst happens. The CO's training kept him topside during storms. The command required the crew to learn how to work in rough weather. Afterward, I experienced storms more powerful, making my first tempest feel like a light-squall in comparison. I experienced fierce gales so powerful they presented a threat to the ships going through them. Storms so violent they caused shipboard damage and gave a risk—loss of the ship, loss of all hands—with no chance of anyone saving us.

After consideration, I must admit that I am thankful for this instance of possible poor leadership. If sent below safe from the sea, I would have missed the experience from this storm, the sting of salt spray, the salt blanket covering me, the dread of the unknown power of the sea. I would have missed seeing massive waves attacking us, missing the opportunity to appreciate the exciting action. Nor, I wouldn't have gained the confidence in the boat's ability to make this an exciting journey removing fear and renewed trust in the *Spikefish*, her officers, Chiefs, and shipmates. I would have missed this adventure.

One conclusion from this event that makes me proud, and the Nation should likewise be full of pride, and the Navy's history reinforces this judgment. When threatened, the U.S. Navy defends our Nation. When defending our country, Navy ships and crews without hesitation sail into harm's way, regardless of the threat—foe or storm. This is what sailors do. It's our duty.

NORFOLK

The first time putting into a significant naval port was fun standing lookout as the *Spikefish* approached Norfolk. On our way in, we passed Carriers, Cruisers, Oilers, Destroyers, and ships I couldn't recognize. Examining the vessels as they went by, I'm amazed seeing the Navy's might. Someone commented, "Most of the fleet has a blockade around Cuba." The warships we passed were enough to whip any nation's navy, and we have most of our ships at sea. As we entered the harbor, I'm observing more warships, realizing it's a minor part of the US Navy's sea power, and viewing the warships, inspired me we're ready for war.

No time to ponder my thoughts, with all those ships around us, we lookouts kept busy tracking each ship, tracking all contacts became impossible—too many ships. To maintain contact tracking to reasonable surveying, we altered tracking contacts, tracking the vessels closest to us. Our ability to track contacts became hampered because many vessels were heading to sea or entering port with uncountable small craft adding to the ship assortment. Then lookouts concentrated on contacts ahead and coming towards us, conducting safety sweeps every ten minutes, making certain no one was running us down. Also, we tracked navigational markers: buoys, rocks, and shoals, changing current signs, and all else imposing a threat.

In the bay, we meet a turbulent harbor. Waves are rising about six feet, then cresting with a slim ribbon of foam, rolling close together, making a nasty choppy sea condition. The bay's turbulence didn't disturb the boat much or cause a problem for the lookouts, but the turbulence made it unpleasant for anyone on deck topside. More massive waves passed over the topside deck, sprayed a wash over the deck, submerging the superstructure from bow to stern.

Before entering the harbor, the CO set the maneuvering watch. The Number One Line Handling Party was my maneuvering watch station assignment, handling the forward most mooring line. Bob relieved me as lookout even though I wanted to stay as a lookout; there was so much to see. Reluctantly, I moved forward, heading towards the line locker. A massive wave washed the deck with frosty foam wetting my feet with a wash of the frigid cold sea, right away my feet were freezing. A fierce, steady cold wind chilled me to the bones, making me uncomfortable.

When we left Key West, Florida, the temperatures were warm in the 80 to 100-degrees range. But in Norfolk, the *Spikefish* wasn't prepared or outfitted for the cold. I suspected no one aboard was ready, either, discovering temperatures lower than 35 degrees—it was bitter cold. A solid gray overcast sky prevented the sun from offering warmth, making this worst. The weather appeared as if at any moment, it would rain or snow. Everyone topside lacked cold-weather outfits and suffered in our freezing conditions.

Before mooring, we made topside ready, getting the mooring lines out of line lockers, flaking the lines down on deck prepared to send to the dock without tangling up and creating a dangerous topside condition.

With waves washing over the deck, pulling the mooring lines out of the forward line-locker presented a dilemma. After I climbed down under the deck into the superstructure into the forward line-locker, I found the mooring line in a rat's nest—all messed up in a heap. The rough seas going through the line-locker had its way with the mooring line. The seas jumbled up the line and made a tangled rat's mess. I had to untangle the heap before sending the line topside.

After freeing the last knot, I passed the line to the deck, then a massive wave washed over topside, flooding the superstructure, including the forward line locker, and drenching me. Suddenly, I'm caught underwater in a confined space under the deck. Ice-Cold water immersed me; the shocking cold gave me a freeze. A cold, as if a quarter of a degree colder, it would have turned me into a block of ice. I'm underwater long enough to freeze me to my core. It frightened me, even so, I had to pass the line topside. As I'm handing the line out of the line locker, my fingers became numb, making work more difficult because I was cold and wet. Frozen fingers made getting the rest of that mooring line out of that line locker difficult.

Another big wave passed through, flooding the line-locker, immersing me up to my neck, yet the sea is warmer than the surrounding air. At least it seemed that way. At last, the line is topside. I go topside as quickly as I could. Then, a biting wind assailed into me; a chill reached me—I'm cold.

The COB asked, "Are you all right?"

"Yeah, I'm OK," I wasn't, I'm cold to the bone.

"Go below if you want."

"COB, I'll stay topside." Despite being cold, I stayed topside. Too much to see, considering what an adventure besides, it was exciting. Because I'm cold, I can't shirk my duties. Wasn't I an Old Salt? But staying topside was a mistake. The cold wind attacked, giving me unbearable discomfort. More than once, I wished I had gone below. The cold affected my abilities, making me ineffective. As we approached the pier, I missed throwing a heaving line to the dock. In frustration, I took three more tries to get the heaving line across. Regularly, one throw was all I needed. To tie-up, I required help to tie the heaving line to the mooring line. Then, my cold hands couldn't grip the mooring line while sending it to the pier. Shipmates worked harder, helping me, but I'm embarrassed because I needed the help.

After the boat is tied up, I was shaking from the cold. I'm chilled clear through. The COB noticed my shivering condition and ordered me below. The COB must have informed the Doc because Doc captured me as soon as I entered the mess decks. Doc draped a wool blanket around me, gave me a shot of brandy, and ordered me to take a long hot shower. The Doc chewed my ass on our way to the showers for being so foolish. "What's the matter with you? Hell, you haven't any sense to get out of the cold. Look at you; you're so cold you're useless...." With the *Spikefish* hooked up to shore power and freshwater as we tied up, I took a long hot shower without causing problems, a rare event on diesel submarines, undoubtedly getting that hot shower saved my life. The cold didn't make me sick. The statement is true—God protects drunkards and fools. During the Norfolk visit, I believed God worked overtime.

The *Spikefish* tied up at the Amphibious Base, Little Creek. Most of the crew didn't understand why we moored there instead of the submarine piers. Later, I find out that all the sub-piers had submarines using them—the submarine force was getting ready for war. I was disappointed with the *Spikefish* moored away from the fighting Navy. All around us were amphibious boats and two white ships. The white ships were Seaplane Tenders. With the *Spikefish* tied at the Amphibious Base, it made me disappointed until I discovered this mooring provided our reason for being here—our mission—changing disappointment to pride, once, I figured it out.

After tying up at the amphibious base, an all-hands working party loaded stores—fresh fruit, vegetables, meat, and the needed warm clothing. As soon as we discovered the warm clothing, work stopped while we downed long sleeve shirts, sweaters, wool socks, and foul-weather jackets. After a quick uniform change, the working-party took nearly three hours of continuous work. Then, we completed squaring away topside. The crew worked extra hard because there was a rumor—liberty is likely.

After finishing our topside work, the COB had us muster in the mess decks and instructed, "You will have two nights of liberty, have fun, but be careful, don't get yourselves into trouble. Remember, conditions are developing fast, expect little liberty. This conflict with Cuba and the Soviets may cause the nation to go to war, resulting in the Navy fighting the Soviets with the *Spikefish* in that fight. I don't know our mission; it may be the forward edge of a blockade or scouting for the fleet. We may be the first US warship to confront the Soviets, or we may do something else like a special mission. The *Spikefish* must be ready for anything. On liberty, control your drinking, and be ready to respond to any change, expect to have liberty canceled on a moment's notice. When your liberty is over, do your duties without someone reminding you, and remember to restrain your drinking. Have fun while you can."

Several of the crew left their dress winter uniforms back in Key West. Issued raincoats were their only weather protection in Norfolk. Raincoats are not good at keeping warm when it's cold—Norfolk was cold. The new foul-weather gear was for working aboard the boat and base only, not allowed as a liberty uniform.

I had duty the first day, and I was one of the unlucky ones staying aboard. Bob used my dress uniform. After celebrating my birthday, Bob's packing wasn't up to par. He left his winter dress-blues in Key West. As soon as possible, I hit my rack, because I had the topside mid-watch that night, later, while on watch, I couldn't believe what took place—what a night.

The liberty-party arrived back aboard and provided rare entertainment, making the mid-watch to be most enjoyable. The shipmates returning made a surprising sight. *Spikefish* sailors sought to compress weeks at sea into a one-night of play. The liberty-party did all they could do in port, doing fun-stuff drinking, dating, and fighting, things they would not do at sea. But controlling their drinking didn't happen. Not knowing when they would get another liberty, they made the best of the opportunity—they had fun, taking the occasion looking for women and finding booze. All returned in various stages of drunkenness. The worst drunks made one hell of a racket, laughing, crying, and telling about their escapades. I scarcely made out what they were saying. From their chatter, I guessed most of the fleet at sea, making liberty great! Anxiously, I looked forward to hitting the beach.

The COB provided my best entertainment, the funniest occurrence when a cab pulled up to the head of the pier. Outcomes the COB staggering down the dock, stopping just before the brow, and farting–a deep, loud, long boom like the blast of a tug's horn when getting underway. Thankfully, the wind was blowing away from me. The COB marches over the brow, marching unstable as if he would fall. Saluted me mumbling, "Re-quest-request-fully permission to come aboard!" Wobbly, holding the salute, he keeps on marching, holding that salute, marching right across the deck, across the boat heading right over to the other side, the COB did not change direction, and didn't stop.

To catch the COB's attention, I yelled, "COB!" Yelling didn't work.

The COB didn't stop, just dropped out of sight. Then a loud splash, the COB grumbles, "Shit, damn, it's cold."

The light beam from my flashlight illuminates the drunken COB. The COB is treading water, looking to be all right, just a wet drunk in trouble, in a situation he couldn't control, getting dangerously cold. As I throw him a lifeline, I yell, "hang on!" Then, I announced on the

1-MC, "MAN OVERBOARD!" In seconds, the whole duty section was topside, helping me. With their support, we pulled a wet, freezing, shivering COB out of that water, wrapped him in a blanket, and sent him below. After he bathed in that icy water, the COB sobered up a bit. The below decks watch told me later that once he got below, he talked the Doc into giving him two shots of brandy to warm him. Then he proceeded to bed. No one saw the COB until noon the next day.

The next day, our duty section rushed to finish our clean-up. A sorry looking duty section relieved us. Most with hangovers, two displayed black eyes while wearing big smiles, and a few exposed sleepy, shit-eating grins on their faces, what they accomplished the night before, I speculated. The oncoming duty section looked tired but happy.

Bob returned my dress uniform in perfect condition. As I dressed for liberty, I'm impatient because it's my first time in a large port like Norfolk. The stories about last night's liberty indicated how good it was, making me eager.

My first liberty away from homeport made a memorable time in Norfolk. In a day of exciting action, starting early, bonding with a senior shipmate and his boatswain friends, I almost get the shit kicked out of me, and fell in and out of love in one night. Then becoming drunk and finishing the night with little sleep by getting sick the following morning—I haven't figured out if it was seasickness or a hangover—perhaps both were at play.

I don't understand why, but Machinist Mate Second Class Hitfirst took a liking to me. Remember, he is the guy who dropped Barf-bucket with one punch. A muscular Hitfirst is one of the strongest men I have known. Hitfirst appointed himself to be my sea daddy, taking it on himself to see I stayed up on my qualifications, helping me understand the complicated systems, and giving me a painful direction when I became behind in quals. When I was behind in my qualifications, he made my life miserable. As expected, Hitfirst had to show me how to have a proper sailor's liberty.

That morning, our first stop was a bar just outside the main gate, a noisy place, nothing fancy about it except it had ships' plaques on its walls—hundreds, representing most ships in the Navy. Also, many pictures of naval ships of all types set in frames of macramé arranged in decorative patterns of macramé lace forming the picture frame decocted the walls. Hitfirst told me, "This bar is a Boatswains' hangout, a dangerous place for anyone else unless you were a submarine sailor. Boatswains like submarine sailors because we were just as mean and as raunchy as they are. Boatswains and submariners consider everyone else in the Navy just a bunch of candy-asses."

As we enter the bar, Hitfirst recognizes friends not seen for a while and orders a round of beers for everyone in the bar. Another reason, Boatswains likes submarine sailors. Submariners get extra money each month in sub pay having more cash than Boatswains. Sub sailors are generous to our friends.

Hitfirst introduced me to the Boatswains as if I was his best friend. They offered a warm, friendly welcome, making me believe I'm part of their group, enjoying my new-found notoriety. As I got to know the Boatswains, I developed a new understanding and respect for them, and I took a liking to them.

Watching the groups of Boatswains sitting at round tables, drinking beers, laughing, and telling sea stories, I imagined many sailors entering this place found it dangerous. If a Boatswain identified an unknown sailor new to this bar, the regular would call the stranger a pussy, checking him out. If the newcomer sensed insult and took offense, a fight would happen, he would prove he wasn't a wimp. Many a brawl occurred in that bar just to rectify the insults.

A Barmaid, a small, nice-looking sexy blonde, arrives at our table, ogling me, showing a welcoming flirting smile. "I'm Suzy," then she snuggles up and puts one arm around my waist, rubbing her body on mine. The sensation of her body was arousing, and the smell of her perfume was stimulating. I liked what she was doing, wanting her near me, but wished we could do this somewhere more private. With an audience, I regarded this erotic display awkward. Suzy keeps it up, getting more audacious shamelessly, caressing me, more than I imagined.

Then, without warning, Suzy reaches down, grasps my nuts and crank, holding them, fondly massaging them, asking, "Hey sailor, how's it hanging?"

Shocked, I practically died of embarrassment.

Hitfirst laughing informed me, "you're as red as an overripe tomato.

Stunned, I couldn't speak and wasn't aware of a proper reaction to my situation. Nothing like this ever happened before. Suzy playing with me was getting me hard. Embarrassed, I wanted to climb under a table. New friends watching my predicament laughed unrestrained.

Not knowing what to do, I responded, trying to be like a tough rough-and-tumble sailor, even though I didn't know what that entailed. With as much macho as possible, I reply, "It's hanging all right. If you go to bed with me tonight, we will see how long we can make it hang."

Suzy stopped what she was doing, stating, "Sounds like a good idea, honey, maybe tonight if you can keep it up." Suzy kissed me on the cheek, patted me on the butt, and departed to attend other tables.

New friends laughed hard and chuckled with tears in their eyes. Hitfirst told me, "One barmaid will do something like what Suzy did to you to about every young sailor who enters this bar. It's an initiation, making the stay in the bar enjoyable unless the victim can't handle that playing around, because of religious or other reasons. The barmaids get more tips fooling around with us sailors than if they acted properly."

A first-class Boatswain spoke, "You're all right. Come on, join us." Calls, "Suzy, give us another round!" We drank our round of beer and emptied another. Just as I became hungry, I realized everyone else was getting hungry, too, because the Boatswain asked, "Have you ever had chicken gizzards?"

"Yeah, I like them a lot."

"Good," then he called Suzy, "Bring us a platter of chicken gizzards."

Shortly, on our table, Suzy placed a full platter of deep-fried chicken gizzards heaping high, virtually overflowing. Suzy gives me a promising look. Not following up on it, I focus on the gizzards, steaming hot and crispy golden-brown. We got right into eating chicken gizzards and washing them down with beer. Chicken gizzards taste good. If you ever get the chance, try them.

In the bar, we stayed until 1700, shooting pool, drinking beer, eating chicken gizzards, dancing with the barmaids, and having fun, I thought liberty should always start like this. As I began to sense my drinking, someone suggested, "Let's go into town."

Boatswains and submariners climbed in two cabs that took us to Norfolk's strip. Many times, later, I have been back to Norfolk and never found the places where I enjoyed my first Norfolk liberty. City Fathers changed the site. The City Fathers in making progress made down-town habitable for responsible citizens. In doing so, they destroyed a liberty district thousands of sailors and marines used for tension release. The strip wasn't bad; it was an excellent place to have fun hurting nobody.

A cab dropped us off at the strip, the main drag full of bars, dance clubs, and restaurants. Our group, on the sidewalk, hungry again, agreed to get something to eat before we did anything else. Then, we proceeded to an elegant restaurant. Opposite the bar, we left. Soft background music added to a pleasant atmosphere. White linen covered tables already set up with the fancy hardware. A few couples are sitting at tables, enjoying meals, drinks, and whatever.

We bring in our noise, loud talking, laughing, telling jokes or sea stories, unaware that others wanted quiet, and not mindful that we're rude to the patrons. Perhaps, we interrupted their enjoyment, making them susceptible to our presence. We detected the patrons' display of perturbed behavior, suggesting that the patrons did not want us there. I realized the management shares the patrons' attitude.

As expected, our meals arrived, excellently prepared, and presented my order, a steak plate, looked appetizing, precisely what I requested, but I didn't enjoy it. The patron's unwarranted complaints about our playfulness prompted the manager to act, at first, to reduce our noise level and not cause trouble. Not wanting trouble, we whispered, but for the snobs in the place, whispering was not acceptable—the elitists whined as soon as one of us murmured. The snobs stared at us with hostile expressions, nitpicking that we were making too much noise. The manager supported the patrons. They interrupted our meal any time one of us spoke.

The manager reacted without verifying the criticisms. As the meal continued, the elitists complained about any noise or anything else they thought wrong about us. Then with evident resentment, the manager directed his judgments towards us, "You're making too much noise, keep it quiet," taking their side. To defend ourselves, we told the manager the complaints were unreasonable. He didn't listen. They were against us.

When we responded to the patron's requests for quiet, our efforts to quiet-down didn't work, except we received more outrage from them. The patrons' actions caused our enjoyment to change to anger. Their false appraisal of us and offensive behavior created our reaction and provoked misbehavior. Collectively, we believed the patrons are wrong mistreating us. We thought the Navy, including us, was ready to go to war, to protect these good people of Norfolk who scorned and snubbed us, displaying an attitude that aggravated our composure. Their resentment created our rudeness, where we became socially unacceptable and disrespectful. We reacted to the patrons' aggressive unacceptable action, and became louder and obnoxious against these folks, behaving ill-mannered, acting and flaunting our contempt rudely towards them.

Earlier, old-timers told me about Norfolk, revealing that some Norfolk folks don't like sailors. They displayed signs on lawns confirming that, "Dogs and sailors keep off the grass." I considered this is disrespectful, unwarranted, and unpatriotic, and I resented anyone who would convey this contempt. Then, as the snobs continued acting rude, I'm convinced that these people were the source of Norfolk's impudence. Not realizing that our conduct supported the cause of the lousy sentiment the citizens of Norfolk had towards sailors, I joined in the reactionary harassment of this establishment and their patrons.

Eventually, the manager rudely invited us to leave. Rowdily, we became. This group of clienteles might not have ill feelings towards sailors before we entered. But when we left, I don't think they liked us much, coming close to blows. Those well-mannered upright people warranted giving us an apology for their conduct, but we didn't get one.

With an irritable attitude, feeling sorry for ourselves, believing the citizens of Norfolk were to blame, well, that put a damper to our party. Therefore, we separated.

The Boatswains left, saying, "We will catch you later. Good luck."

Hitfirst and I started bar hopping, traveling from one bar to another, having a beer in each, checking out the places, seeking something, looking for something unknown to me. Finding girls and a good time was my mission, but bar hopping was not entertaining.

After examining a dozen places, Hitfirst guides me down a darkened side street with no traffic on it. I wondered why we are were going down it.

Hitfirst exclaimed, "I knew I would find it." He cheered up.

"Find what?" I inquired.

"The SUB BAR, the SUB BAR, is the Norfolk bar for us submariners. The sub sailors home-ported here hang out there. It's the finest liberty in Norfolk," he replied.

Down the street, I looked, not seeing the bar. The SUB BAR hid about a third way down the street with no clues for its presence. After a short walk, we're standing in the bar's front and ready to enter, the name in red letters, "SUB BAR," painted on a front window, told us it was a bar.

A dark, dense smoke-filled the place. I could barely see through the smoke, but enough to see the back wall of the bar, making the impression that this bar extended forever. I scanned the room and saw many sailors with sexy looking barmaids attending them, carrying trays of beers to tables, and removing empties. Sailors are sitting around the tables talking to one another. A loud rock-and-roll song was coming from the jute box. As our eyes adjusted to the darkness, we saw that this bar was full of skimmers—surface craft and shore duty sailors.

Hitfirst stared at the skimmers, and his face became vivid red and angry looking. Not realizing what he would do, I perceived we would be doing something we would regret later. The skimmers outnumbered us about 200 to two. Not liking the odds, discovering shortly, I was right.

A sexy, good-looking waitress wearing a short tight red dress displaying lovely legs and a white blouse half unbuttoned in the front, exposing inviting curves came over smiling, asking, "What can I get for you, handsome sailors?"

I would have welcomed a beer, but Hitfirst curtly answers, "Nothing!" Startled, the waitress frowned and left to attend another table.

For what seems like an hour, we stand watching the crowd. Hitfirst is building up a head of steam scowling at a group of twelve skimmers sitting at a large round table at the back of the bar. Not paying any attention to us, they were enjoying their beers and a waitress's attention. There were two pitchers of beer, beer bottles, and glasses partially filled with beer on the table. At random, a sailor would lift his glass, sip his beer, and place it back on the table.

Without warning, Hitfirst saunters over to that table and picks up a chair. I assumed he would join that group, but I'm mistaken. Hitfirst picked the chair high over his right shoulder and then swung the chair as if you would swing a ball bat. The swinging chair hit the table's contents sweeping off the pitchers of beer, beer glasses, and beer bottles, spilling beer and broken glass on most of the skimmers. Yelling, "All of you f--king, candy-asses, surface skimming, ass-hole, landlubbers get the f--k out! This submarine bar is not for f--kers like you!"

Astonished, I had to marvel at his bravery, but not his wisdom. I considered his attack, and language was the dumbest spectacle I ever saw. No one aboard used that language. No chance to linger on my thoughts, I think the only reason we are alive today was that Hitfirst frightened those skimmers. The skimmers became flabbergasted and confused by his hitting the beers on the table. The skimmers glared at us with confusion, with a seeking look—why did you do that unbelievable act? A moment of dead silence filled the bar. Sailors glared at Hitfirst, and he is staring back, looking menacing, wanting a fight. Not willing, they scowled, looking uncertain what would happen next. Not knowing how many submarine sailors were with us made them cautious. No matter, the surrounding group of skimmers regrouped, picked me up, hoisting me in the air, and handed me to a crowd of sailors who passed me hand-to-hand above their heads towards the door. I was helpless to do anything to stop them.

Without slowing down, the skimmers brought me towards the door then flung me airborne out through the door. Falling about halfway into the street, I landed in a heap. As I picked myself up, expecting, that mob will kill Hitfirst, and worriedly thought how I might help him. Then, Hitfirst came flying out through the door. He missed me before he struck the pavement, rolling like a ball and halted in a heap. Hitfirst gets up and brushes himself off, and he declares, "Shit, that didn't work, we need help. Let's find our crew. We will get those skimmers out of that shithole tonight; skimmers make it a shithole."

Off we went to locate our crew. Before the night's over, I expect it would end in a brawl. But I'm not looking forward to fighting, realizing we're outnumbered even with the rest of our crew. Hitfirst is determined. Fearless he may be, but he's acting dumber than a shit can. Hitfirst is behaving like he's furious at something with a rage that was growing worse since we left the SUB BAR, after seeing it full of skimmers. Hitfirst was heading for trouble.

As we went bar hopping hunting for our crew, I slowed down my drinking. Hitfirst keeps drinking from bar-to-bar, drinking too much, making his displeasure come out in a fury. On a short fuse, and with the slightest irritation, Hitfirst would let out a torrent of profanities, not happy like, or joking like, but utterances that were mean, vicious, and crude. I didn't like being with him in his condition, worrying that he might turn on me. Yet, he's my shipmate. Since I'm his shipmate and would support him, yet I didn't see how I would keep him out of trouble, lacking experience in such matters. I'm determined to follow Hitfirst back into that SUB BAR with only the two of us to clean it out.

Later, we found our crew at a bar and dance club at the center of the strip across the street where the cab first dropped us off. As we enter, our friends greet us. Someone bought a round of beers. Hitfirst moved to a rear table talking to other senior petty officers, guessing to get support for the fight I expected. It took a little time until Hitfirst appeared happy. Hitfirst chugged his beer and ordered a pitcher for the table. Those sailors knew how Hitfirst got when drinking, and they were experts on keeping him under control. The senior petty officers knew he contained anger when sober, knowing it builds inside him, coming out when drinking—too much.

As I finished my beer, I noticed Hitfirst asleep—harmless. Now, I saw that he was all right; I relaxed and ordered another beer.

The music coming from the dance club upstairs was inviting. To check it out, I had to pay $2.00 admission cost to join this club. At the time, $2.00 was a lot of money. I wouldn't pay it at first, but I saw many sexy-looking girls with members of our crew, all having fun, dancing, and socializing. The admission charge was club dues for one night. To get the pleasure I wanted, I became a member and proceeded in the club.

The ladies in the club were "B" Girls. Without any knowledge about "B" Girls, I'm primed for the worst. Club owners paid "B" Girls to act as hostesses and waitresses for customers, us sailors. "B" Girls work as hostesses with their main job is getting sailors, Marines, and anyone foolish enough to give quarters for the jute box, to buy many drinks. Buying drinks for himself, for his friends, and especially buying special expensive drinks with fancy names for the hostesses.

The "B" Girls' exclusive cocktails were colored water, soda, and tea, but all the girl's drinks were pricey. The hostesses increased their pay by being expert at getting their customer's tips as high as possible—their chosen prey were naïve sailors like me. "B" Girls became shrewd, using their charms, capturing victims without the patsy realizing what was happening.

For their pay, "B" Girls would give their intended victims, the customers, a good time and friendly conversation, a dance partner, and an imagined assurance to erotic rewards to come. To get great tips, "B" Girls would sit with prey, like a willing sailor, suggesting hints of a sincere desire. Others will tell targets their family hardships, working on the victim's sympathy to help. "B" Girls will do anything sexy with their victims holding their bodies tight while dancing, allowing a sailor to fondle private places, and giving short kisses anything stimulating to become successful in taking an unsuspecting sailor's pay. Specialists had talents so good that before an evening was over, the "B" Girl's prey is too drunk to get his hinted reward. Or, when it came time to collect false promises, the girls would be with someone else, leave unnoticeably, have a husband or boyfriend show up, breaking the implied promises. After paydays, many victims were eager for return visits but getting an unfilled dream on the dupe's part. Many a sailor with a just cashed paycheck entered that establishment and departed it without bus fare to their ship. Several never figured it out and fell in love, nightly, bringing money for their nightly entertainment. Most sailors wised up to the treatment and chalked up their pay loss to their education. "B" Girls didn't hurt sailors significantly; most victims were not aware that a "B" Girl duped them. In this business, "B" Girls were experts, and they were most prosperous with the *Spikefish's* new crew.

Into the club I go, oblivious to anything about "B" Girls, and join Ferguson sitting at a table with an attractive sexy looking blond.

Ferguson has a big grin, loving the attention the blond is giving him. Ferguson introduces her, "this is Sherry." She talks him into buying a round of drinks. Also, Sherry was coming on to me while acting as if she's also Ferguson 's girl. Unsuspecting, he was unaware of what she was doing. Sherry's advances caused suggestive stimulating sensations yet made me uneasy at the same time. That girl made me believe I was a stud or something. I'm so ecstatic; I bought a round of beers.

Then the most beautiful gorgeous girl I have ever seen walks in, looking prettier and more appealing and sexier than any model or pinup from Playboy or any other man's magazine I checked out. Couldn't keep my eyes off her, a real, walking, talking beautiful sweetheart. Short jet-black hair framed a lovely face of this voluptuous girl whose dark eyes looked directly at mine and beckoned I want you—now. That young woman's alluring and inviting red lips beckoned—kiss me passionately. The beautiful girl's sexy body was sensuous. A stunning looking figure with flawless light olive smooth skin, with an exquisite shape so dazzling that a sailor after looking at her one time would dream about her many times at sea—from one look to many a wet dream. The gorgeous girl was wearing a tight short red dress that surrounded the most inviting of curves; a slit along its side displayed much of her limbs, showing long sexy smooth looking legs attached to the rest of her sexy parts. She was eye candy—the hottest looking girl my eyes have ever scrutinized.

This gorgeous girl captured me, showing the sexiest lovely, alluring smile, informing me—I want you now. Beautiful eyes of an angel locked on mine, pierced into me, and changed all brain cells that controlled responsibility and wisdom into a mush of silliness. A brain that no longer keeps any reasonable control allowed my penis to take complete control of all brain cells with prospects of wanting lust, craving her.

Without any intelligent control, my penis dominates rational brain cell functions.

With an appealing sensual manner of walking, she's striking, astonishing, and eye-catching in her charms, watching her floating sexually toward our table. She's stunning, dignified, and proper in her manners. Melted, smitten—entirely for me, I realized love at first sight. The senses tell me I'm solely in love, completely in love, thoroughly, undoubtedly in love. I'm smitten—she's for me. But it 's only my penis thinking I'm in love. To my joy, she asks in a most charming, voluptuous, inviting way, "Can I join you, sailor?"

Nervously, with rubber leg and shaking feet, I stood up, knocking over my beer, babbling, "Sure, most welcome, oops, sorry about that— yes, please join us; my name is Gary," then stammering, "Awe—can I get you a drink?" I'm silly meeting her, yet happy that I had a wonderful, beautiful sexy woman giving me attention. This dazzling girl had a way about her beyond any other young woman I had known. In her approaches with a sexy way of speaking, she was making me believe I was the most handsome man in the world, and that I would be her man tonight. I couldn't believe my luck.

"Nice to meet you, Gary, my name is Collette."

In a pleasant sensual way, this ravishing girl orders drinks for us, a beer for me and a virgin-My-Tai, the most expensive drink for her—I pay for them. A virgin cocktail of any kind means a concoction without alcohol; I didn't know that. Quickly, this delightful girl gulps hers. With suggestive pleasures to happen, I order her another. We get up to dance—a slow dance. With Collette in my arms, I'm in paradise, holding her tight close, sensing her body, sensing her perfume. This exciting exquisite girl embraces me snugly, and she's stimulating as I sense breathing caressing my neck. I seize her closer, invigorating pleasure, becoming delirious. After the song is over, we float back to our table. With conviction, I buy drinks—beers and a virgin-My-Tai drained, more ordered.

Collette, with a pleading smile, pleads, "That was a good drink, I was thirsty, thanks, may have another?" With suggestive pleasures awaiting me, I order another round.

Sherry acts cold towards my true love, unwelcoming her presence. I ignore her.

Another song, we dance. A slow song, a slow dance, we grip each other tighter. Lips meet in a kiss, I'm in paradise, holding her tightly, feeling her body; my hands touch her backside; she lets me explore. Collette's sensual figure presses into mine, swaying with the rhythm. Thighs are holding my hardness, erotic, arousing, intensifying, and passionate; I'm in ecstasy. While dancing, we fondle one another with slow, gentle caressing, liking the foreplay more than we should while dancing, Collette feels delightful in my arms, making me feel marvelous. Now, I fully realize I'm in love. We dance to every slow song. With each dance, I become passionate about kisses, with sensual caressing suggesting possibilities to come. Between dances, with passion, I'm buying drinks.

Then, the worst happened, I'm broke, not possessing enough money to buy my future wife another drink. To ask Collette to marry me later that night, well, I was waiting for the right moment. Embarrassed, I created an excuse to go to the head. Instead, I left to borrow money from my shipmates. My friends were in the same financial condition as I. As I realized later, the "B" girls were experts. I proceeded downstairs to see if I could borrow money from the senior sailors who already underwent what was transpiring, they had the cash but pretended they didn't. They knew better and wouldn't give me any. Upstairs, I'm humiliated, trying to explain to my true love, "I'm broke. I cannot buy you another drink tonight, but many more nights we'll have later…"

Collette looks at me and declares, "That's OK honey, I'll see you around." Collette gets up, leaving me, going over to sailors who have just entered, and selects her new victim. Then, Collette carries out the same scam on him as she executed on me.

Watching her in shock, not accepting what I'm looking at, I go to her and plead, "Let's dance."

Collette politely replies, "Not now, honey," looking affectionately at the guy she is with. "I'm with someone. Maybe later, we'll get together."

The sailor with her commands, "Move on shipmate, she is with me."

My love rejected me. I'm devastated. While watching her laughing and flirting, I'm thinking—hurting. Then, hell no! Damn, she used me. She robbed me. Anger built I wanted to hurt someone. Her new boyfriend, shit! I wanted to rip his head off, stick it up his ass, and then piss down his windpipe. I stared into his eyes, letting him know I'll harm him. In his stare, looking back at me, I saw fear. Before I acted, two big bouncers came over and suggested that I sit down and not bother anyone or leave. I was about to take them on, but Sherry calls me over to join her. Barf-bucket was asleep snoring softly, using the table for his head. Sherry saw what happened, and I suppose she was genuinely sorry for me. Grudgingly, I join Sherry, who orders us drinks. Sherry paid. A fast dance started. Sherry asked, "Let's Dance." Halfheartedly, I get up to dance with her, moving like a plank leaning on a wall. Not wanting to dance, I ached so much.

Sherry studies me with a radiant grin and says, "Come on, sailor, get with it." Then wiggling her body to the beat of the music, moving sexily, laughing, she urges, "Dance with me." Forgetting my disappointment, I grin and start dancing. After a few rock-and-roll dances, I'm enjoying fast dancing. In high school, I never danced during the fast rock-and-roll songs, but I'm doing it—liking dancing—making fast dancing moves. Sherry would dance slow dances with other sailors, but she saved the fast dances with me and supplied me with beers. I'm enjoying myself, dancing fast, having fun. The blond probably saved my life, saved me from a beating, or, at least, kept me out of jail.

A law of nature exists that trained science professors never explain. You will not find this law's subject taught in a schools' approved class schedule. However, many students understand this rule. It's as authentic as Newton's law of gravity's effect on falling objects. It's the "Law of Boozing." I realized this law with too many experiences. The Law of Boozing applies to any young sailor drinking alcohol over a prolonged duration. After continuous drinking, the sailor drinking will ultimately become intoxicated and exhibit a drunk's behavior—woozy, befuddled, tipsy, unsteady, nauseous, gross, disgusting, detestable, smashed—performing socially unacceptable actions. A sailor's continuous drinking results in the sailor falling asleep, becoming angry—the mean drunk, or a happy, outgoing friend to all he meets—the happy drunk. The drunk's condition may also result in him getting sick—with vomit spewing uncontrollably.

This law applies to everybody, not just sailors. The law of boozing applied to me. I underwent the effects of this law after all those beers, acting silly, happy, and carefree. Likely, I looked and acted unsocial and ridiculous. Most sailors in the club, end their evening in the same condition as me, but many acted differently. I neglected Sherry. From our crew, we bunched up, recounting tales that only we consider funny, laughing over nothing. Others rudely touched and caressed the ladies without their welcome. While others drunkenly verbally degraded the women with obscenities. The drunks vocally attacked humiliating by cussing at anyone they didn't recognize. The night of drinking culminates about closing time when the bouncers encouraged us to leave.

Cheerfully, we leave, but with a final farewell, we nearly killed ourselves playing a game called, "catch me." In our group, one would stand at rigid attention and yell, "Catch me!" Suddenly the drunk would fall either forward or backward stiff as a board, expecting the surrounding sailors to catch him before he hit the floor. Don't know why we considered this entertaining, but we did, doing our "Catch me" often without warning. Each time, someone would seize the fallen fool before he struck the floor. As we were leaving, on the top of the stairs, I yell, "Catch me!" and fall forward. No one was in front of me. A group, six steps below me, pivoted around, scrambled up, and grabbed me in time, stopping my face just one inch from a stair tread. The group pulled me up, laughing.

Someone said, "You dumb shit for brains." We loudly chuckled.

As we made it to the first floor and were leaving, I hear, "Catch me."

Facing forward at the top of the stairs, Seamen Apprentice New-guy, stiff as a board, falls forward as I previously did. But there was no one near enough to catch him. New-guy hits the stairs making a loud crunch sound. New-guy turns into a ball and rolls down the stairs, and he gets up as if he stepped down the stairs as if nothing happened. He grins at us with blood running out of his nose. A bloody nose for his fall is his only injury. In amazement, we stare at New-guy. Someone in our group laughing announced, "God helps drunks and fools, and we're having him working overtime tonight."

To get back to the boat, we seek a cab. Cabbies pulled to the curb, looked at us, and pulled away without us. As they drove off, we profusely cussed at them. I suppose they figured we would be more trouble than the fare was worth. The cabbies were correct.

Next to a corner, we gathered when a bus pulls up to its stop. We rushed in, boarding the bus before the driver stopped us.

Later, I bore the world exploding like a massive earthquake. My head was throbbing so severe, giving such pain, I wanted to rip it off. I wanted to weep. Loud shouting worsened my pain. I wanted to cry, but the roaring was not the world's annihilation, because no one was shouting. It was the Shore Patrol shaking me, waking me up, trying to identify me to find out where I should be. The shore patrol talking wasn't loud, but their questions seemed like cannons firing.

After I open my eyes, everything appears fuzzy, moving—the pain in my head increases.

"Sailor wake up. You cannot sleep here. What ship are you attached?"

Fixated on the closest one, was there more shore patrol? No idea, nor did I care, sitting up, I asked, "Where is the head? I'm going to throw up."

A hand points. The way he's pointing, I go, finding the head, rushing inside, throwing open a shitter door, getting to the toilet, and making it in time to fill the toilet bowl with green, yellow vomit. I puke until nothing more comes out. Still sick, I flushed that toilet, wishing I didn't do that—the flushing noise hurt. That toilet's sound caused more head pain. I rush to a sink, fill the basin, and wash my face. The water felt good. I immerse my head into the bowl. Coldwater soothed my headache and made suffering slightly less, I leave the head, overhearing someone declare, "Man, he must have tied one on last night."

Someone else, in disgust, replies, "Yeah, the young sailors can't hold their booze. They do this every chance they get until they grow up." I'm assuming these guys did not like me, but I didn't know what I did wrong.

Inquiring, "Where are the white boats?" Oddly they stared at me as if I didn't understand what I was requesting, demanding, "The white boats, the white boats, where are they?" They peered at me as if I lost my mind.

Someone suggests, "That dumb son-of-a-bitch means the seaplane tenders that are painted white. The drunk doesn't know the difference between a boat and a ship."

I inquired again, "Well, where are they?"

"Why, are you stationed on them?" Someone asks.

As I look at one of the shore pratol, with a look that questions their assessment of me, I replied, "Hell no, I'm a submarine sailor off the USS Spikefish (AGSS 404), and we're tied up close to those white ships." In my condition, I bet the CO would have rather me keep my command private.

"A submarine sailor," someone replied. "No wonder he's messed up," he jokingly stated. They treated me with a little more respect, though, giving me directions to get the Spikefish.

"When you leave the front door, take your first right, and follow the road to the bay, then turn left and follow the shoreline. Keep walking, and you will get there," someone instructed.

With their directions, I walked and walked for more than an hour, and started thinking they lied. The shore patrol didn't know where the seaplane tenders were, or they sent me in the wrong direction just to give me a hard time and to be mean. Later, I realized if I were in a better condition, I would have tried to get the Shore Patrol to give me a ride to the boat, but I didn't think about it at the time.

The coming day was gradually changing from the night's black darkness. The sky is getting brighter, even though the sunrise was yet to happen, I could see around me better, spotting landing craft of all sorts. The site made me understand a little better; at least I was at Little Creek, the Amphibious Base. Then, I spot the seaplane tenders in the direction I was walking. The shore patrol didn't lie, and they gave me the right instructions. I quickened my pace. As I cross the brow, I'm watching a blazing red sky. Soon I would find out about a sailor's warning, "Red sky at night, a sailors' delight. Red sky in the morning, sailors take warning."

Finally, I'm aboard and head below, enter berthing, undress, and climb into my rack. Before I can close my eyes for sleep, a cook comes in and shakes me, yelling, "get up, it's time to get up. You start mess cooking in five minutes. So, you get your dumb-ass moving."

"That can't be right. I'm the senior lookout. I wasn't informed about mess cooking."

The cook angrily glaring down at me, orders, "Get your ass going. I don't have time to argue with you. The COB told me you're my new mess-cook. You work for me now. We got breakfast to prepare, and we are running behind. Now, get your ass going. You got two minutes to get to the mess decks."

My headache violently returned—a constant throbbing headache as I climbed out of my rack. Thinking as I dress, "Damn, this day will be a good day, one of my better ones. Gosh darn, I don't deserve this." When dressed, I move unhurriedly to the mess decks to join new pleasures, feeling sorry for myself.

MESS COOKING

Every sailor should have at least one tour of mess-cooking because mess-cooking builds character, develops a strong work ethic, allows the mess-cook to learn something about everyone in the crew. Mess-cooking produces humility more than any other job I experienced. But when I was too tired to move, I didn't grasp this concept. I moved anyway, shuffling towards the mess decks to start mess-cooking. I arrived in time to receive a million orders from the night cook. Cookie wore a white apron that covered a white t-shirt. The apron with splattered with foodstuff over it bulged over his waistline displaying his overweight condition. Cookie expected I should have been getting the breakfast setup done or should have it already set. At this blissful moment, I didn't understand how to do the tasks Cookie demanded. Mess-cooking started like this. This ain't no shit.

"Get the coffee made," orders Cookie.

"How do I make the coffee?"

A red face answered with impatience, "Don't you know anything? Drain and clean the coffee urn first and fill the urn to its full mark. That will put five gallons of cold water in it; next, you fill the coffee basket with coffee to its full level mark."

"How do I clean and fill the coffeepot, and where's the coffee?"

With his red sweating face showing irritation, Cookie answers. "Shit, you know nothing. You damn well better pay attention, because

I'll only show you how to make coffee this once. And, if you don't get it right, the crew will keelhaul you. Every single morning, while mess-cooking, you will make the coffee hot and strong—that's the way the crew likes it." Then, Cookie tells me how to make my first pot of coffee. Cookie instructed me in every step and made me repeat to him each step as I did it. As he scoops coffee grounds from the coffee bin, the scoop scraped the bin's bottom. Cookie orders, "The coffee bin is getting empty. After breakfast, get two cans of coffee and fill this bin."

"Where's the coffee cans?"

"The coffee is stored in the forward engine room outboard of the starboard diesel." Cookie replied with growing annoyance. "Before you get it, inform the engine room-watch about what you're doing. If you're lucky, the watch will help you get it."

As the coffee brews, Cookie directs, "Get this mess decks ready for breakfast, wipe down, all the tables and benches, and set up the tables. The table setups are in the benches and scrub the deck. You have twenty minutes to get everything done. As soon as you're finished, you see me—got it!"

"Got it, where's the cleaning gear?"

"Shit, what a boot camp. How long have you been aboard?" Before I can answer, he continues, "You've been here long enough to know this."

"Pay attention, while I give you a brief qualification instruction on the mess decks and galley; you damn well better learn this. We have breakfast to serve, because of you, we're behind. When we get through, you hustle your ass, get the mess decks cleaned up, and make it ready for dinner." Then, Cookie gives me the five-minute college course—a tour of the mess decks and galley.

Holy shit, I couldn't believe how much information he gave me in five minutes—an information overload. What was faster? The rate of the information he presented me or how fast I forgot that info. Overwhelmed, all I could remember was the galley sink and the scullery location, and I knew that before he started his lessons.

While he's heading into the galley, Cookie ordered, "get a move-on and catch-up; we've got a crew to feed."

My main job in the Navy so far was cleaning, so I knew how to clean. I found the cleaning gear in lockers and rushed wiping down the tables and benches, scrubbed the deck, then set-up the tables for breakfast. Table-benches held everything required, napkins, salt, pepper, jelly, ketchup, sugar, and hot sauce. After placing the condiments on each table, in the reefer, I found butter for toast and cream for coffee, then I put the butter on saucers and poured the cream into pictures one for each table.

Cookie comes out of the galley, inspecting my progress. Cookie seems pleased and surprised, remarking, "Holy shit, we're ready for breakfast, good job, we're on schedule. Make the toast; put a plate full on each table."

"How do I make the toast?"

After a ten-second lesson on toast making, Cookie heads back into the galley.

As I was making toast, feeling sorry for myself, assuming I shouldn't be mess-cooking, thinking about what has been happening, shit, I'm in this dilemma with no way to get out of it. How am I going to do this? Damn, I understood nothing about mess-cooking. Cookie, what a shithead, he is so damn demanding, getting me up when I had no sleep. Cookie allowed me only five minutes to learn my job, but I showed him. Cookie was surprised when I got the mess decks cleaned and setup. It was easy, finding everything Cookie showed me earlier—everything I needed, locating the table set up stuff arranged and stored in a logical order for setting up convenience.

Afterward, Cookie praised me for doing a good job—what's happening? Possibly I'm wrong about the Cookie. How the cooks prepare the food, bake bread, and sticky-buns, and how the mess cooks serve all the food family style is a wonder. The *Spikefish* is a great feeder, and I haven't had a bad meal since I came aboard, the chow is superb. Maybe Cookie has qualities I'm unaware of, and he's better than I thought.

With Cookie's balding head and boyish face, I can't tell if he's young or old. Look at his spotted white apron over his bulging white t-shirt. Cookie is moving like a fanatic ensign on an imminent mission, baking bacon, frosting sticky-buns, cooking shit on the shingle, frying potatoes, and scrambling eggs, doing this all simultaneously. Cookie is enjoying himself, contented as a pig wallowing in shit, happier than a boot-camp coming out of a cathouse for his first time with a shit-eating grin on his face, as if he was lucky for the first time—ecstatic in happiness. I wondered why Cookie is so cheerful doing all that cooking and food preparations, and he's so skillful at it.

Cookie interrupts my toast making and orders, "Knife, take these sticky-buns and coffee topside for the Topside Watch, to the Belowdecks Watch, and the wardroom for the OOD. Get your ass back here promptly. We start breakfast in fifteen minutes."

As I hear "Knife," I cringe with embarrassment and respond, "Aye-Aye, bread is in the toaster, just to let you know."

"I'll finish the toast, get moving."

While delivering the coffee and sticky-buns topside, I realized he is the guy who has been making coffee and sticky-buns when I've been on watch. Cookie provided the goodies at the right time, preventing me from falling asleep and getting in serious trouble. Damn, I didn't realize, recalling my first sticky-bun tasting so good with coffee is a fond memory. A sticky-bun so delicious, I would have shipped over to get another one, man that's good eating! Cookie is the guy making those sticky-buns, making sure the watches got one before anyone else, I wonder, why did he give us such enjoyable delights? What a great memorable experience he provided us watch-standers, making pleasurable duty days. Cookie must be one of the Navy's top cooks. I judged that he's the most excellent cook.

As soon as I step into the mess decks, Cookie orders, "Get the chow out. Place a bowl of minced meat, eggs, and a platter of bacon with toast on each table."

As I carried my first bowl of the meat sauce, I brought it gently, struggling not to spill any. Then Granny Knot, the day mess cook, shows up, grabs the bowl out of my hand, and slings it on the Chief's table without spilling a drop. In amazement, I saw it slide to its position.

"Hey, get your ass moving, get the food out, we don't have all day," Granny Knot orders.

Stunned by the order, and pissed off at the one giving it, I recover heading into the Galley, collecting the food, and passing it out to Granny Knot. The task was demanding, and I struggled to keep up with him. With no pause, he filled each table. Anytime I was too slow to keep him from setting up the tables, he showed his displeasure, bugging me to move faster, "Knife, get another plate of toast, get more eggs, move your ass! You're missing a bowl of sauce."

As rapidly as I could move to keep up, I'm thinking, who died and left behind that boot camp shit-for-brains in charge? Shit, two weeks ago, he couldn't tie his shoes. Granny Knot was so screwed up; he couldn't get ready for war, making him the last one on the boat before we left Key West. That's the reason he is mess-cooking now. The COB kept his promise. "The last one aboard will start mess-cooking." Shit! I damn well don't like Admiral Granny Knot bossing me.

I had no time to ponder on this further because the mess decks filled up with a hungry, noisy crew. As they consumed dishes of food, we returned the empties to the galley for a refill and got the food back promptly to the tables. As diners finished their meal, we cleaned and reset the tables with bowls and platters full of food. The sailors, who finished eating, took their dirty dishes and fighting gear to the mess deck's scullery, where I'm the one who washed all those dirty dishes.

Before the second wave of eaters could sit at a table, a dozen underwater demolition sailors came down from topside into the mess decks lugging a pile of equipment. The divers created complete chaos, interrupting and delaying breakfast. The COB suddenly shows up with First-Class Sewell, the forward torpedo room-watch. Pointing to Sewell, he addressed the newcomers, "Follow Sewell here to the forward room. Take your equipment with you. Sewell will get you set up with berthing and help you get the rest of your gear below through the forward access hatch. After stowing your gear, get back here for breakfast. Cookie will keep the galley open for you."

Sewell commands, "Follow me," as he heads forward with the divers following him. The divers inspect the boat as they left the mess decks and looked uncertain about their new home.

The COB steps into the Galley, "Cookie, keep the mess decks open to feed this group. The boat is getting underway soon, get as much trash removed as you can. The crew increased by these twelve divers, and four new boots right out of sub school. You need to adjust to feeding the extra people."

Cookie replies, grinning, "Aye-Aye, will do, I'll take good care of them." Looking at me, Cookie orders, "Knife, get the trash together and take it to the dumpsters topside, and be quick about it."

After I got all the trash in plastic bags placed under the after-battery access hatch, I had a considerable trash pile blocking the passage aft from the mess decks. As I stare at the garbage, I wondered, how am I going to get that crap topside.

A First-Class engineman, waiting in line for breakfast with a dozen shipmates, sees my difficulty. With a big smile, he orders the crew behind him, "The Knife needs help to get this trash topside. Get in a line and pass this trash topside." Within seconds, all the trash was topside, two engine-men and a second-class electrician helped me carry the trash to the dumpster making the trash removal easy and quick work.

Relieved and surprised for the help, as I left the dumpster, heading back to the boat, suddenly, I understood our next mission. The United States will invade Cuba. But the *Spikefish* won't be part of the blockade to prevent Soviet ships from reaching Cuba. The *Spikefish* will play a more significant role, being the first to strike Cuba by taking the divers to Cuba. The divers will be the first ones in, doing the initial groundwork necessary to invade Cuba, making a landing site ready for an invasion, and making history. I grasped, shit! I'm mess-cooking. When this happens, I'll miss the action.

With disappointment, I kept my insight quiet as I head below. In the mess decks, I observed the divers finishing their breakfast, acting like submariners. The divers laughed together at unknown matters and interacted with their mannerisms, cocky, arrogant, and confident. They displayed a physical difference from our crew. They were in physically good shape—looking muscular, showing hard muscles like bulging rocks compared with the *Spikefish* crew's soft muscle tone.

While I'm finishing the morning cleanup, the ship's motion lets me realize we're underway. I'm saddened because I'm mess-cooking, missing the excitement topside, missing the bustle getting ready for combat. The moment in history, when the battle happens, I won't play a fighting part. Yet, time did not allow further thought about my self-felt misfortune—dinner preparation was next. As soon as we started cleaning the mess decks, the divers, and some of the crew joined us in the cleaning, making the cleanup faster than the breakfast set-up. As we're cleaning, I'm thinking, that's why I like riding submarines, everyone helps one another.

After the breakfast cleanup, the mess-decks became a lounge for off-watch-qualified crew with divers joining them. As the *Spikefish* greeted the open Ocean, new crewmembers became sick, sensing increasing ship movement. By attaching one end of a large sausage to the overhead, the old salts found amusement watching the sailors get seasick when they saw the horse-cock swaying. We called the sausage horse-cock because it was huge six inches in diameter and three feet long. Mess cooks sliced horse-cock to make sandwiches. The sausage dangled like a plumb bob. As the boat moved, it appeared swinging as if it were moving. Everyone seeing the horse-cock became more aware of the ship's movement, causing those prone to seasickness to become sick. The old salts disregarded the ill suffering they were creating. Before long, the mess decks were empty except for the old salts laughing from their mischief.

As the dinner cleanup was winding down, I was washing dishes in the deep sink. Ship motion increased; the seas were getting more robust like a storm is brewing. This motion made simple work challenging. Then it happened, the boat rolled to starboard with a larger down pitch angle. I'm facing aft, looking at the water level in the deep sink rise towards the sink's top, away from me. The boat's pitch angle shifted to an up-angle causing the sink water to drop until I could see the deep sink's bottom two inches. At the next down-angle, the sink water rose again. The moment this happened, the contents of my stomach, this morning's breakfast, followed the sink's water level. Stomach juices filled my mouth with a foul-tasting liquid, giving me a nauseating sickness. With the next up angle, this mess dropped back into my stomach. Unexpectedly, another pitch down angle happened; this time, my stomach's contents stayed in my mouth, forcing me to vomit over the closest container next to me, a filled trash can where plate scrapping of uneaten food collected. Barf filled to the top, and vomit overflowed it, making an unpleasant sight, providing a more unpleasant odor. Vomiting removed my nauseating sickness. Enjoyment at someone else's misfortune backfired, green-faced old salts fled the mess decks, giving me the mess decks to enjoy all by myself.

As the day progressed, my sickness did not return. I'm glad the boat's motion was not so severe to prevent completing our regular routines, just enough to keep those prone to seasickness sick sufficient to keep them out of the mess decks.

After the dinner cleanup, Granny Knot and I made breakouts for the evening meal, finding everything quickly and getting it without searching or moving stuff in its way. How fast we got the job done amazed me. Granny Knot gave me an insight into why this happened. "You understand I started mess-cooking before we got underway in Key West. Like you, I didn't know shit about mess-cooking. I was lucky, though. I worked with Wingnut, who was the leading mess cook, now he is in 'A' division. He showed me the ropes. The first mess-cooking job I had was loading stores before getting underway. That task gave me a revelation, and there's more to cooking than just cooking food."

"Caldas, the senior cook, was on the pier with his menu for the next two months. Caldas directed the loading using a store's loading plan, sending the last meal's menu ingredients belowdecks to stow first, followed by the next day's meal ingredients. The store's load continued until we stowed all the stores. Properly stowed food made breakouts accessible without digging through piles of unneeded supplies. Caldas's plan changed my opinion of the cooks and seniors on this boat. The senior people realize what they are doing, and they consider the crew when deciding what meals and desserts to prepare. The cooks realize their job is much more than preparing a meal. They understand their primary job is upholding crew's high morale—this was a revelation. You'll learn a lot while mess-cooking."

In bewilderment, I listen to Granny Knot. Holy shit, how did he become so smart and gung-ho in such a short time? Before we left Key West, he couldn't even tie his shoes without knotting them up into a tripping hazard—hell. He couldn't even fart correctly without shitting his pants. The COB was on Granny Knot's ass every time he screwed up, calling him a slacker, requiring someone else to finish everything he messed up—too many times. But I was the one who saved his ass, fixing his screw-ups. Because he was cumbersome completing the simplest of tasks, he got by doing the minimum to stay out of trouble. Granny Knot displayed no leadership skill, and I never heard him express an original opinion, but sure, he's a great guy to hit the beach with and to hunt for girls. Now I'm listening to Admiral Granny Knot explains why it's easy locating what I needed for dinner, telling the cook's ability made it simple for us. This abrupt shift in his manner, and his new skill, how did that develop?

Next, we prepared for the noon meal, the main meal the galley served every day. First, I made another pot of coffee. For Caldas, I peeled fifty pounds of potatoes, peeled and chopped ten pounds of onions, washed fifteen pounds of carrots, and sliced them thin, and chopped ten bunches of celery. For a salad, I peeled and chopped more onions, washed carrots slicing them on the diagonal, sliced celery, cucumbers, and radishes, and diced up a dozen tomatoes, chopped up a bag of parsley and ten heads of lettuce. After I mixed all this in a large tub, I added black and green olives and stored the salad in the reefer.

During a short break, Caldas gave me my new berthing assignment, giving me my rack in a section assigned only for the cooks and mess cooks—no more hot-bunking while mess-cooking. With the break over, the cooks and mess cooks did their part in setting up and preparing for the next meal, doing multiple tasks I never thought about, details crucial to feed the crew.

The cooks' challenge: they must prepare various dishes of different foods made in large quantities that take different times to cook and make sure the food tastes good and is ready on time. The mess cooks helped the cooks, having meal setups completed on time. The mess cooks washed pots and pans, filled bowls and platters with grub, cleaned up the messes, set up the tables, and kept food available for every table during every meal. The cooks and mess cooks did this while the boat pitched and rolled.

In shifts, the crew ate meals; the first set was for the ongoing-watch section and Chiefs who sat at a table reserved only for them. Chiefs never waited in line. Chiefs came into the mess decks any time they wanted. The second set was a hungry group of off going watch-standers mixed with anyone who joined them if space allowed. The third setting was for stragglers, mess cooks, and cooks. During this setting, the divers filled the mess decks.

Everyone left full and expressed enjoyment of the food: a meal that included meatloaf, roasted vegetables, beans, soup, and the salad I made, followed by desserts of a chocolate fudge cake. Cookie baked the cake while I was falling in and out of love the previous night. The mess cooks served the cake with ice cream—the *Spikefish* always had plenty of ice cream. The noon meal ended after everyone ate.

Later, through the scuttlebutt, we hear the message, the war is over, the Soviets backed down, and their ships are heading home. Afterward, the 1 MC barks, "The naval situation has changed, and our orders have changed. The *Spikefish* is heading back to port. Keep the maneuvering-watch set while in port because we will head back to Key West as soon as the divers disembark." The *Spikefish* got underway to Key West, leaving the divers in Norfolk.

LIBERTY IN KEY WEST

For a young couple, Key West, Florida, is an ideal location as a romantic paradise. For a sailor under twenty-one on liberty, I found Key West a lonely place. When I had liberty, I strolled down Duval Street, passed bars full of gorgeous young ladies dancing to sounds of merriment luring me in, but I had to be twenty-one to enter.

So many evenings, I passed the time at a pool hall, playing snooker or eight-ball. Snooker required more skill using smaller balls and larger pool tables. I honed my pool skills by playing snooker. Eight-ball was a faster game that was easy to play with larger pockets and smaller pool tables. Most players liked playing eight-ball. Then playing eight-ball, I made wagers to make the games challenging and striving to make the night more enjoyable. The snooker practices paid off; some nights were profitable.

On weekends during the day, shipmates and I fished or went scuba diving. Other days and nights alone, I would walk around the side streets and back alleys exploring Key West. Since I'm under twenty-one and wanting a female friendship, but it seemed impossible to find female companionship, finding there wasn't a girl for me. In Key West, I'm miserable with so little to do. Not accepting hopelessness, I never gave up my search for enjoyment.

Fun wasn't in the local bars, but I discovered pleasure with a curiosity for exploring local cuisine eateries. Locally prepared food, so different from Michigan, was available for sampling. One Key West restaurant, where local families and fishermen were patrons, served my first sampling of sea turtle and key lime pie. There was a moment of enjoyment as I savored an excellent sea turtle. As he would prepare a pork cutlet, the chef fixed the turtle; it tasted scrumptious. You can't get turtle today; sea turtles are on the extinct critical species list. For dessert, I had my first bite of key lime pie—it was yummy. Key limes are smaller and have a different flavor than limes found in the stores in Michigan. In that restaurant, the owners treated me like family; their hospitality prompted me to return many times. I found a home away from home. That experience gave me the passion for discovering unique, delicious food found in local eateries today.

Key West provides excellent fishing and diving prospects. Every time I could have someone to go with me, I enjoyed fishing and diving. On one of our fishing trips, Ferguson, Bob, Charlie, and I got a boat from the parks-recreation department with help from Billy-Bob. He was a second-class petty officer who had a car. Billy-Bob took a liking to us and welcomed us as diving and fishing companions. Outdoor activity is where Key West is spectacular. Clear waters surround Key West, with sunlight reflecting off the bottom presenting displays of various light blue, dark blue, and bright green colors.

After diving off the boat and swimming, we fished. That's when the excitement happened when we discovered that Bob was afraid of sharks. Charlie caught a shark about five feet long. Charlie hoisted the shark into the boat. Then, the shark dropped to the bottom of the boat and thrashed around. Charlie and I tried grabbing it to get the hook out of its mouth. The shark squirmed out of our hands when we struggled to catch it. That shark didn't like our company, flailing, trying to get back into the water. Bob acted as if he knew the vicious shark was after him and wanted to take a bite out of him in a panic, he jumped up and stood on the aft boat seat holding a spear gun. He made the boat rock back and forth, making everything unstable. That made grabbing the shark impossible. Bob then shot at the shark, missed, but his arrow punched a small hole in the boat's bottom. Charlie demanded, "What the hell! Bob, why did you do that?" I had to tease him more, saying, "You dumb shit. The boat is flooding, and if it sinks, you'll be in the water with that angry shark. Think about it."

Anyway, we didn't sink but made it back to shore. Later, Bob told us why he has a fear of sharks. "Before my father's Air Force retirement, our family accompanied him to the Azores for two years of supper duty. For a kid, the Azores is a great place to grow up, lots to do. We went swimming almost every day. I made friends with many of the local kids.

One day, I'm sitting on the beach, when I hear screams of pain. My friend's father rushed down the beach, dived into the bay and swam franticly towards his daughter. A shark attacked her while she was swimming. I saw the attack's aftermath as her father carried her out of the water. She's crying in pain while blood flows from a gash on her leg. I watched as her father gives her emergency first aid. I could see the worry in her tearful eyes as her father carries her to his car, rushing for further help. I have never forgotten the pain, the wounds, and the later scars from her injuries."

Now, I understood how Bob's watching this event reinforced his fear of sharks.

One Saturday morning, as I departed the base, through the main gate, I saw a sexy-looking babe standing next to a tent across the street. The pretty gal caught my eye. With an attractive smile and eyes beaming at me, she indicated she had something to show me. She motioned for me to join her while encouraging me to talk to her.

Thinking my search for a female is over, I rushed to the tent to join her. The lovely gal welcomed me and invited me into the open canopy.

The tent is a sailor's trap. About sailors' traps, I knew nothing. I'm primed for being conned in the enclosure that provided shade. The good-looking babe is the bate that caught me. Inside the tent, an older overweight guy sat on a stool behind a table full of books. Sweat dripping off his forehead dropped onto his bright red-faced bulging cheeks and dripped off a bright red nose. He's smiling at me as I enter. The guy greets me as if he found his best friend's son. With a sweaty paw, he shakes my hand, giving me the sensation as if I grabbed a warm wet diaper. The guy invites me to sit on a fold-up chair.

As I'm sitting, he asks questions, "What books have you been reading? Who is your favorite author? What books do you own?"

"I don't have favorite author, and I own none," I answered. I inspected the table showing interest in the books. The table had stacks of new books for sale. The piles of books to sell on the table established a sailor's trap. I wasn't aware of a sales pitch that was coming, but I'm about to be taken.

The lovely sweetheart with charming smiles gave suggestions of future meetings, says, "I admire smart men who enjoy reading a lot. You sound like a scholar. You must be a reader." The babe is buttering me up, but I'm clueless about the reason for her charms, not knowing she is setting me up to buy something.

The guy started his sales pitch, "To be kept up on events, this set of encyclopedias will allow you to do just that.... Oh, you need to be thinking ahead, you will have children, and one of the best ways to develop the children's mind is to read to them. This set of children's books has all the classic children's stories. Think about it; your children will pass on these books to their children.... A bible, just you look at this beautiful bible. It will be your family's bible. It has a place to record all your family members...." I'm gullible with his sales pitch, I bought a set of encyclopedias, a collection of children's storybooks, and one large, fancy-looking Bible. The books weren't a complete rip-off, they were of good quality, but expensive. I paid three times the price I would have if I bought the same books elsewhere. Adding to the cost, because I had no place to store the books, I had to ship the books to Michigan. After these purchases, the hopeful follow-up date with the lovely girl never materialized.

The sailor's trap got me. I became a victim of vermin, the parasites that prey on young military unsuspecting service members, and used my youthful foolishness to con me, to steal from me legally. As a victim, I overpaid for books I didn't need.

Afterward, I realized this was a hard-knocks college lesson. The lesson's tuition was the book's excessive price, and the embarrassment I endured after discovering a parasite duped me. Afterward, I'm more cautious in dealings with questionable salesmanship tactics.

A HOT BOURBON

Torpedoman First-Class Blackheart was an excellent section leader. Blackheart was consistently fair in making out the watch-bill, ensuring that he equally treated everyone miserably. Blackheart was hard on nonquals but took many hours every duty night explaining the aft torpedo room to help us qualify.

Blackheart took the Chief's test and was waiting for the test results. Blackheart demanded everyone in the duty section to do their duty, and he was quick to set anyone straight. I couldn't figure him out. Blackheart surprised me one-weekend duty day. After the noon meal, I was working topside. The Key West's heat was roasting me. Then, Blackheart coming from the aft hatch ordered me to follow him. Off the boat, we head down the pier and stop at his car. Blackheart ordered, "Get in." I'm wondering what's this about. As I opened the passenger's side door, the heat from a blast furnace seared me. Sitting in that hot sun, made the inside of Blackheart's car a hot dry-heat oven. After I sat down, the dry-heat feels like I'm bread baking. I got a burning sensation because the seats are searing, making me speculate the heated seats might burn me. What's this about, I wonder?

Blackheart opens the rear door and pulls a paper bag from the ledge behind the back seat. The rear window was like a magnifier setting the bag as a heat target as a magnifier used to start a fire. I discovered shortly that the bag's content was as hot as a freshly poured cup of coffee.

Blackheart gets in on the driver's side, looks at me, studying me, and then with a grin, orders, "Roll down the windows." Then, he startles me with, "I hear you like a drink occasionally."

"Yeah, I drink when I can."

Blackheart exposes the head of a bottle from the bag, removes the cap, and hands me the open bottle hiding within the bag. "Try this; you'll appreciate it."

As I bring the bottle to my lips, I get a strong aroma whiff of bourbon whiskey. I take a generous gulp—a colossal mistake. That bourbon was burning hot. Hot bourbon ignited my mouth, scorched my throat, heated my stomach, making me gasp, causing me to cough. From my toes to the top of my head, I suffered like I'm on fire.

Blackheart comments while controlling laughter, "That's sipping whiskey. Slow down. You don't gulp sipping whiskey, you savor it, sipping it to enjoy the flavor. Haven't been drinking much, have you?"

"Don't drink much, but enjoy it when I can get a good bottle." I'm unable to prevent sputtering my response, with tears in my eyes and fire in my mouth.

Blackheart takes the bottle from me, and takes a sip, holds it in his mouth, and acts as he's savoring the hot bourbon. "That's good," passing the bottle back.

This time, I took a cautious sip, holding bourbon in my mouth, savoring the flavor, finding the hot bourbon essence intense and exceptional. "Man, that bourbon tasted good," I declared. After we shared one more enjoyable sip, Blackheart puts the bourbon away, and we headed back to the boat. Friendship is developing; I'm amazed, considering I'm exclusive that he included me with his drink, knowing to drink while on duty is against regulations. Blackheart is acting like an older brother, teaching me the proper ways to drink. I learned how to enjoy drinking, be mischievous while being responsible for not drinking to excess. Blackheart showed me how it's acceptable to bend the rules at times to add enjoyment. And he stressed we must uphold responsibility for doing one's duty. After many years, I remembered the bourbon flavor is so good, I've enjoyed bourbon since.

THE SPANKING

Four qualified crewmembers conducted a cruel act of near-criminal perspectives to a Nonqual named Rocky. Seaman Apprentice Rocky reported aboard about a month after me. He left Boot Camp, went to Sub-school, and then to the *Spikefish*. From the start, Rocky did not fit into the submarine lifestyle. He took three weeks to become dink, and five weeks to become incredibly behind in his qualification. The expected time to qualify topside security-watch was two weeks. After six weeks, Rocky didn't qualify topside security-watch. The COB put Rocky on port and starboard watch-standing until he became a qualified topside security-watch. Rocky took another week to qualify the watch. He was a load because he caused other watchstanders to stand more watches without him.

Rocky was a know-it-all, you recognize the kind, a wise guy, a sailor whose leaders and no one else can tell him anything—a real mental midget with a rock-hard attitude. He thinks he knows everything, but Rocky would need to add ten pounds of knowledge to his brain to get a vacuum. During his brief time aboard, he engaged in three fights. Because of his abrasive manner, everyone aboard was ready to punch his lights out. Rocky did not fit into submarine life from the moment he first crossed the brow—no salute to the Ensign or the Topside-Watch. He dropped his seabag on deck and demanded help to get it belowdecks.

Rocky was always getting into trouble, nothing serious, but he annoyed the COB, his section leaders, and anyone else in authority the most. One night, while standing a mid-watch, Rocky's first topside security-watch by himself, he played with his sidearm, a Colt .45 Automatic. You guessed it; Rocky dropped his weapon over the side. Rocky told the below-decks-watch who woke up the section leader to inform him of the problem. The Section Leader had to wake up the Duty Torpedo-man to issue a new weapon to Rocky. The Section Leader also reported the issue to the Duty Chief, who woke up the Duty Officer telling him Rocky's carelessness.

There was a discussion about whether to shoot Rocky on the spot or throw him overboard and not let him back aboard until he had the weapon. Those were the nicest considerations they desired. The Duty Officer saved him. I guess the Duty Officer could have supported the worst for Rocky if it resulted in no paperwork. If someone killed Rocky or worse, he might have to explain it in writing and triplicate.

Divers got that weapon the next morning, not taking long finding it. When they brought it up, it looked like an old rusty gun. Saltwater was quick to damage the gunmetal. You guessed it. Rocky wouldn't get off easy, just because no one killed him.

TM1 (SS) Sewell, the leading torpedo-man, in charge of the ship's small-arms weapons, took great pride in how well he kept the boat's guns like new. Sewell took it personally if someone mistreated a weapon.

The following day before the evening meal, in the Forward Torpedo Room, Sewell ordered, "Rocky, you clean up that .45 until it's like new. You will not get any liberty until you get this weapon looking as if it had never touched seawater." Sewell handed Rocky the rusted gun, a cleaning kit, rags, solvent, towels, and a Colt .45 manual. Then Sewell left for chow.

First, Rocky fieldstrips the .45 as far as he could without using tools. He has the weapon's pieces placed in a tidy order on a towel on top of a workbench.

Sewell comes into the room and sees what Rocky is doing. "You better not drop any parts into the bilges. If you put those parts in a can of solvent, it will help you stay out of further trouble. First, you will not lose the parts, and second, the solvent will clean the parts faster."

"I can manage it, don't you worry about it," replied Rocky, his words angered Sewell.

Instantly pissed, Sewell says, "If one-piece falls into the bilges, not only will you get it, but you will clean the torpedo room bilges. Do you understand me?"

Rocky had to have the last word, and said, "I've got it under control, don't worry, I know what I'm doing. You think this job is hard. I'll have this weapon cleaned shortly. See, it's already field-stripped with only a little more cleaning to do."

Sewell goes to the workbench and picks up one of the weapon pieces. A crimson-faced Sewell's yelled. "You call that clean! That weapon was in seawater. Take it apart further than field stripping. You remove, scrub, and clean each part!" Sewell was angry, big-time.

Rocky glaring back at Sewell cries, "How in the hell can I do that? You didn't give me any tools," as if it was Sewell's fault.

Not used to a seamen apprentice giving him any lip, Sewell startled for a moment, then he recovered with anger. His face was beet red as he pointed to his toolbox, "The tools you need are in my toolbox over there. Use them but put them back when done."

Rocky turned and walked towards the toolbox. Somehow, when Rocky moved to get tools, the towel holding the weapon parts went with him. Gun parts dropped to the deck, parts bouncing off the torpedo under the workbench and fell into the bilge. Loud crashing noises were from the big pieces hitting the deck and bilges. Tinkling sounds as small springs, pins, screws, and parts bounced downwards, bouncing off obstacles on the way to the bilges.

After the last sound from those falling gun parts, Rocky yelled, "I didn't mean it!"

Sewell exploded. "You shit for brains! You ass wipe! You're a dumb shit! How in the hell can you be so stupid? Get one of your rags and cover the bilge strainer before those parts get sucked into the Drain System. And find all those parts! You start forward and work aft until you find the parts. You clean each section of the bilge so clean you can eat off of it—because you will eat off of it! Shit for brains, you're not doing anything until you find all those parts and clean that weapon." He handed Rocky a number 10 can and ordered, "Put the gun parts in this!"

With a can in hand, Rocky climbed down into the aft-bilge while Sewell stared at Rocky in growing anger and waited until Rocky was in the bilge. Then Sewell yelled, "Hey shit for brains. I said, start forward, then work aft. What the hell! Why are you down there? You're dumber than a rock. You're doing another half-assed job! Well, I got news for you; you will do this right, even if it kills you. If you don't, I will rip off your head, stick it up your ass, and piss down your windpipe! Now, Rock, get your dumb ass forward, and do as you're told!"

With his new title, Rock climbed out of that bilge and started forward between the torpedo tubes. He mumbled, "Why should I have to clean this far forward? The parts couldn't get up here."

Sewell yelled at him, "Rock, shut, you're an asshole! If I wanted more crap out of you, I would squeeze your head. I had enough out of you. Rock, you don't quit until you get the bilges, and the weapon cleaned correctly. Rock, do you understand me?"

The Rock took three days toiling, to find the gun parts, and finish the bilge cleaning. He took another two days and nights, getting the weapon cleaned enough to meet Sewell's standards. Rock handed Sewell the cleaned revolver, then Sewell inspected the pistol, and found parts dirtied with salt residue. He made Rock take the weapon apart and clean it again. His weapon re-cleaning happened too many times to count. After the Rock finished cleaning the gun, meeting Sewell's requirements, he could field strip a .45 Cal faster than anybody.

The Rock's irresponsibility resulted in five days making the seamen gang one man short. He was unavailable for his everyday topside duties. We worked long hours, getting our jobs done; during this time, the Rock appeared unconcerned.

After the weapon incident, the Rock's manner didn't change. He was a no-load and troublemaker. A week after the gun incident, the COB sent the Rock mess cooking. Before he finished mess cooking, the Rock had most of the crew ready to keelhaul him. Also, the cooks threatened to kill him daily. He was continually doing wrong or annoying.

One day, while washing dishes, the Rock didn't rinse the cups good enough, leaving a soap film on the cups. The Rock's negligence gave most of the crew the shits for two days. Several had nauseous stomach aches and were unable to work, and a few were severely sick. The Doc sent them to the base sickbay for a doctor's treatment. Rock made mealtime an ordeal instead of a pleasurable event by getting into ridiculous arguments with everybody over nothing important. The Rock knew it all, not listening to anybody.

After the crew had enough of the Rock's nonsense, then direct hostilities started. The senior petty officers began actions to make his life miserable. It looked like a downhill slide for his stay in submarines.

Because of his slovenly performance, and to keep him out of everybody's way so he wouldn't cause anyone harm, the cooks kept the Rock away from the other mess cooks. The cooks gave the Rock the least desirable of duties, cleaning out the freeze box, the reefer, and dirty cleaning jobs in the pantry where they could watch him. He created problems there too.

The Rock messed up big time, putting frozen food in the reefer and fresh vegetables in the freeze box. When the cooks detected the error, the ice cream melted, cases of steaks thawed, and lettuce, eggs, and milk froze, by making a quick menu change saved the meat, but much lettuce was uneatable. The cooks wanted to barbecue him—thought this solution through—realized that grilling him would be counterproductive to their careers. Politicians and wimps might cause trouble from such action. Instead, they asked the COB to replace him, but the COB would not take the Rock back.

The Rock's fellow mess-cooks disliked working with him, because most work he performed, he did wrong. With irritation, the cooks and the other mess cooks redid the Rock's tasks. The mess-cooks working with the Rock finished or resumed their duties without his help, and they found it easier and faster without the Rock's help. He was a load. No one wanted to work with him. No matter the cause, the Rock's miserable performance caused the cooks and mess-cooks to work harder and longer.

I couldn't understand how Rock got away with what he did without someone setting him straight. I thought something must happen to the Rock to correct his performance flaws. Unknown to me were the methods the command and crew used, expecting someone like the COB to place the Rock on report, or kick him out of submarines. Great forces were in motion—corrections would happen soon. I did not expect the viciousness and cruelty given to the Rock. I did not see it happen, but I heard about it. Swift, cruel, and vicious were the Rock's treatments, but most effective. Four crewmembers did this to the Rock. This ain't no shit.

During the end of his third week of mess cooking, one late morning after breakfast clean up, the breakfast cook sent the Rock to the After-Engine Room to get coffee. We store five-gallon coffee cans outboard between the pressure hull and the main engines. Maybe, the cook assumed the Rock might get coffee without getting into trouble.

That morning, going aft, the Rock climbed outboard and got the coffee as ordered. True to his nature, instead of taking that coffee back to the mess decks, he stopped to chew the fat with the engine room gang.

The engine room gang comprising four qualified enginemen stood around their workbench located port side aft when the Rock, carrying the coffee can, invited himself to their group. As with most groups with an unwanted intruder, their topic discussion switched. The enginemen continued talking but chatted as if they were talking on a different matter before the Rock showed up, conversing as if no topic changed. The Rock was oblivious of the topic change as he struts up to the gang, placed the coffee-can on the deck, and said, "Hey guys, what's happening?"

The gang didn't want the Rock, but the Rock was unaware he wasn't wanted. Because the enginemen acted friendly towards him, they were not rude regarding him as they typically were. They included him in their discussions and told their sea stories. The enginemen welcomed him to their game to set him up, and he didn't realize it.

The enginemen look at him, grinning with a greeting approval. One replied, "Not much, we're preparing to set up a bravery test."

"A bravery test, what's a bravery test? I never heard of anyone having to do a bravery test. Who will you test? What is a bravery test?" The Rock said in his typical rude manner.

"You wouldn't have heard of a bravery test since you're not qualified. A bravery test is a submariners' secret test and not for skimmers and landlubbers. Only qualified submariners know about bravery tests because they had to pass one," one engineman replied.

"When you become ready, you will be allowed a bravery test. I don't think you're ready now." Another added.

The Rock acting insulted, utters, "What do you mean I'm not ready? I'm ready for any test anyone can give me. I can handle your wimpy bravery test."

A different member of that group stated. "Bull shit! After you understand what you must do, you wouldn't take the test. You wouldn't prove your bravery. You would cry to the COB for help because you couldn't take it. A guy like you would give away the secret of the Submariners' bravery test."

Brashly the Rock replies, "What do you mean? I'm a submariner. I'm—I'm almost qualified. I even want to become an engineman. I wouldn't ever tell. I can take your bravery test right now if you get it ready." And then, "Hell, I can pass any bravery test you can give me. I wouldn't tell a soul about your wimpy test. I promise." The Rock stated with conviction.

For several minutes, the engine room gang and the Rock continued their conversation. The group expressed, "The test is scary, hard, and dangerous."

The Rock stated, "I can do it."

They replied, "Rock, you would tell the world about the bravery test."

The Rock promised, "If any knowledge about the test got leaked, it wouldn't come from me."

This exchange finished with the Rock pleading to take this test. That's what the group expected. The cook must have been in on the

Rock's setup because he didn't check on him. The Rock was away from the mess decks longer than it takes to get coffee.

After the Rock's ample pleading and promising, the engine room gang agreed to give him the submarine bravery test. The Rock didn't realize what the engine-men were planning for him and what he agreed to.

An engineman stated, "Rock, you can't tell anyone about this test, not even a little bit about it. Once we start the test, you can't stop it. There's no turning back for you." The enginemen expressed what they would do if he told anyone about this test. They warned him of the pain and agony he would have if he let one word concerning this test slip out.

Before they started, the enginemen gave the Rock one last chance to leave without doing the test.

"I'm ready for any wimpy bravery test." Not realizing what he was getting into, but with the foolishness of youth, the Rock begged, "Please give me the bravery test. I promise never to tell anyone about it."

An engineman replied, "We will give you the bravery test."

"What must I do," asked the Rock.

"You will know soon enough," snapped another engineman.

The Rock appeared eager while the enginemen carried out test preparations. They cleared the engine room workbench except the large machine vise bolted to the workbench. They created a passage around three sides of the bench. Next, they placed a blanket over the benchtop, so only the vise was showing. The enginemen positioned the Rock on the opposite side of the vise. Then ordered, "lean across the benchtop towards the vise."

Virtually lying on the benchtop, the Rock obeyed the order. Then two of the engine room gang grabbed the Rock's arms and yanked his hands towards that vise, and command, "Stick out your index finger from each hand." Again, the Rock followed the order. Next, each enginemen holding a hand positioned Rock's fingers between the vise's jaws. They kept the Rock's fingers in position between the vice jaws. Another engineman gradually turned the vise's handle one full turn, closing the jaws.

The Rock didn't move to struggle. Then the engineman made another turn. The Rock held steady. Turn after turn the Rock held steady, this continued until the vise jaws were touching the Rock's fingers. The engineman stopped turning the vise handle, looked at the Rock, and declared, "Now the test begins. There's no stopping this test." The engineman turned a half-turn more. The Rock sensed the pressure of the vise jaws on his fingers. Beads of sweat formed on the Rock's forehead, but the Rock did not cower. His hands held steady.

One engineman blindfolded the Rock, as another stated, "Unworthy sailors failing this test will go out of their mind watching their fingers get crushed in the vise."

The Rock moved his hands, but the jaws clenched his fingers. He sensed more pressure on his fingers as the jaws closed on them. He believed, "Oh God, they will crush my fingers." The Rock looked worried as sweat flowed from his brow, and his hands shook. He couldn't pull his hands from the vise that gripped his fingers.

The engine-men sensed the vise held the Rock fast to it. They released his arms. They asked him, "Can you pull your fingers out?"

"No, I can't." The Rock replied, looking worried with a quivering voice.

Let's give it another quarter turn just to make sure," someone suggested.

The Rock underwent increased pressure and then pain. He yelled, "That hurts like hell!" The Rock tried in vain to pull his hands from that vise, believing the vise would crush his fingers, but that was not their plan.

The vise held the Rock, so the engine-men did nothing further with the vise. They kept the Rock caught in the vise.

The Rock tried to pull his hands free, but the vise held his fingers. He cried out, "Let me loose, I quit, I don't want to do this anymore."

"Tough shit! You're committed," someone in the group replied.

"The test has started—too late. A tough guy like you should be brave, but you're just a pussy," another added.

The Rock tried to regain his composure. He must have reasoned that they would not crush his fingers because they would be in trouble if they did. He realized he was in a predicament, expecting he would live through it without harm. The Rock relaxed somewhat.

The Rock felt hands raise his belly off the workbench and felt someone unbuckling his belt, and his pants loosened. Next, he sensed fresh air on his backside as someone pulled his pants and underpants down to his ankles. There was a pause of no action while his bare backside lay exposed to the group. Worried, he was—helpless, trapped at their mercy. The Rock suspected anxiety for what he thought they might do to him. He tried to thrash and move his body, but it was no use. With hands locked-in the vise, the Rock only squirmed. Next, with a loud slap, the Rock suffered extreme sharp pain on his backside. After another slap with intense pain, followed by another, the engine-men continued spanking him and striking him hard, hurting him as if he previously never felt throbbing before—like torture.

The enginemen used a leather belt to spank him because they knew of his misdeeds. While striking him, they declared each of his unwanted troublesome deeds the Rock had done, a smack for each case perceived.

"You got most of the crew sick"—whack! "You're a lazy ass-hole."—whack! "You're a dink…"—Whack! "You do nothing right."—Whack! "You're a load."—Whack! They had enough incidents on the Rock to give him a harsh spanking. They spanked him until he had welts on his backside—large bright red ones. The enginemen smacked the Rock until welts bled. Before they stopped, the Rock sobbed like a baby.

As abruptly as it started, the spanking stopped. The Rock's backside pain felt as if his ass was burning. In his agony, the Rock calmed as he imagined this was the nastiest, that they might do to him. Then he sensed a coldness on his backside. Again, he envisioned the worst when he realized that they were greasing him. Someone slapped grease over the Rock's backside, brutally pushing green-brown globs of grease into his most private of parts. The Rock, with a sense of intense humiliation, cried harder—with long, loud sobs. His helplessness added extreme misery. The Rock's agony made him so sick, he vomited.

When the Rock vomited, the engine-room gang stopped their torture. Then the enginemen removed the Rock's blindfold and watched tears flowing down the Rock's cheeks. After they freed his hands, the Rock sobbed as he slid down to the deck. His humiliation carried out.

They watched the Rock uncontrolled sobbing. Thoughts were in the minds of that engine room gang, "Did we give punishment too severe, making punishment—torture?" Did the Rock's conduct justify such an act? They realized their game progressed too far—their game turned vicious.

As they looked at the Rock sobbing, two enginemen became ashamed of their actions and bore sorrow for what they did, suffering revulsion for their shameful deeds. The enginemen wanted to console the Rock and rectify matters, but they realized this wouldn't take place—they gave the Rock too much pain. They didn't understand how to undo what they had recently carried out. They doubted but hoped Rocky would forgive the horrid treatment they induced.

The two other enginemen intend the spanking to be humiliating, but for it to become a beating wasn't their propose. They wished to retool the Rock—turn him around and make a good sailor out of him. The enginemen didn't expect their actions to get out of control, turning to abuse. These men experienced no shame because the Rock deserved his punishment. No matter, the enginemen gang were fearful if higher authority found out what they did, afraid of the punishment they would receive for their shocking acts.

The Rock now suffered violated with a crushed spirit.

The enginemen watched the Rock weeping. Complete sadness filled the engine room—sorrow that drowned out the noise from the equipment, fans, and other machinery—grief so intense that each of the engine-men suffered. They only heard the Rock's sobbing. While watching the Rock's feeble and painful moaning made their conscience, amplify the sobbing so deafening it reached deep within their souls—saddening them—too late to rectify what they have done.

One of the engine room gang tried to help the Rock.

Bawling, sobbing, and then screaming, "Don't—don't you touch me." Next, glaring with deep, intensive hatred towards them, he bellowed, "Don't you dare touch me!"

Helping hands drew back.

Another gave the Rock towels. He took the towels and wiped the grease off himself. As towels became full of grease, the Rock threw them at his tormentors. They did not flinch, as a towel hit them, leaving oil spots on dungarees where they hit. The Rock changed the moment he threw towels at his tormentors.

Not finished cleaning himself, the Rock pulled up his pants, tucked in his shirt, and buckled up his belt. He picked up the coffee can and left the engine room without saying a word.

In shame and worry, the engine room gang watched him leave.

The Rock left the engine room to the mess decks and emptied the can of coffee into the coffee bin. While working, with a subdued spirit, he accomplished tasks, performed chores silently, and toiled without humor. He finished the day's work with no one telling him what to do, later that night, he considered what he must do.

Events, good or bad, horrible or astonishing, shape lives as people react to them. A few individuals renew their strength, yet for others, the incident destroys them, or they become broken in spirit. A change happened to the Rock, like the few people who turn their lives around forever. He assumed the crew liked his antics. Now he realized they despised him for them.

The Rock had to decide; he could leave submarines, that's easy, merely non-volunteer. Many other sailors quit subs for less treatment. But to stay in subs, he couldn't stay with affairs as they were. The Rock understood his previous conditions must change to remain in submarines. The Rock realized it was the wise-guy character that he must replace. Yes, he had a shattered spirit, but deep within his soul, he found inner strength and decided to improve with a different attitude and not quit.

Rapidly, everyone in the crew realized something had happened to the Rock. We did not get the details, but we sensed the extent. A silent, humorless, dejected Rock performed duties with new efficiency, but without enthusiasm or reaction—not within his past nature.

Several individuals on board hoped the Rock would give up, but he didn't. The Rock was a constant reminder to those that hurt him. He kept his pledge, telling no one about what happened. He held revulsion towards each one of the engine room gang. The enginemen were helpless to change his feelings or to have Rocky forgive them. Over time, the tortures suffered more than the Rocky. The engine-men were fearful because information regarding their cruelty might get out—they underwent shame and fear of punishment.

Later, I discovered the details concerning the spanking and greasing. On different nights when drinking, the enginemen cried their stories. By telling me, they hoped it would remove their shame, but it didn't. That tragic event haunts them, for there was no glory, no fun, no joy, only suffering a never-ending disgrace and fear of punishment from that fateful beating.

The Rock qualified while the *Spikefish* headed for Norfolk. He started striking for torpedoman. Because he worked hard, every working party welcomed him from loading stores to loading weapons. The Rock kept himself distant from the crew. Perhaps the Rock lost something that may never return. Maybe the Rock lost the ability to have fun—to enjoy life to its fullest. Possibly, he never again trusted a shipmate for anything. Finding friends aboard did not happen until he changed; he thought all were against him. However, after the Rock adjusted, he then found friends, success, and contentment.

THE SAILOR EATING MORAY EEL

As a non-qualified seaman, submarine weekend duty days get crammed with actions my section leader and the qualified crew considered mandatory to make my life miserable, seeking to motivate me. Blackheart, my section leader, kept me busy, standing topside-watch, cleaning, and maintaining topside shipshape. During off time, the experienced crew expected me to qualify in submarines. The duty nights were uneventful, comprising boring watches or sleeping, but no movies. For me, standing topside-watch at night with little for me to do, except staying alert for any abnormality, and being the first line of defense against attack or incident which never happened was boring. One duty weekend started like any other weekend duty. On this duty weekend, my topside-watch was different, exciting, and made me an observer of mischief—that was hilarious.

On weekend duty days, the duty section took it easy, doing simple tasks during the day, possibly a little letter writing, goofing off, and later watching the evening movie in the mess decks that provided nightly entertainment. On most duty nights, my section leader Blackheart, with his selected gang Machinist Mate First-Class Sacher, Hitfirst—my sea daddy, Quartermaster Third-Class Snatch, and Torpedoman Third-Class Miller would meet topside. They met when the mess decks cleanup takes place, the time between the end of the evening meal and when the movie starts. On the smoking deck, lounging aft of the bridge, they enjoyed the evenings, feeling refreshing tropical breezes, a pleasant relief from the hot daytime Key West sun, making their duty days as enjoyable as possible.

Submarine sailors are never content to see the world drift by without assisting it; sailors will give the world a little push making it spin faster. Sub sailors intend to do one's duty, yet make work exciting and fun, living life to its fullest. In like manner, Blackheart's gang broke up the boredom.

One of my duty nights, I'm the topside-watch, making my safety inspection. I stopped aft of the sail under the smoking deck, where I accidentally overheard Blackheart's gang developing a plan. I'm below them, and they were unaware of my presence, because they spoke freely, disclosing their conniving details. I heard their conversation without the gang, knowing I was spying on them. As I listened to their plan, it kept my interest because I discovered that they were contriving mischief. On the following duty nights, I would return to the hiding place and learned more about their scheme.

While on the smoking deck, sitting topside, the gang scrutinized the pier, studying a fisherman's actions setting and recovering his lobster traps. The group spied on the fisherman, monitored his fishing, noted his catch, and followed his movements. Like planning for a military mission, the group acted like Admiral-Strategists. The Strategists discussed the fisherman and developed their plan, a good idea, a thought-out plan, giving each gang member given a critical assignment. As Admirals understand, not all projects are successful—something goes amiss because they didn't consider something, or they missed an unknown factor. The gang's plan overlooked some details, causing them considerable embarrassment. It happened like this. This ain't no shit.

"Blackheart, you have been inspecting that lobsterman every duty day since before we went to Norfolk. What's with that, are you in love with him?" Sacher asks while chuckling.

"Hell no, I'm not interested in him in that way." Acting insulted for the implied query, letting Sacher know his challenge was fruitful, getting under Blackheart's iron armor. Blackheart surprised Sacher with his response. "I'm studying his fishing methods. Along these piers, he's the most successful fisherman. I'm thinking we should get a few traps and try lobstering. During a movie, a lobster meal would be excellent—they're damn good eating. I bet it would make officers jealous of seeing us eat lobsters."

"That won't work; if we had traps, we would lose them when we went to sea. Someone would steal them. We have no place to store them." Hitfirst Commented.

Without a sound, they see the fisherman set his last trap and leave the pier heading towards his car.

"What's he doing?" Snatch asks.

"He'll return. He sets his traps, and then he leaves and returns four to five hours later to recover his catch. The fisherman does this every night." Replies Blackheart.

"Wouldn't he be worried that someone would steal his catch while he is away?" Miller asks.

"Hell no, nobody messes with the Key West fishermen. The fishermen have a reputation; they'll make fish bait out of anyone who messes with their livelihood." Blackheart answers.

Sacher listens to that exchange—Oh shit! With a big grin, he declares, "We'll have lobster on a duty weekend. I know how we can get them. I have a plan, but I will need your help to pull this off."

Like preparing for a military mission, setting the gang's pinpoint objectives, they begin their scheme, assigning mission tasks for each one. Sacher orders, "Snatch, you're the timekeeper. Find out when that fisherman first gets here, how long he stays baiting his traps, and how long he stays away. Get the time it takes Miller and Hitfirst to walk down the pier to the traps and then return. Hitfirst and I will make friends with the fisherman and learn how to pull up a trap and reset it. Snatch, you need to time how long it takes to pull up a trap, remove the lobsters, and reset it. Miller, you can also make friends with the fisherman, bring him a coffee, or find out what we can give him he could use."

Blackheart seeing the plan has merit, adds, "We cannot be topside at the same time all the time. Everyone rotates, someone must be topside every time that fisherman shows up to check his traps. I'll adjust the watch bills to keep one of us topside as much as possible. Keep this secret if caught, we must vow not to rat on a teammate." The gang members promise to hold their secrets private.

Snatch, the timekeeper, stalked the fisherman's pier-side actions every night before the next duty weekend. Snatch recognized the fisherman would arrive just before sunset. He recorded the time it took for the fisherman to bait and set his lobster traps off the piers or quay wall. After everything was ready, he left. Four hours and forty minutes was the shortest time he was away. Snatch estimated it would take thirty to forty-five minutes to retrieve the traps, collect the Spiny Lobsters, then re-bait the traps. Snatch saw the longest the fisherman was away from them—five hours and ten minutes was the longest time.

Hitfirst, Miller, and Sacher made acquaintances with the fisherman, showing their interest in lobstering. Miller was the most successful in winning the fisherman's trust, perhaps being younger with eager curiosity, prompted the fisherman to help him.

Miller bragged to the gang after the second night into the plan, "I strolled down to the fisherman, and ask him, what are you doing?"

"I'm getting lobsters from my traps and resetting the traps." The fisherman told me as he pulled out a lobster from a trap.

"I never saw a lobster without claws, like that one. I'm from Maine, and we get lobster with big claws. Are your lobsters good eating?" I asked.

The fisherman grabbed a lobster and held the lobster's back, picking it up, displaying it for my inspection, and explained. "It's a spiny lobster. Spiny lobsters have no claws and grow throughout the Caribbean. In Key West, we call them langoustes. Langoustes have a harder shell and large antenna compared with Maine lobsters. The tails like the Maine lobsters are dam-good eating."

"You're getting lobsters right off this pier. In Maine, we must set our traps off boats; it seems we must travel further out every year. You're getting a good catch right here. Dam, that's amazing. I would like to know how you do it, if you teach me, I will help you in retrieving and setting traps?"

"Glad to get help. Give me a hand, and I will show you the tricks I use. Pull up that trap." The fisherman points to a trap line next to me.

The fisherman showed me how to bag the lobsters, bait, and reset the traps. When we finished, he thanks me, "Thanks a lot. The two of us working made short work getting this done. Tonight, I can get more sleep before getting back to reset the traps."

"Glad to help, and I learned a lot. When I can, I'll help you. See you later."

While Miller bragged about his lobster fishing—mischievous minds were working, developing their plan details, making it ready for implementation, because the gang understood the fisherman's pattern. The group noted he took three minutes to retrieve a trap, two minutes to get the lobsters out, and another four minutes to reset the trap with bait and place it back in the water. The gang identified the most time the fisherman took to set and re-bait the traps—ten minutes. The group saw how long he was away from the pier—four to six hours.

Like any good strategist, they measured their weaknesses and strengths. By testing, they determined the time they took to walk from the boat to the pier—both walking and running. The gang also established their best and worst times to pull a trap, empty and re-bait it. Blackheart added safety measures. "We won't take any chances; we'll use the Fisherman's shortest time away from the pier minus ten minutes as our window to complete tasks, giving us three hours and fifty minutes to get the lobsters."

Sacher added, "We have less time than that. We must give a chance to allow the lobsters to get into the traps. Also, the traps should be back in the water to allow the dock to dry off to prevent the fisherman from discovering someone was messing with them."

"Wow, I wouldn't have thought of that, good thinking." Miller is applying praise and feeling they considered everything—nothing could go wrong, he thought. But they missed something.

With expectation, the group looked forward to the next duty weekend. The gang was ready. As predicted, the fisherman arrived just before sunset and set his traps. As soon as the fisherman left the pier, Blackheart assembled his working party, told Snatch, the timekeeper, to let him know when two hours had passed. Blackheart then assigned the rest specific duties and expressed that they only had forty-five minutes to carry out their plan. Any longer, they would risk discovery. The misfits rush to the pier, pull up every other trap, and took the lobsters dumping them into a sack. After robbing the traps, they dropped the empty traps overboard. Some traps they returned with lobsters because the sailors didn't steal from every trap.

On his return inspection, the fisherman would find an empty or low yield trap and consider like most fisherman it was just a meager day of fishing. The fisherman never envisioned someone was messing with his traps. The sailors took the eatable crustaceans belowdecks for an evening feast sharing with the rest of the duty section, including the duty officer who did not realize where these Spiny Lobsters came from. The duty section may have considered the crewmembers who were fishing off the boat were sharing their catch. If they thought otherwise, they made no issue, enjoying the lobster treat. The duty section enjoyed a lobster feast Saturday afternoon and night.

Sunday evening, the same lobster trap robbers continued until they received a wake-up call that taught them to realize what they were doing was wrong. The fisherman did not catch them; if discovered, it might have been life-threatening for them. We all understood Key West fishermen did not fool around. What happened next scared the misfits more than what a fisherman would have done to them.

After they had pulled up the third lobster trap, they found a terrifying surprise. After opening the hatch to get at lobsters, inside the trap, was a giant angry moray eel. I'm not sure of the enraged condition, but the eel acted like it didn't like the lobster trap. The eel jumped out of the trap, attacking. Startled sailors jumped back to get away from it. The moray eel acted dangerously out of the water, thrashed about trying to bite the sailors, looking vicious as it was trying to chomp its teeth into anything. Trap-robbing sailors thought the moray was attacking them, scaring out their daring. The startled, scared sailors ran frantically away from the eel towards the boat. The giant green-brown thrashing sailor-eating eel chased them, looking like it would get them. Just before the eel could bite them, the eel flopped over the pier into the harbor, hitting the water with a splash. The sailors kept on running anyway, not taking chances that the eel would get them.

Blackheart's gang running out of time to replace the traps before the fisherman returned created a problem. But, no one was brave enough for trap replacement. As the topside-watch, looking at this action, I could not help them. Anyhow, I was out of commission laughing. With two buckets, two brave robbers left the safety of the boat and got the traps back in the water just in time to avoid the fisherman catching them—thus ending the lobster robberies. After that night, the fisherman had successfully caught lobsters.

Every time I tell this story, I wonder how did that moray eel get into that trap? Perhaps, the fisherman placed the eel in the trap, knowing it would stop any trap robberies. It was a better solution for protecting his traps than killing robbing sailors.

A SEAMAN IN CHARGE

New Year's Eve 1962 started unremarkably but concluded as an astonishing holiday I would never forget. Because I'm close to completing my submarine qualification, I allowed time to celebrate the New Year. My buddies met me on a fishing pier where we could drink without someone bothering us. We shared a rum and coke, but my intention was not getting smashed. After two drinks, I left my friends early. On New Year's Day, I had the duty. So, I returned to the boat to sleep instead of the barracks, wanting as much sleep as possible before starting my duty day—I had qualifying to-do. Yet qualifying did not happen. On New Year's Eve around 2300 hours, I found myself a non-qualified seaman in charge of the USS *Spikefish*—a position I'm not prepared to hold. Never dreaming I would shoulder the responsibility for a submarine. Perceiving no one of any intellect would let a non-qualified seaman like me take the accountability of a sub. But that night, I had full responsibility for the *Spikefish*. It transpired like this. This ain't no shit.

As I arrived at the boat, I discovered a disturbing situation, because I'm the only one aboard sober enough to do anything. As I crossed the brow, I saluted towards the Topside-Watch station. But I don't see him. After I stepped off the brow, I spotted the Topside Watch lying on the deck aft of the sail. Something is amiss, I investigated the Topside Watch's condition, considering he might have fallen and may need help.

Instead, I discovered the watch in a heap, sleeping and snoring in a drunken coma. The watch stank like a bar's men's bathroom just before closing—a horrible stench surrounded him. Attempts to wake him didn't work. In his drunken state, I couldn't arouse him. The Topside Watch did not respond to my shaking and yelling. What caused his condition, I wondered? Shouldn't someone else be on watch?

Puzzled, I headed down the after-battery hatch to the mess-decks. There, I viewed an amusing sight—after I recognized what I saw made it an upsetting spectacle. As I examined the mess-decks, I wondered what happened. Everyone there was sound asleep. The Duty Officer had a gorgeous woman snuggled up next to him with his arms holding her snug. The girlfriend, wearing a short skirt, pulled up high, exposed her long smooth legs, postured for enjoyable eye medicine. Both asleep, I guessed, sleeping in a drunken stupor, they would never allow themselves to gain such a condition. The Duty Chief was snoring loudly, wearing debris of spattered food all over himself. The Chief likewise appeared sleeping in a drunken coma. I struggled to wake both, but I can't arouse them. As I examined the space, I saw the section leader under a table, sleeping on the deck in a pool of vomit. The movie projector was running with a reel full of the film still spinning around and-around, producing a slapping, flopping slap with each turn. The projector beamed a stream of sputtering light, illuminating a white movie-screen, adding a flickering glow to the mess deck. Mystified at what happened, I shut off the projector.

In the mess-decks, the intense stench of old rum told the story. The room was a mess, bowls full of uneaten chili, and partly filled cups of rum smelling liquid, looking like cream, assembled next to everyone sleeping. No matter how much noise I made didn't awaken anyone from their drunken slumber. I tried everything to wake them, but nothing worked. When I banged a metal serving spoon and hit a sizable empty pan, making a loud clanging noise, no one awakened. Additional shaking them and yelling at them didn't succeed either. As plastered drunks, everyone in the mess-decks slept profoundly—all oblivious of doing duties. No matter how I tried or what I did, I can't wake them. In the mess-decks, everyone is smashed—out of commission.

I searched through the boat for someone who would explain what happened. In Control, I find the below-decks-watch. He, too, was unconscious in an intoxicated stupor—I couldn't wake him. In berthing, everyone in a rack was sleeping in the same smashed like condition—I can't wake anybody—recognizing something was gravely wrong. Still, I didn't know what to do.

The *Spikefish* is in serious trouble if war broke out and needed our response—she couldn't respond; I grasped! If an emergency condition took place, the duty section couldn't give any correct reaction to deal with it. Everyone aboard was out of commission, plastered, and worthless. Boot camp training taught when in combat or emergency, as leaders fall, the next in line takes charge. Accepting that fact, I realized I'm the only one aboard sober enough to walk and be awake—that put me in charge. **Holy shit! The *Spikefish* is in danger!** No one can function. Who's in charge? I'm the only one aboard able to perform. This makes me the one to take charge. **Damn! I'm in charge!** What must I do? I worried.

With the duty section out of commission, I can't go to sleep, because I'm the only one sober. I must keep the boat safe—it's my duty. In Control, I took over the belowdecks-watch, taking the belowdecks' clipboard I made the rounds, making the belowdecks-watch checks. Fortunately, last week, I finished my belowdecks-watch quals learning how to make the rounds and what to look for to detect danger. So, after completing the rounds, I verified the *Spikefish* was safe from flooding or other shipboard danger—no rising water in the bilges, no leaking air, and no fire. Then, I went topside and read the draft readings that verified the *Spikefish* was not sinking.

Between rounds, I cleaned up the mess-decks and covered the girl with a blanket. Each time I moved through the mess-decks, I tried to wake someone up—again without success. Then, I put on a pot of coffee to start the breakfast setup.

While investigating the mess-decks, I discovered an enormous pot containing a cream looking stuff smelling like rum and something else I can't identify. The cream stuff filed less than one-fourth of the container. I tasted the cream. It savored like rum with a blend of strange sweet flavors. Not an authority on hard liquor, so I wasn't sure what the concoction was. Nevertheless, I recognized booze was the leading cause for everyone's drunkenness. I wondered how this happened.

About 0500, the duty cook arrived to start breakfast. The cook is more successful than I in waking up drunken duty section members, including the Duty Officer. When the Duty Officer saw the condition of everyone in the mess-decks and his girlfriend, he sobers up a little. The Duty Officer wakes up his girlfriend. With difficulty, he woke the Duty Chief and got more sleeping crew awake. Everyone they woke up acted messed up, showing all the results of a night's boozing. The leaders couldn't wake up everyone; many of the duty section was still too drunk. The Duty Officer, the Duty Chief, and the section leader were not in the best alert condition either.

When she awakens, the duty officer's girlfriend, ashen-faced and with bloodshot eyes, appeared to be sick. As she looked at her watch, her face showed alarm. Without a goodbye, she clambers up the ladder to the topside. Because I appreciate the beauty of a flower in full bloom, the welcome of a fantastic sunset or sunrise, or the allure of fine art, all exceptional beauty captures my attention. Her beauty compelled me to stop and enjoy the view. As the eye candy slowly climbed the ladder, a lovely young lady with more loveliness than those made by man and found in nature. I can't help myself watching the beautiful vision climb the ladder topside.

In hysteria, the Duty Officer and Duty Chief continued awakening the duty-section. They then supervised the boat's clean up before the relieving watch showed up, expecting them before 0600 hours. Clean up didn't happen fast enough because they couldn't wake most of the duty section from their drunkenness. But everyone they awakened showed symptoms of hangovers with varying degrees of severity, all were slow moving, feeling sick, and some rushed to the head to puke. As he opened his eyes, one third-class sleeping on the mess deck barfed all over himself. Most complained of extreme headaches. The duty section can't move fast enough to avoid the awaiting trouble when the oncoming watch discovered their unacceptable state and the boat's deplorable condition.

At first, no one realized everyone else in the duty section was plastered. Each drunken duty section member declared it was not his fault—an accident must have caused the problem. Duty section members were unaware of how this transpired. Investigations discovered the reason. The day before, on New Year's Eve, about 1500, the CO had the cooks prepare eggnog for the duty section. The CO granted permission for a movie marathon, including the non-qualified, intending to give the duty section a fun day. With the best of intents, the CO spiked the eggnog with a bottle of rum, sharing the first drink with everyone not on watch, knowing this wouldn't cause a drunken duty section. The CO expected his rum would be the only booze given. Then he left the boat to enjoy the day with his family. The CO was not aware others would add to his spiked eggnog.

The COB feeling the duty section should have a drink to start the New Year, and not knowing about the CO's present, also spiked the eggnog around 1530. Around 1600, the XO delivered a similar gift. They were followed soon after by each of the officers and the Chiefs wandering in, bringing drinks of cheer, pouring rum, whiskey, or brandy into the already spiked eggnog. Each duty section member joyfully joined the toasts of joy toasting in the New Year. None of these well-intended leaders knew others previously acted the same—spiked many times—the eggnog was.

With celebration, each duty section member drank the spiked eggnog that grew into high alcohol strength. No one on duty understood what was developing, therefore utterly unaware of what the party-drink would do to them. New Year's eve was the choicest of duty days, and they enjoyed the holiday spirit. The booze in the sweet eggnog went down smoothly and in vast quantities; drink after drink, and over time, the effects of the alcohol took over and culminated in everyone aboard falling into a deep drunken sleep.

The impaired duty section slowly recovered, but not without issues. All had hangovers that slowed completing cleanup and delayed the section turnover. Drunken watchstanders did not keep up the logs—inadequate explanations they made. How does one explain, with no acceptable justifications, safety checks the watch did not make? The duty section can't clean up the boat in time, delaying the watch turnover, adding to the dilemma.

I wondered about the Duty Officer's report to the CO. Did the CO find out about the drunken out-of-commission duty section? If a drunken account reached higher, what was the CO's response to the squadron commander if intoxicated news reached that high? All who realized they avoided a major problem, kept the incident quiet and thanked me for keeping the boat safe, and for keeping the event subdued. When most needed, I helped them out, keeping them out of a tight spot—for them, most embarrassing, and perhaps career-ending. All involved kept this occurrence private.

"How can this be true?" You ask. "If such a condition happened, Subschool and Sub Vets would still talk about the drunken out-of-commission duty section. The Navy would have warnings preventing this from ever happening. Heads would have rolled—Court Martial and condition reports would ruin careers."

All kept this event concealed, not grasping the severity of the issue until later, after probing the reasons for the missed watch rounds. The leaders would not put themselves on report. At the time it happened, I'm the only one who saw the danger. Yet, I didn't report it, not realizing its full significance until I had more experience to understand how dangerous this could have been. This ain't no shit. Think about it!

In the morning, when coming aboard, the cook didn't see the drunken topside watch asleep on the deck aft of the sail. The cook had breakfast to prepare, and the mess-decks made ready. The cook wasn't aware of the duty section watchstanders' disabled conditions. All he saw was the mess deck's chaotic state and only the duty section members' deplorable conditions in the mess deck. The cook woke the drunks because they had more hours of sleep to recover from their drunkenness. Yes, the cook was unhappy with the duty section's irresponsible behavior, but they were his friends. The cook knew the duty section had to make conditions right before the on-coming duty section would relieve them. As fast as possible, the cook made those in the mess-decks clean up after themselves and prepared the space ready for breakfast. Therefore, he didn't destroy their careers for misbehaving by raising an issue of the mess-decks disorders.

After waking up, the Duty Officer, the Duty Chief, and the Section Leader were not aware of the boat's dangerous condition. The leaders didn't realize everyone in the duty section was out of commission until later. During the section turnover, inspection results disclosed the boat's condition. Only then, the leaders realized the boat's precarious state, and they might be in trouble for allowing it to happen.

Ask yourself, would the Topside-Watch, Belowdecks-watch, Section Leader, Duty Officer, and the Duty Chief brag to anyone about the duty section's drunkenness. Uncontrolled drunkenness got themselves into ineptness. Their lack of function causes the *Spikefish* danger by the duty section being out of commission during their drunken stupor— the drunks couldn't do their duties. The leaders wouldn't brag about the duty section's irresponsible behavior. It would have been a career- ending or other grave results that would have been painful for them. The excellent leaders unknowingly allowed this to occur. They are casualties of careless behaviors, yet smart enough to keep this event silent, protecting themselves, the command, and the duty section. Yes, they invented reasons for not maintaining the logs up-to-date and not making rounds on time. The rest of the duty section after awaking found belowdecks a mess from the drunken state they made. With hangovers, they cleaned the heads, mess-decks, and berthing then the rest of the boat's spaces. When they finished their end of the duty-day cleanup, the boat was inspection ready forward to aft. The cleanup took much longer than usual. All duty section members were unaware that they had become useless because of their drunkenness, and that their combined worthless drunken ability put the Spikefish out-of-commission.

The on-coming duty section, the Duty Officer, and Duty Chief were unaware of the-out-of- commission status of the crew they were to relieve. These leaders only saw the unsatisfactory boat's condition and the ongoing cleanup. The on-coming duty section wouldn't relieve irresponsible shipmates until they cleaned up the boat—bow to stern and made the boat acceptable, with the promise that this would never happen again.

Only afterward, the Duty Officer and Duty Chief realized how severe the conditions had become on their watch. They put the *Spikefish* in danger because no one aboard could save her if a casualty occurred. If word got out about this, they would face serious trouble. Realizing this they accepted the humiliation for allowing unacceptable boat conditions but kept the seriousness of this subdued.

No doubt, the CO learned about this as bits and pieces told the story. The CO did not advance this issue to a higher authority because the *Spikefish* and crew had no harm. The CO conducted no further public inquiry—it might have affected his career goals. The CO supplied the first bottle of joy. Privately, he made changes and corrections to prevent this from ever happening again. Each leader involved thanked me later for keeping the *Spikefish* safe and for keeping the event quiet—this event was private.

QUALIFYING

After finishing Subschool, awaiting schooling in the Polaris school pipeline, I felt fortunate getting orders to my first submarine, the *USS Spikefish (AGSS 404)* homeported in Key West Florida. With an eager attitude, I reported aboard the *Spikefish*, I'm pleased about my first boat and expected my first-at-sea duty to be an adventure. However, I didn't realize what I was getting into. From the first day, I noticed submarine qualifying was challenging. Also complicating my efforts, I'm the nonqual—the lowest life-form on a submarine. The submarine start turned into difficulty as qualifying strained my abilities, losing momentum, and causing me to doubt staying in subs.

Adding to this, I found the *Spikefish* unfit to live in, work in, or relax in at least for us new crewmembers—the nonquals. Intense discomfort I felt being on the *Spikefish*. Anywhere I worked or when qualifying turned into frustration. Basic tasks are challenging because overcrowding made my living and workspaces congested—the closeness in cramped spaces made working and qualifying a challenge. No matter what I was doing, someone wanted to get by me interrupting work, or somebody was in my way, slowing me down. Sleep was infrequent and interrupted, sharing a rack, hot-bunking with Bob, and Ferguson was a pain in the ass because there weren't enough bunks in berthing for each crewmember. In shifts, we ate meals, slept, stood watch, and living with watch-shifts dictating everything we did wasn't fun. A secluded place to collect one's thoughts wasn't available because a submarine has no spot for privacy; there's no space for this luxury.

From day one, I had difficulties. Many times, later, I wished I paid better attention to my Subschool instructors. I squandered the opportunity to learn the know-how needed on Subs. Because of my Subschool neglect, I added extra effort to learn the boat's systems and equipment. For obscure reasons, I couldn't grasp anything about a fighting submarine. I discovered qualifying was drudgery, studying the boat's systems, understanding how they worked, and learning to use the equipment in normal and emergency modes, there was too much to learn. The effort to learn the boat's systems and equipment was grueling. After I studied a system or a watch's duty requirements, I then had a greater struggle convincing a senior, a system's expert, that I understood the systems' arrangements, the equipment's use, or a watch's requirements.

The system's expert was usually a qualified first- or second-class petty officer responsible for maintaining his system or equipment. They gave me demanding questions. With correct answers, I confirmed that I acquired the system know-how. Afterward, he would sign-off the system's stipulation on my qual-card. If my answers lacked detail, the responsible sailor would make me record my missed questions. The seniors called missed questions, look-ups. Later, I had to find the answers to my look-ups that involved researching the system to get the correct answers. The seniors became irritated by my wasting their time, showing I didn't grasp the material during my first effort. Once I had look-ups to obtain, getting the answers became more laborious than the first system research. The system's expert made sure I understood the system's specifics before they would sign my qual card. For me, as a nonqual crewmember, submarine qualification became an unremitting painstaking pain-in-the-ass task. A few of my answers caused humiliation because they showed how little I grasped about the boat or the Navy.

I don't recall how and when it happened, but maybe I enjoyed the beach too much or believed I'm smarter than the other seamen. Anyway, the worst happened when I became delinquent in my quals—a big No-No aboard the *Spikefish*. On the dink-list, I had to stay aboard extra hours without any early-liberty. On the boat, I couldn't take part in anything that had fun or relaxation, but qualifying, standing watches, or working was my submarine reality. Every day, someone was on my ass about qualifying, making my life miserable. On the delinquent list was a massive pain, no matter how hard I struggled to catch-up wasn't working. I must declare, I didn't try too hard, resulting in becoming further behind scheduled progress. Quickly, I'm aware of being inadequate, trying to qualify, and getting my tasks accomplished. Subsequently, after falling behind in qualifications, my life became more miserable, making me question my decision to volunteer for submarines—I didn't fit into the submarine life, is submarine life for me, I wondered?

The old-timers, attempting encouragement, expressed a submariner must move fast, reacting to the many life-threatening emergencies. Old-timers gave me their lesson every time I had to get a sign-off. On a sub, you often experience dangerous conditions. Do your duty; you must do your job and support other shipmates when needed. On subs, you must make friends with the crew, work as a team, and don't create problems for other crewmembers—always do your duty.

Nonqual harassment added misery to my time aboard. No qualified crew liked any nonqual, and the qualified submariners detested dinks. Without exceptions, the old-timers enjoyed making our lives miserable. Well, let me tell you, the old-farts were expert at providing subtle harassment, ensuring my life was miserable. The old-timers knew what nerves to pinch to cause upset, and used my youthful foolishness, my pride, and my values against me. The skillful harassment schemes they pulled were funny, but not so to us victims. On rare occasions, bullying methods might have been against regulations, vicious and mean, but all had a purpose. For the old-timers, adding harassment was entertaining while training nonquals. I wasted time making my life worse, searching for stuff, finding out after a considerable time hunting, the things didn't exist. As for me, I was easy prey. The old-farts' bullying made my life hell while I was qualifying. Let me tell you about it. This ain't no shit.

For the Forward Torpedo Room signature, Sewell, another old-time WWII warrior, a First-Class Torpedo-man, asked me a bunch of questions about the torpedo room. Not knowing the answers, I had to list my unknowns as lookups. Sewell expected me to find the answers for each of his questions I didn't answer correctly and then explain my answers. Sewell demanded of me to understand this stuff before I went on liberty the coming weekend. Just before he concludes his inquisition, he rolled a torpedo skid roller and looked perturbed, "This roller needs greasing." Suddenly he orders, "Get a can of relative bearing grease. It's in a locker, find it, I need the grease before the weapon load. We have a weapon load this week, got to grease the skids."

After I searched every locker in the room without success, with frustration, I told Sewell, "I can't find the relative bearing grease anywhere in this room."

"It's in this room, maybe someone stowed the relative bearing grease in the wrong place, or they dropped the grease into the bilges the last time someone used it. It's a small green-can check the bilges." Sewell commanded.

Down in the bilges, I go, searching everywhere, among frame bays, bilge pockets, under torpedo skids, but didn't locate the relative bearing grease. I spent most of the day exploring the torpedo room, looking for the grease, I tell Sewell with frustration, "There's no relative bearing grease in this room."

"Maybe the Aft Torpedo Room has the grease, Chase knows where it's stowed, go get it from him, tell him, I'll replace it later."

A critical mission, off to the Aft Torpedo Room I go. Sewell needs that relative bearing grease. In the aft room, I meet Chase, a second-class torpedo man. Chase looks younger than Sewell. After I ask him for relative bearing grease, his response pissed me off.

"I'm busy getting ready for the weapon load, and I don't know where it's stored. Look through the lockers; it should be in one," Chase commanded, displaying a grouchy arrogance, and telling me that I'm bothering him.

"The weapon load is why I need the relative bearing grease. Sewell told me to get it for him; I didn't find it in the Forward Room. Sewell needs it today."

Chase with an insolent manner ordered, "then look for it."

Not knowing why Chase wouldn't help me find the relative bearing grease, I became irritated with him, thinking what a lazy son-of-a-bitch. Looking for the relative bearing grease, I checked every locker in the Aft Torpedo Room, hunted in the bilges, searched under weapons, looked between frame bays, but I didn't find the relative bearing grease. In frustration, I reported to Chase, "Shit, I can't find the relative bearing grease."

"Check A-Gang; they have the most assortment of grease. A-Gangers keep their supply in the Pump Room. Hurry, shit, we need that grease." Yeah, I criticized under my breath, shit-head, you need that grease, like, I'm going to help you when you wouldn't give me a hand.

At the Pump Room, I ask the A-Ganger on watch if I can get relative bearing grease for Sewell. The old fart responded like Chase, pointing at a group of small lockers, "I'm on watch, so I can't help you now, look for the grease in one of those lockers."

After another thorough search, I couldn't find any damn relative bearing grease. Discouraged, as I come out of the pump room, I overhear Sam one of the new seamen qualifying for lookout, asking, "What is the difference between Relative Bearing and True Bearing?"

Ah-shit! It hit me, making me feel foolish, stupid, embarrassed, and angry. As a qualified lookout, I understood what Relative Bearing is, and Relative Bearings needs no grease, but I missed that important fact. I'm angry as I rush to the forward torpedo room and report to Sewell, "I discovered Relative Bearing has no grease. You're pulling my chain. You're not respecting me. You can't treat me that way. I won't allow it. It ain't right. I'm pissed."

Sewell's reply startled me, "Don't take it too hard, consider how much qualifying you made. Now you're more familiar with both torpedo rooms and the pump room, better than most nonquals aboard," giving me a big grin.

The old-fart group effort made me pissed because I didn't realize they jerked me around and made me suffer humiliation, hunting for something that didn't exist. I should have known better, for them, setting me up was too easy embarrassing it was.

Then, it happened again with another qual question I was unable to answer. Sewell asked me, "What's the *Spikefish's* longest line.?" For a lookup, I searched for the answer, getting the same runaround. Because I realized the old-farts were setting me up, I showed them. On a duty day, I found the longest line aboard by pulling out each line from the topside line-lockers and measured each line. I have the line measurements. Line-one is the longest line. No matter, finding out later that I was wrong. Line-one isn't the longest line. Puzzled, I didn't find the longest line.

Later while qualifying with me, Bob told me, "You're a dumb shit. The longest line is the waterline."

How did this happen again, now, I'm looking foolish, and my failure after I figure it out, embarrassed me?

I wasn't the only nonqual on a mission that sought after a bucket of steam, relative bearing grease, or the longest line on the boat. Nonquals would spend hours looking for items like these. When we didn't find them, we would eventually ask for help from one of the qualified sailors. They acted eager to help, taking the nonqual through their compartment hunting for the item. When the nonqual didn't find the thing hunted for, the submariner called a shipmate in another compartment, and send the nonqual to him. The nonqual would repeat a similar search in that compartment. The item still not found; the senior petty officer would direct the nonqual to another space. Nonqual searching happened until the nonqual explored each compartment, never locating the searched for items because the items didn't exist.

At first, I didn't realize the purpose, but the result of the nonqual's search was helpful. The nonqual would study each compartment and working space, and meet the crew members, firsthand. The nonqual would receive a qualification lecture on compartmentation without noticing it. Also, this search added a few days' worth of humor for the crew. Once the nonqual figured out what was happening to him, he would feel stupid—at least, I felt foolish when it occurred.

After the COB posted my name on the dink list, all the qualified crewmembers took a particular interest in my qualification, seeking to motivate me, helping me out, whenever I showed interest to learn or not, and no matter if I called for help or not. When I didn't respond to the aid, the results were painful for me.

Even the XO got involved in my qualification, motivating me, helping me out, and trying to change my direction. After finding out I wrestled in high school, he volunteered my services at the gym for conditioning. The XO was a champion wrestler in college and maintained his ability by wrestling college teams every chance he could get. This provided experience to those he wrestled and kept him in shape. Believing I was a good wrestler but found out otherwise after the XO whipped me. He pinned me anytime he wished—more than once, any time the XO thought I wasn't doing my best. The XO taught me a lot about wrestling. The first few times after a hard workout, when I almost upchucked my guts, told me I'm out of shape. After getting back in shape, I enjoyed the wrestling because it kept me in shape and off the beach while improving my wrestling skills. After showing qualification improvement, the XO and I developed a friendship. The more I knew about the XO, the more I respected him and admired his leadership ability. Learning more from him than qualification requirements, I noticed his leadership skills.

Fun times kept me going. The day the XO advanced to Lt. Commander, I was in the torpedo room qualifying when Hitfirst, Sewell, Sacher, Miller, and the XO all drenching wet came below, laughing like kids in a playground on a rainy day. A dripping XO heads aft to his stateroom. Puzzled, I ask Sewell, "How did you all get soaked, and what happened that's so funny?"

Sewell replied, "On the *Spikefish*, when someone advances in rank or rate, and for any other good reason, we throw him overboard like a baptism of sorts. The XO made Lt. Commander today. The officers aren't immune from a dunking. What happened, we ambushed the XO on the side of the sail. Three torpedomen prevented him from going forward, while three machinist's mates with two enginemen blocked him from going aft. We had him trapped. With determination, we'll throw the XO overboard, but our strategy didn't work. Hitfirst grabs him, but he ends up overboard. Hitfirst wasn't able to delay the XO long enough to get help. Instead, he's treading water. In like manner, Blackheart is bathing. Shortly, most everyone topside is treading water except the XO. More help arrives. The CO watching realizes that someone might get hurt, but it wouldn't be the XO. The CO orders, 'XO jump.'"

'Jump, Aye-Aye.' The XO takes off his hat, shoes and removes his wallet, setting them safely on the deck. Then he jumps overboard. Followed by the rest of the crew jumping overboard. Good fun today, we enjoyed a brief swim."

December 1, 1962, was the day our leaders recognized the Soviets removed all their nuclear weapons from Cuba. The following day, the COB got Bob, Ferguson, and I together in the mess decks, and gave us the news. "Your orders came in; the Navy is sending you to Polaris Fire Control School at Dam Neck, Virginia, to report before January 29, 1963. From now on, because you're transferring off the *Spikefish*, you don't have to continue qualifications—don't have enough time to finish. The crew will no longer treat you as nonquals; you can watch movies, hit the beach, enjoy your short time aboard, and enjoy your time off."

Granny Knot and Barf Bucket appeared happy about the news, more than just delighted. With big grins on their faces, they reacted, showing happy smiles. The kind you would see if an attractive barmaid changed her mind and suggestively told them she wanted them to take her home at the end of her shift—they at once took the fun path.

Bob and Ferguson surprised me when they expressed delight in their decision to stop qualifying—even though they were further ahead of me in their quals. I was the dink way behind in my quals, yet I'm disappointed in their quitting. Oblivious as to why my buddies gave up, after what we went through together. For them, finishing qualifying would be easy.

The news was a jolt, after receiving the orders to the Polaris Fire Control School I'm taken aback not knowing I would be leaving so soon. The announcement woke me up, grasping I might leave the boat unqualified. I don't understand why I believed qualifying was so important, but I desired to qualify. I stared at the COB looking steadily into his eyes with determination as I responded, "COB, I will qualify."

Bob, with his mouth open, stared at me with astonishment. Ferguson gawked in hushed awe.

The COB paused a moment looked surprised as he advised, "With only a month and two weeks to finish, you don't have enough time to qualify. You're dink, way behind in your qualification. It's almost impossible for anyone to qualify in the short time available. Even if you were current with signatures, I don't believe you can do it. Don't make it hard for yourself. After you finish mess cooking, you will stay in the seaman gang until transferred, so enjoy as much liberty as you can. You're no longer on the dink list."

I sensed a compelling desire to finish qualifying, feeling different than my past attitude, and realizing that I might leave the boat unqualified gave me determination. The COB's words told me he lost confidence in me and made me regretful. To rectify this, I must prove he's mistaken in his judgment of me. Confirming the COB is wrong reinforced my resolve as I repeated. "COB, I will qualify."

In astonishment, the COB studied me for a lengthy time, his eyes locked on mine as if he was trying to read my mind. Then he spoke, "How can you qualify? For anyone up in quals, like Bob and Ferguson, qualifying would-be challenging. In your case, you're dink, way behind schedule, need the at-sea requirements completed, and you have too many systems to learn and not enough time to learn them. Don't think you can do it, and I admire your attempt, but you don't have to qualify. If you don't qualify, I will hold nothing against you."

IT'S YOUR DUTY

The COB's judgment of me shocked me. How do I respond to him when he doesn't believe I'm capable, I'm thinking. Usually, the COB is encouraging, giving positive motivation, but in my case, he's mistaken, misjudging me, giving up on me. I'm troubled, angry, and irritated at myself because I caused this, unintentionally I let him down by not doing my duty. Yes, I have been goofing off, but now I'm determined. After I considered my situation, my beliefs made me answer with purpose and tenacious determination, "The Navy sent me to the *Spikefish* to qualify, and qualifying is what I will do. I know I can do this; you'll see. COB, I will leave the boat qualified."

"I don't believe you can do it. You're confronting an almost unfeasible undertaking to qualify, but we'll see," replied the COB shaking his head, showing disbelief. "You haven't taken qualifying seriously, so why are you determined now?"

Not answering right away, I probed the COB eye-to-eye, gathering my thoughts, seeking the correct response, selecting my words, I responded with resolve, "The Navy assigned me to the *Spikefish* to qualify. Up to now, I was enjoying liberty, having as much fun as possible, and not paying any attention to the national news or the Navy's role in defending the country. I didn't realize how short of time I would have to get qualifying done. Afterward, when we're preparing for war, with everyone getting ready for battle, it showed the crew doing their duties. That action made me think about how close we came to combat. The war preparations made me reflect on my responsibilities. The Navy's main mission isn't creating a playground for sailors; its mission is to defend our country. Therefore, from now on, I must do my part, I'll qualify on the *Spikefish*. I know it's difficult, but I'll make it happen. It's my duty."

"When I see it, I'll believe it. Anyway, for the rest of your stay, it's your call. Don't need to get signatures, you can stop anytime you wish, but if you're serious, you will find the crew will help you if you show them that becoming qualified is your primary mission. If you don't do that, you will have a rough time getting it done. Here is a piece of advice, get all at sea requirements done before we return to Key West. The *Spikefish* will go into a holiday routine after we return. If you don't have those signatures, it will be impossible to qualify. If you're serious about this, good luck," The COB replies.

I had little more than a month to learn by memory submarine knowledge. Was I facing an impossible task? As I tried not to show it, I worried. Afterward, my qualifying became a seamless never-ending task that tested my resolve to stay in submarines and qualify.

Mess cooking was the choicest job when qualifying. When delivering baked goodies, I took the time to chat with everyone who receives them. While passing out sticky buns, cookies, and snacks, I learned about the crew and their work, showing an interest in their equipment, and showing them I wanted to learn all about their gear helped me more than I envisaged. When the crew discovered that I would qualify when I didn't have to, their support surprised me. After the crew saw I was serious about qualifying and believed that I was trying, their treatment towards me changed. Without the silly harassment, the crew took extra effort, interrupting their schedules, and teaching me their systems. Senior petty officers described system operations, asked questions, and made me clarify my vague answers. The leading petty officers showed me items, valves, and piping locations and explained their functions. Later they required me to find them again and explain the details about their use. Quickly, I added signatures to my qual card, getting me off the dink list even though I did not have to, I kept on anyway.

Sewell, the forward torpedo room's senior torpedoman, astonished me when he took painstaking effort to teach me the forward torpedo room. Sewell's instructions included lining up and shooting a water-slug.

Sewell told me what-to-do for each step in lining up and making a tube ready to shoot.

After four days of concentrated torpedo room instruction, Sewell and I took most of another day to fire a water-slug. Sewell calls Control, "Request permission to make Tube 3 ready in all respects and shoot a water-slug for training and maintenance. The WEPS will verify the return to rig-for-dive after we're through."

Control must have given permission, because he hung up the phone and ordered me, "Tell me all the steps to make Tube 3 ready in all respects to shoot a water-slug."

"Open Tube 3's vent, flood the tube, close the vent when the tube is full, equalize the tube to sea pressure, and then open the muzzle door," I reply, hoping I didn't forget something.

"You didn't check to verify that Tube 3 is empty. Tell me all the steps you would do to check that Tube 3 is empty."

"I checked it empty; Tube 3 has an 'EMPTY' metal sign hanging over the tube's breech door, showing the tube is empty," I answered while pointing to the sign.

"You didn't check the tube is empty. You don't want to be the one who shoots a torpedo instead of a water-slug. More than once in this man's Navy, some shit-for-brains shot a torpedo instead of a water-slug. A career-ending brain fart for the one who does it, shooting a torpedo into a pier, is command embarrassing. Never give blind trust to a sign hanging on a tube, always check the tube first. If you shot a torpedo instead of a water-slug from this room, I will rip off your head, stick it up your ass, and piss down your windpipe—got it." Sewell cautioned.

"Got it," I answer with understanding, "I'll always check first." Next, I tell Sewell I must do the steps that check Tube 3 empty.

Sewell ordered, "OK, tell me the steps to verify Tube 3 is empty. Start with the first step and tell me all the following steps." I go through the steps to verify Tube 3 is empty. Sewell seems satisfied.

Then Sewell orders, "Line up and shoot a water-slug from Tube 3. Follow the same method used for checking the tube empty. Tell me each step, then perform the action, and report to me after you completed each step."

I go through the steps and verify Tube 3 is empty. While I'm doing this lineup, Sewell explains each step's purpose while pointing to the valve or item he is talking about, "That is the tube's vent-valve. The tube's vent-valve vents the tube inboard when opened." Pointing to the stop-bolt, "The stop-bolt is a solid metal bar that holds a torpedo in position while in the tube. The stop-bolt prevents the torpedo from sliding forward or aft, preventing damage to the torpedo or the tube when the boat makes steep angles. When the tube fires, part of its firing sequence raises the stop bolt. If the stop-bolt didn't raise, the torpedo couldn't leave the tube."

The following morning, I meet Sewell in the forward room, Sewell commands, "You're the Torpedoman in charge of this compartment, and the WEPS orders you to shoot a water-slug from Tube 4 for training and maintenance. Go through all the steps required to shoot a water-slug from Tube 4. Before you begin a step, tell me what you will do before starting each step—got it."

Can I remember all the steps? I worry as I tell Sewell, "First, I must call control and get permission to break rig-for-dive, flood Tube 4 from sea, make ready Tube 4 to fire a water-slug, fire the water-slug, and then restore the Tube to its rig-for-dive condition. After I fire the water-slug, I get an officer to verify the tube's rig-for-dive condition."

"Good, shoot a water-slug from tube 4," Sewell commands.

I call Control and ask, "for training, request permission to make Tube 4 ready in all respects to shoot a water-slug from Tube 4. Shooting a water-slug requires breaking the rig-for-dive in the torpedo room to open tube's breach breech door to inspect Tube 4 before flooding it down, making it ready for firing the water-slug. The WEPS will verify rig-for-dive after Tube 4 is secured.

After a brief pause, Control calls back, "Make Tube 4 ready to shoot a water-slug in all respects. After the Tube 4 is lined up, report to Control when Tube 4 is ready to shoot a water-slug in all respects before you fire the water-slug."

"Report to Control when Tube 4 is ready before firing the water-slug—Aye—Aye," I answer.

Then I tell Sewell, "First, I must verify that tube 4 is empty."

"How do you do that?"

"I inspect the tube's sight-level on the breech door," I reply, looking at the tube's sight-level's glass tubes, showing a dry tube. "Tube 4 is dry."

"What's next?"

"Before I open the breech door, I must vent and equalize the pressure in the tube with the torpedo room's pressure," I respond.

"Make it so."

As I open the tube's vent, I hear air noise. When the sound stops, I report, "The tube's pressure is equalized."

"Next."

"Drain the tube."

"Make it so."

I slowly open Tube 4's drain valve, I hear a trickle of water draining into the bilges. The water noise stopped by the time the valve is opened. Then, I reported, "Tube 4 is dry."

"Next."

"I must open the breech door."

"Make it so."

I open the breech door, looking into the tube, into a twenty-one-inch diameter pipe, looking into a dark dreadness towards the muzzle end. With a flashlight, I inspect the tube, inspecting all the way towards the muzzle and report. "Tube 4 is empty."

"Good next."

"I must shut the breech door, shut the tube's drain valve, open the sea valve, and flood the tube."

"Make it so."

After I shut and lock the breech door, I open the sea valve and flood the tube from the sea until water flowed from the tube's vent. Next, I shut the sea valve. When Tube 4's sight-level glass tubes show a flooded tube, I report, "Tube 4 is flooded."

"Good next."

"I must open the muzzle door."

"Make it so."

I open the muzzle door, inspect the muzzle door indicator, and report, "Tube 4's muzzle door is open."

"Good next."

I report to control, "Tube 4 is flooded and is ready in all respects for shooting a water-slug—request permission to shoot Tube 4 locally."

Control soon commands, "Shoot Tube 4, locally."

"Shoot Tube 4, locally—Aye-Aye Sir," I respond.

I reach up to the local firing panel and shoot Tube 4. When the tube fired, the loud noise of high-pressure air blasted into Tube 4, pushing water out of the tube as if the water was a torpedo. The loud noise told me the tube fired. Then I shut the muzzle door, vent and drain down the tube, open the breech door and inspect the tube for debris, shut the breech door, and then lined up Tube 4 for rig-for-dive.

"What must you do next?" asked Sewell.

"Call control and report successfully fired a water-slug from Tube 4. Also, report that Tube 4 is empty and lined up for rig-for-dive."

"Almost correct, you also request that an officer checks the rig-for-dive condition," Sewell replies, "Make it so."

I reported to control, "Successfully fired a water-slug from Tube 4. Tube 4 is empty and lined up for rig-for-dive. Request the WEPS to check Tube 4's rig-for-dive."

Sewell commands me, "Let me see your quall Card." Sewell studies it for a moment, then signs off the tube firing practical and the forward torpedo room compartment signature. Sewell smiles at me with approval, "I don't know what changed you, but you are a better sailor now compared to when you first came aboard. You still have challenges to finish, but at the pace you are going, you'll make it. Keep up the good work. You showed me you are knowledgeable about this room. Good job."

"Thank you," I reply, thinking, Holy shit, getting praise from Sewell, I didn't believe it would ever happen, assuming he hated me. Sewell was consistently on my ass, making my life miserable. Maybe he is not as bad as I believed. I wondered.

Later, the same happened in the aft torpedo room; Blackheart made me understand everything about the aft room. My searching lookups in the aft room took me four days until Blackheart's satisfied. I had to walk Blackheart through all the steps to shoot a flare, but we didn't shoot one.

One night, Hitfirst unexpectedly shakes me awake, "Get up, get up, we're about to do a battery charge tonight; it'll be your last chance to get your at sea qual sign-off to light off diesel and conduct a battery charge. Meet me in the forward engine room. Hurry, we'll be starting soon. You'll light off the diesel engines tonight."

On my way to the engine room, I stopped at the head, pumped bulges, then entered the forward engine room. Hitfirst orders me, "You'll start all four engines tonight, start by lining up number one engine. You had better remember what I showed you. Now tell me every step you do before you do it."

In my mind, I go through the steps, remembering that diesel engines on a submarine need air, fuel, and exhaust before they can start. Exactly like I did for Sewell in the forward room, I tell Hitfirst what I plan to-do pointing to each valve, lever, and gauge, explaining what it's for and why I need to open or shut a valve.

"Line engine one up," commands Hitfirst.

As I lineup the diesel, I report each step to Hitfirst.

"Start engine one," orders Hitfirst.

After I start the engine, a deep, roar tells me the engine is running, giving me confidence. In like manner, I repeat lighting off the other engines.

"Good job. You know your shit," comments Hitfirst with an approving grin, studying my qual card. "I'll sign off your qual card later, head to Maneuvering, and get that at-sea qual sign-off. You won't get much of a chance later."

In Maneuvering, the senior electrician had me perform all the lineup steps to conduct a battery charge, use the sticks to make speed changes, and transfer power to the different buses. While doing this, he drills me about Maneuvering and the Motor Room.

Two at sea practical factors and three compartments qual sign-offs in one night was an accomplishment. I'm pleased with the achievement, but it made one tired mess-cook the following morning.

Later, the "A" Gang Chief, one of the old-time warriors, took me through the pump room, the air systems, and hydraulic systems. The Chief concentrated on the control room. He described the installed equipment's purpose, showing how to read equipment's instruments and gauges, and demonstrating their controls and operation. When he had the dive, with me under instruction, he made me pump water from the forward trim tank to the aft trim tank, then pump the water from aft trim to aux 1, and then pump water from aux 1 tank to the forward trim tank. I had to operate the planes in normal. Easy for me, I already qualified as helmsman and planesman. He had me switch to manual, which was also easy because I have done that many times. Next, he had me shift to emergency. The emergency operations line up was simple, but using the planes in emergency was hard work.

After mess cooking, back in the seamen gang, I found qualifying a laborious continual mission to finish, learning everything about the *Spikefish*, learning more than a system's equipment location, and operational knowledge, but learning how to do everyone's job. On a moment's notice, I had to fire torpedoes, blow sanitary tanks, and start the main engines, lighting off any of the four diesel engines. In an emergency, I used the sticks in maneuvering, pumped bilges, transferred water from tank to tank, used the planes to control the ship's depth and the bubble, steer the boat, and get the *Spikefish* ready to get underway by myself if that became necessary. Besides knowing the locations, I understood the purpose of every light switch, valve, meter, alarm, fire extinguisher, fire hose, and damage control equipment. I had to understand the function of all the emergency equipment, tell why the *Spikefish* needed it, and how to use it. In each compartment, I had to rig it for dive, and rig for emergencies, flooding, fire, depth charge, and collision.

The qualified crew didn't give me a free ride; they made me work hard and required me to learn. At a valve, I followed pipes attached to it in both directions, sometimes to the next valve or pipe ends. Qualifying made me find every pipe and valve's location in a compartment. With that method, I made a system drawing that identified all the system elements, parts, and interfaces. The drawing had to show how each piece connects to equipment and other systems. I had to learn each system so well I drew it in such a manner that using my drawing. I explained each part, pipe, valve, and gauge identified on my drawing. For the hydraulics, air, and ventilation systems, I had to describe normal and emergency operations. When I got the sanitary tank sign-off, I had better knowledge about it than the petty officer who drilled me for information—he was never inside a sanitary-tank. As I'm getting qual signatures, my confidence builds.

All levels gave me help. The officers, the XO to the supply officer, the Chiefs, and the LPOs, all would give me their walk-through on systems or compartments. Crew-members stayed late on watch and took their free time at sea helping me. Before arriving in Key West, I had all-at-sea requirements completed.

On duty nights in port, the qualified crew continued teaching me. A Chief followed by an officer repeating my examination. The crew's action encouraged me. Before getting a system sign off, they made me learn and prove that I knew the system. The qualified crew drilled me with questions—detailed answers I had to give correctly. For my ventilation system requirement, I described the different ventilation lineups, normal operation, battery-charge, and emergency venting for each compartment. I received the same treatment, getting the other systems. Without my knowledge, the officers helped me by having at sea events happen when I was off-watch mess cooking. The officers delayed a battery charge start until I was off-watch to line up the ventilation system for a battery charge and light off a diesel engine, allowing me to get these at-sea requirements completed. The officers and Chiefs helped me, making themselves available and scheduling events when I was able to do them. That support made qualifying possible.

I earned every signature except one on my qual card, showing I mastered the required knowledge and proved my ability to use all equipment, learning the information, and showing all equipment operation. Subsequently, I had the final walk-through with the engineer. The engineer's signature was the one I needed to complete my qualification. To get it, the engineer required all nonquals to make a final walk-through the boat with him, showing him, they mastered enough knowledge. The COB gave me a heads-up that the engineer would leave the boat the week after the coming weekend. Later, I asked the engineer, "As soon as possible, sir, because your signature is the last one required, please take me through my final walk-through?"

"When I have the duty this coming weekend, I will take you through your walk-through. I'm going on leave the following Monday. You must be ready. It's your only chance to get my walk-through, I'll see you after I take over as duty officer. We will start as soon as possible after I make my first duty officer's inspection." The engineer answered with authority and concern.

Little sleep I had in the past week added to my difficulty, every free moment I used for qualifying, getting my last required signatures. Lack of sleep made me so tired; I wanted to sleep after working around the clock to get signatures. I worried realizing it's difficult going through the rigors of a final walk-through. In the mess decks, I cornered the DOC, explaining my physical condition, asking for help.

"Doc, I'm so tired I can't remember how to spell my name, let alone go through my final walk-through with the Engineer. Can you help me? How much coffee must I drink to stay awake?"

The Doc peers at me with interest and understanding, "Wait right here. I'll be right back." Returning, he hands me a little pill. "Take this, remember, I didn't give it to you. This pill should keep you awake long enough for your walk-through."

"Thanks, Doc, I appreciate it," as I pop the pill in my mouth and follow it with a big gulp of coffee.

"I didn't give you anything."

Not grasping what he was talking about, why the warning? Was taking this drug illegal? Couldn't be, I thought, only the medical profession can administer medicines. The DOC gave it to me. At the time, I didn't have knowledge about drugs, nor about anyone using drugs for recreation—like drinking booze. No matter, whatever the pill was, the little pill worked. I'm wide-awake and ready as I met the Engineer in the forward torpedo room—and wide awake for the next three days.

The Engineer kept his promise of giving me final qualification walk-through, using his weekend duty, taking most of it testing me. On an early January morning in 1963, I start my final qualification walk-through. With only one shot to pass my walk-through, I was anxious, knowing the Engineer would go on leave the following Monday and won't return to the boat until after I'm transferred. I had my orders.

On the topside deck, we met to start. Subsequently, I follow the Engineer to the pier, beginning at the bow, we walked aft, checking out the boat. The Engineer points at a boat's feature and asks, "What is the purpose for that?" I answered all of his questions. Next, we went back topside, starting at the stern we headed towards the bow. The Engineer repeated the examining questions. Except he wanted me to describe in detail each item he pointed to or asked about. My responses included the name and function of each item. We devoted an extended time in the sail, where I identified the masts and antennas.

Subsequently, we headed below through the Forward Torpedo Room access hatch, stopping in the escape trunk. You guessed it. I had to explain how to make an emergency escape using the escape trunk.

When the Engineer was satisfied that I could help the crew in escaping from a sunken sub, we head into the Forward Torpedo Room.

In the Forward Torpedo Room, The Engineer looks at the tubes. Tube 2, the upper starboard one, had a metal sign hanging on its breech-door that displayed painted large red-letters, "EMPTY." The Engineer orders me, "Line up and shoot a water-slug from Tube 2 and explain what you need to do before you do it."

"First, I must verify that Tube 2 is empty," I tell him.

"The tube's sign shows empty. Why do you need to do that?" The Engineer asks.

"Sewell would rip my head off if I ever shot a torpedo by mistake. He stated many times, 'Always verify the tube empty before you shoot water-slugs. Too many officers and Torpedomen fire torpedoes from supposedly empty tubes; those who fire a torpedo into a pier find its career-ending.' So, I will check Tube 2 to verify it's empty— merely a caution—unless you order me otherwise." I reply.

As if he didn't think about that check, the Engineer looked surprised and ordered. "OK, now verify that Tube 2 is empty and complete all the steps to shoot a water-slug."

After I lined up and shot the water-slug, the Engineer had me line up and pump the torpedo room bilges, and then blow sanitary tank 1. Afterward, I rigged the Torpedo Room for dive, emergency, and collision.

Next, we started working aft, I lined up the forward battery compartment for a battery charge and emergency ventilation and rigged the compartment for dive, emergency, and collision. And then I returned the compartment to its normal in-port lineup.

In the control room, I rigged the compartment for dive, emergency, and collision, then pumped bilges. I explained to the Engineer all the ship's alarms. After using the trim system, to transfer water between the forward and aft trim tanks, bow buoyancy, and Aux tanks, and returned the compartment to its normal in-port lineup, I finished this compartment.

In the after-battery compartment, I electrically secured the galley, rigged the compartment for ventilation, dive, battery-charge, and emergency. Then I pumped Sanitary Tank 2. Finishing, I returned the compartment to its normal in-port lineup.

In the forward engine room, the Engineer ordered, "Line up and start a diesel engine, rig the compartment for dive and make all the emergency lineups, and afterward restore the compartment to its normal in-port lineup. I accomplished his request with no issues.

In maneuvering, I explained controlling the sticks providing power to the screws driving the boat forward and back.

Finishing in the after-torpedo room, I lined up and blew the aft sanitary tank and explained how I would shoot a flare. I had to tell the Engineer how to escape using the Aft Emergency Escape Trunk. I rigged the aft torpedo room for dive and continued lining up ventilation in normal and emergency operation. I returned the compartment to its normal in-port lineup that concluded this compartment.

In the aft room, smiling at me, the Engineer comments, "I'm impressed that you know this boat so well." He takes my qual card, sets it on a torpedo warhead, and signs the last signature, saying, "Well done. No one aboard believed you would qualify, but you proved us wrong. I will see you tomorrow at morning-quarters."

The January 9, 1963 morning quarters, the COB calls me out of ranks. I'm with the CO standing in front of the crew. The COB is at his side. The CO, LT CMDR Fox, presented me with my dolphins—pinning the submarine insignia pin on my work shirt for me to display on my chest, showing the Navy and everyone else that I qualified in submarines. Once below with everyone congratulating me, I hear the

CO making the 1MC announcement, "Seaman Goeschel has qualified on the *Spikefish*, well done Seaman Goeschel." The CO's announcement gave me one of my proudest moments—qualified in submarines, providing me with the most excellent sense of satisfaction. Qualifying was an experience I never forget, and one I'm proud and pleased I went through. one of the old-timers said, while congratulating me while shaking my hand, "Qualifying builds character—good job."

Qualifying provided me with the highest sentiment of pride and one of my most rewarding moments—qualified in submarines. In my final walk-through, I explained the ability to take over any watch station at any unexpected time. The *Spikefish* had four diesel engines, and I lit off each one; I worked the sticks in maneuvering, pumped bilges, transferred water from tank to tank, operated the planes to control the ship's depth and the bubble or steered the boat, fired torpedoes. I could keep the submarine safe by myself—already proved that. After I had qualified, I realized that those old-time warriors were not my problem—I was the problem—I made it tough for me.

UNDEFINED QUAL PROCESS

After I qualified, I learned that qualified submarine crewmembers reporting aboard must re-qualify their selected watch-stations and systems without receiving harassment. One day, I observed a seaman about a year younger than I, struggling to find the ship's longest line. The boot appeared frustrated after many attempts at measuring the mooring lines and yet wrong in discovering the longest one. To help him out, I told him it was the waterline. The COB, one of the old-time warriors, overheard our conversation. The COB called me aside, so no one else could hear. With a red face showing anger, eyes locked onto mine making a critical inspection of my thoughts, the COB's deep stern voice ordered, "We've got to talk. Meet me in the mess decks in five minutes."

"What did I do wrong? What made the COB pissed?" I thought, worrying as I headed towards the mess decks.

In the mess decks, as I'm pouring myself a coffee, the COB arrived. Thoroughly confusing me, his disposition had changed back to his usual friendly self. He smiled as he poured himself a coffee and invited me to join him at the chief's table.

The COB took a sip of coffee, locked his eyes to mine, pierced my thoughts with questions, holding my attention with a grin. "Why were you helping Jones out by answering his qual lookups for him?"

"Thought I was helping him out. I remember having the same frustrating aggravation happening when I was qualifying."

"Did any qualified crew give you a free ride while you qualified?"

"No, no-one ever did. Everyone gave me a hard time. Friends qualifying with me helped when able. We helped one another."

"Did anyone ever explain the reasons we treat the nonquals like we do?" The COB asked.

"No, I don't understand why everyone qualified treated us like shit. I guessed it was the Navy's way to get us qualified as fast as possible."

"You're correct, but there's more to it. A long time ago, after I qualified, just like you, an Old-Timer enlightened me about qualifying, telling me there was an essential reason for harassing the nonquals. Therefore, I'll give you the same talk the Old-Timer gave me.

The qualifying process is a submarine tradition that started during WWII when there was no way submarine crews would know if a newcomer is suitable for submarines. War experienced crews lived through frightening events during an enemy's depth-charging, causing some sailors to break under strain. The depth-charging causes extreme stress on self-control. When someone fell apart because of the stress, during depth-charging, then the danger became worse. Hazards from uncontrolled sailor's acts added to the enemy's threat. Combatting an enemy or confronting an emergency, an out-of-control sailor caused further danger to the crew and his submarine.

Nonquals lack experience in submarines, knowing little about subs. Experienced submariners consider them a menace to the boat and themselves. Not qualified in submarines means the crew cannot rely on nonquals to help in normal operations, let alone an emergency. The experienced crew treats nonquals severely for their safety and the boat's protection. We test them for submarine knowledge, watch-standing ability, and assess them for submarine compatibility. The qualified submariner examines unqualified crewmembers' strengths and weaknesses because we must live with them in close quarters unfit for living. We must rely on them to do their duty—our lives and theirs depend on it because submarines sail in harm's way.

To protect themselves, sub crews developed a qualification process for all new arrivals to make the nonqual useful as soon as possible, and to determine a newcomer's warfare abilities before they found themselves in a combat crisis with him. The experienced crew starts the submarine qualification method for the nonqual soon after he reports aboard. You will not find the submarine qualification approach in any ship's instruction or directives. Nonquals are unaware of the hidden stipulation but live through its effects while qualifying.

The nonqual qualification process serves a worthy purpose as a proven progression of learning as much as possible in the shortest amount of time. First, when qualifying for selected watch-stations, the nonqual gets increasing responsibility carried out in steps as the nonqual learns the watch's duties and submarine systems. Second, qualification harasses the newcomer taxing his resolve and testing his stamina, weeding out the unsuited who do not belong on submarines.

The submarine qualification method gives nonquals an initiation of long duration, with an essential purpose that is harsh but necessary to weed out the unsuitable. Qualified submariners harass all the nonquals going through ship's qualification because it makes sense. Experienced crews considered that if a youngster couldn't handle a little harassment, then they assumed that he wouldn't survive a real combat or emergency crisis when conditions got rough. If a nonqual cannot handle slight hazing during qualification, then how can he handle the severe crisis and challenges found during submarine missions? Submariners don't allow discovering the answer to that question during rough times. Submariners harass and ridicule all nonquals with a purpose, to learn if the nonqual would fit into the rigors of submarines, to identify the unsuited for riding subs, to uncover their flaws, and to cause the ones who can't handle it quit. Submariners are all volunteers; therefore, nonquals lacking the stamina or other reasons to continue the submarine qualification approach can quit without repercussions for stopping.

After a sailor becomes qualified, the crew accepts him as a welcomed asset and respects him, then his pestering stops. Once qualified, he has a responsibility to give similar harassment to the nonqual newcomers. Qualification is a tradition that crews continue, from boat to boat, from World War II to the present. To follow this tradition is your duty.

Over time, experienced submariners become experts at harassment finding which nerves to pinch, attacking the values that would be most upsetting to the nonqual. The incidents pulled on nonquals are cunning, using the foolishness of a boot's youth and his pride to get his attention. Several harassment methods used on me seem funny now but weren't comical when they happened. A few harassment approaches were brutal and cruel. For the qualified sailor, harassing nonquals was fun with exceptions, but all harassment had an essential purpose.

How the nonqual interacted with the crew while qualifying sets the tone of his stay in submarines. If he sought information with an effort, listened with appreciation, and complied with the submariner's guidance, his chance of finishing his quals and continuing in submarines was high. Disrespectful nonquals or ones who had know-it-all attitudes were in trouble from the onset coming aboard. Their life aboard would be hell; few starting that way ever succeeded.

The submarine profession is for sailors who want to serve on submarines, proven by their qualifying. Submariners are proud of what we accomplish, and we take great pride in wearing our dolphins and surviving the qualification process. Qualified submariners know sailors wearing dolphins are the best shipmates in the Navy. Submariners achieve a lot defending our country—no bullshit—just the truth.

The qualification practice that includes harassment methods the modern Navy may consider as bullying, but that is a mistake. Qualification harassment is not bullying—it has an essential purpose to prove nonquals are compatible within the submarine's environment.

LEAVING THE SPIKEFISH

January 10, 1963, I left the *Spikefish* for the last time, with orders to the Polaris Fire Control School at Dam Neck, Virginia. After saying goodbye to my friends, and thanking those who helped me, I leave the boat with sea-bag in hand. The full sea-bag is cumbersome and gives me one last struggle to push the bag up through the after-battery hatch. As I approach the upper opening, the bag lifts, releasing my burden. The topside watch, Seamen Bruce, saw me struggling, he lifted the sea-bag to the topside deck. Without the bag, it was easy for me to follow the bag topside.

Bruce greats me with a big smile shakes my hand, and speaks, "You're leaving; I can't believe it. Well, good luck. Thanks again for saving my life, and thanks for helping me with my quals. In a short time, we knew each other, you taught me a lot, been a good shipmate and friend, and I know you will do well whatever you do."

I thanked Bruce and downplayed the lifesaving bit. Then we said our goodbyes.... I'm thinking, what did I do to teach him a lot? With the goodbyes over, picking up the sea-bag, I head to the brow. Feeling mighty proud of qualifying, pausing at the brow, and saluting the topside watch, I ask, "request to leave the Spikefish."

Bruce comes to attention, raises his right arm, and returns my salute. Bruce commands, "Permission granted. Good luck."

With the salute over, I stepped on the brow, turned aft, and with honor saluted the ensign, while I held back emotions of happiness.

As I crossed the brow, halfway across, an emotion stopped me. As if the Spikefish was saying goodbye, I delayed departure for another reminiscing look. While I lingered on the brow, I looked the boat over forward to aft. While examining the Spikefish's topside, inspecting the sail, studying the sheers, I remembered with amazement what I experienced. Then, I realized, I must go, but I didn't travel far. At the end of the brow, another sentiment stopped me as if the Spikefish didn't want me to leave—not yet. Before stepping off the brow, I paused for a moment, reflecting on what I achieved—I'm qualified in submarines. During the pause, I'm filled with gratification. I grasp how my Spikefish experience inspired me. With conviction, when I set my mind to do something, it will transpire. I'm convinced I will meet the challenges that await me, with new confidence to take on any responsibility,

At the pier, I inspected the Spikefish again from bow to stern. She's a fine-looking submarine. The lady is showing off, not a rust-spot on her, mooring lines tight—war-ready. Honored, because I served on her, but saddened to leave her, remembering the outstanding sailors who helped me, and the friendships attained. I left the dock, reminiscing adventures, appreciating experiences, marveling at my endurance, and was amazed at how I prevailed.

Later, with the Spikefish out of sight, I wondered what new adventures awaited me, considered what new exploits will challenge me, speculated where new courses might take me, and looked forward to the new ventures that expect me.

EPILOGUE

Later, the youngster who listened to every word every time I told him my stories enters the diner. The seaman flashes a big smile when he sees me. Walking towards my booth, "I got good news. I'm going to a boat in Hawaii; orders came in today, I'm leaving next Friday, taking some leave to see the family." As the youngster sits down, "It's my turn, I'll buy you breakfast. While going through Subschool, your stories helped me a lot." The youngster sits across from me, looking pleased.

"Thanks for the compliment, congratulations on getting through Subschool and getting orders." After ordering breakfast, savoring good black coffee, "There is not enough time to tell you the whole story. I didn't get to tell you everything about my Navy experiences, serving aboard submarines and surface ships, but serving most of my time on submarines—it's rare to experience both. There is much more to tell about serving in the Navy, the great sailors with whom I served, the leaders who taught me, the obstacles I overcome that shaped me, and all awesome adventures I experienced along the way.

"On submarines, our missions were silent and critical. Crews could not talk about the mission's details to anyone off the boat. On patrol, a sub establishes wartime conditions, silently sailing in harm's way— constant dangers. For a submariner, your job was to protect the nation, doing your duty to your country, family, and shipmates. Unfortunately, we do not have enough time before you leave for me to tell you about these experiences."

The youngster looked at me with admiration, "You helped me a lot, and I enjoyed listening to your experiences. Like, you should write a book about your experiences; your stories are that good."

Pausing, thinking about what I told the youngster, and with a smile, "You're correct, that's a good idea to record my experiences. So, you may look forward to more stories. Well, it's my duty."

APPENDIX A: GLOSSARY

GLOSSARY	
TERM	**DEFINITION**
1MC	The submarine's announcing system, includes the collision, diving, and general alarms.
A bust in rate	A reduction in a sailor's rate and pay as punishment for an infraction.
Aft Trim Tank	The ship's after variable ballast tank used to obtain neutral buoyancy and adjust the ship's trim and tilting moment.
A-gang	Slang for the Auxiliary division
A Gangers	Slang for Auxiliary division personnel
Angle on the bow	The angle formed by the longitudinal axis of a ship and the line of sight from the submarine intersecting the ship
At-a-boy	Slang for praise—note, one ah-shit that is slang for a screw-up wipes out ten at-a-boys
Aux-forward	Slang for the Forward Compartment's Auxiliary-man on watch
Auxiliary Tanks	Variable Ballast tanks used to obtain neutral buoyancy and adjust the ship's trim.
Ballast Tanks	Saddle tanks between the pressure hull and outer hull. Blown dry provides positive buoyancy for surfacing and surface operations. Venting these tanks fills the tank and gives negative buoyancy to submerge the submarine.

GLOSSARY	
TERM	DEFINITION
B-Girls	B-Girls are bar girls working on getting customers to buy as many a drink as possible and get many tips for doing just that.
BARF Bucket	Seasick sailors carry a BARF Bucket; a number 10 can holds the vomit.
Berthing	Berthing is the term for the sleeping areas aboard ship
Brass	Slang for officers
Bight of a line	a line with slack curve bending that forms a loop
Bilges	the lower part of the ship or boat where wastewater and seepage collect.
Boat	Submariners use term "Boat" for referring to their submarine
Boatswain— pronounced "bosun,"	A Boatswain Mate (BM), sailors who perform deck duties, manage handling gear, and control small craft. Boatswain mates are part of the few skimmers that submarine sailors find worthy of becoming friends with, having some of the same unsociable behavior and humor of the submariner along with a high commitment to duty
Boot camp	I slang for the initial Navy schooling. Sailors calling someone, "Boot camp" is an insult indicating the sailor lacks basic knowledge
Bow Buoyancy	The ship's forward Main Ballast tank used to obtain positive buoyancy when blown empty and negative buoyancy when flooded.
Bow planes	The bow planes are horizontal diving planes, extending from each side of the submarine near the bow.
Brig	Military jail or prison
Brig time	Military jail or prison time

GLOSSARY	
TERM	**DEFINITION**
Brow	A brow is a gangplank that connects the ship to the pier, allowing sailors to come from ashore and leave the ship while in port.
Brown Speckled Sparrow Club	When someone blows a sanitary tank's contents inboard all over himself, he unwillingly becomes a club member.
Bubble	The slang term for the Pitch Angle
Buying Buicks or hunting for O'-ROARIC	Slang terms for vomiting
A cathouse	Slang for a brothel, a house of prostitution
Cavitate	Screw noise. Increasing shaft turns causes speed increases. When shaft turns are increased too rapidly, it will cause cavitating.
Chief of the Watch	The senior enlisted watch station when the boat is on the surface
Chief Petty Officers	The US Navy gives Chief Petty Officers (CPO) more authority and responsibility than any other equivalent enlisted rating in any other service in the world.
CO	Acronym for a ship's Commanding Officer
COB	Acronym for the Chief of the Boat (COB). The COB is the senior enlisted aboard a submarine who has unique duties and responsibilities.
Captain's mast	A trial that allows a ship's captain to award selective punishment for infractions. CO's Mast is a military trial where the commanding officer assigns punishment.
Coffee Urn	A five-gallon coffee urn is in the crew's mess. A cold-water line supplies water to the coffee pot.
CON	When a watch officer has the Con, he has the authority to direct the ship's course and speed.

GLOSSARY	
TERM	**DEFINITION**
CT	Acronym for the Conning Tower
Conning Tower	Inside a Fleet Boat's sail is the conning tower, a small watertight compartment above the control room and below the bridge, and is the main navigation and firing control station for the submarine. The conning tower contains the steering stand, the gyro repeater, torpedo data computer, firing panel, radar, periscopes and periscope hoist equipment, fathometer, navigation plot, and target bearing transmitter-receivers. The conning tower connects with the control room through a watertight hatch designated as the lower conning tower hatch. The upper conning tower hatch provides access to the bridge from the conning tower. The top of the conning tower in the sail is used as a bridge when on the surface. When submerged: 1. The conning tower is the watch station for the Officer of the Deck (OOD), Helmsman, and Navigator, or Quartermaster. 2. The OOD controls the boat from the conning tower. Periscope operators make observations within the conning tower. 3. During Battle Stations, the Conning Tower is the commanding officer's battle station and gets a target tracking party, periscope operators, fire-control system operator, phone talker, and the Navigator.
Control Room	A submarine's midship compartment that contains diving controls, trim system manifold, the ship's gyrocompasses, aux steering stand, the interior communications switchboard, and radio room.

GLOSSARY	
TERM	**DEFINITION**
Court-martials	Court-martials are military court to trial defendants accused of serious offenses and severe crimes. Court-martials can award long prison time and up to death penalties during the time of war.
Cuban Missile Crisis	The closest time after WWII we came to use nuclear weapons
Davy Jones's locker	The bottom of the ocean
Deep sink	The scullery sink
(DEFCON 3)	Defense Readiness Condition: A Navy increased force readiness above that required for normal readiness
Dink	Slang for delinquent in qualification, a nonqual's status title for not maintaining expected progress. Dink on quals for becoming behind in making expected progress—much frowned upon in the submarine navy
The Dive	Short for the Diving Officer
Doc	Doc is an acronym for the boat's corpsman. A submarine corpsman is highly trained in medical specialties and has exceptional medical training. The Doc is like a doctor assigned to the boat to take care of the crew's medical issues.
ET	Acronym for an Electronic Technician
ENG or Engineer	Acronym for the engineering officer
EOT	Engine Order Telegraph is used to make speed commands from the CONN to maneuvering
Field-day	All hands ship clean-up
Fighting gear	Slang for knives, forks, and spoons

GLOSSARY	
TERM	**DEFINITION**
Flying Cloud	A clipper ship that set the world's sailing record for the fastest passage between New York and San Francisco, 89 days 8 hours. The ship held this record for over 100 years, from 1854 to 1989. Flying Cloud was the most famous of the clippers built by Donald McKay. She was known for her extremely close race with Hornet in 1853
Fwd. Trim Tank	The ship's forward variable ballast tank used to obtain neutral buoyancy and adjust the ship's trim and tilting moment.
Freeze-box	The walk-in freezer
FT	Acronym for Fire Control Technician
FTs	Acronym for Fire Control Technicians
FT B School	The Fire Control Technicians most advanced electronic technical school
Fox Division	The Fire Control Division on combat ships
Galley and scullery sinks	The officers' pantry and the galley have sinks. The crew's mess contains a scullery sink. Each sink's drains connect to the sanitary drainage system.
Goat Locker	Slang for the Chief's quarters and berthing compartment
Guppy submarines	WWII Fleet boats with snorkel, hull, and sail modifications. Adding a bow sonar dome made them a Killer Class designed to hunt for other subs.
Granny Knot	A knot similar to a square knot, but it will not hold under pressure. Also, a derogatory term is given to a sailor to indicate he is not respected and capable.
Head	A space that has toilet facilities, or the Navy's term for a bathroom

GLOSSARY	
TERM	**DEFINITION**
Heaving line	A small line with a weighted monkey fist tied to one end, allowing the monkey-fist to be thrown to a pier or other craft. The heaving line is tied to a more massive mooring line enabling the mooring line to be hauled to the dock or ship.
Helm	The watch station where the rudder is controlled by the helmsman who steers the boat or ship
Helmsman	The sailor who steers the ship
Hollywood-shower	A long-duration water-wasting shower. While underway, taking a Hollywood-shower was not allowed.
Horse-cock	Slang for luncheon sausage before it's sliced
Hot bunking	The condition when there are not enough bunks available for all crewmembers. Junior crewmembers get the luxury of sharing a rack. Two sailors may share one bunk, or three sailors will share two racks. The sailors rotate using the rack—the one-off watch gets the vacated rack while the others are on watch or qualifying.
IC's	IC is an acronym for Interior Communications Electrician. ICs maintain and repair interior communication systems.
Jarheads	Slang for Marines
Keelhaul	**Keelhaul** is a punishment used in the days of sail. Punishers tie lines to the guilty one starboard and one port, then crewmembers pull the unfortunate sailor amidships from port to starboard under the keel. For the gravest offense, the guilty sailor gets dragged from bow to stern under the keel as his ship sails over him.
Landlubber	Anyone who never went to sea

GLOSSARY	
TERM	**DEFINITION**
Leading seamen	The leading seaman has the responsibility for the supervision of the topside gang. He answers directly to the First Lieutenant or COB when the COB has that responsibility.
Lieutenant Always Alert	The nickname for an excellent officer whose name is forgotten
Liberty	Recreation time off the boat and base that is authorized shore leave off a ship or station
LPOs	Acronym for Leading Petty Officers
LPO	Acronym for the Leading Petty Officer in a division
Macramé'	Fancy knots made into many decorative forms
Macnamara lace	Boatswains' handy work, taking canvas apart, forming the cloth into threads, and then making fancywork knotwork and trimming from the canvas threads.
Maneuvering Watch	The special watch using full crew involvement when the boat goes in or out of port or experiences other critical navigating conditions
Mess Cooking	**Mess Cooking** is an assigned temporary duty or job for a junior crew to help the cooks in preparing and serving the crew their meals.
Mess Decks	Even though there is one, the crew calls the eating area **Mess Decks**.
NAV	Short for the Navigator
Navy Hymn	William Whiting 1860, 1869, this is the Navy's web site's version. Note many versions exist

GLOSSARY	
TERM	**DEFINITION**
Negative Tank	The negative tank is a variable ballast tank used to reduce the time required in submerging from the surface condition, to reduce the time needed to increase depth while operating submerged, and to prevent broaching. The negative tank may be filled, blown, or pumped. During diving, a filled negative tank gives the boat a negative ballast that accelerates diving. After diving, the negative tank is blown to its mark, giving the sub a neutral ballast, allowing the submarine to operate submerged in neutral buoyancy.
Nonqual	A crew member that is not qualified in submarines.
On the beach	Slang for liberty ashore
On-report	Formally charged with a violation of regulations, placing someone on-report is making them subject to disciplinary action
O'-ROARIC	Slang for vomiting
On Watch	When a sailor is on duty at his station, lasting four to six hours and at times much longer.
Pitching	The fore-and-aft motion of a ship at sea in the direction of the keel
Port and Starboard Watch	Port and starboard is a watch rotation with no break between the watch. A watch duration was six to twelve hours on watch and six to twelve hours off watch.
Pressure Hull	The submarine's inner hull and conning tower, it's a people tank, built to withstand sea pressure to designed limits.
Pump Bulges	Slang for taking a leak, or urinating
Qual	Slang for qualification
Qualified	A sailor is qualified in submarines, making him a valuable crew member. Qualified sailors are sailors who ware dolphins showing that they qualified in submarines.

GLOSSARY	
TERM	**DEFINITION**
Qual cards	A Qual Card lists all the systems, equipment, and practical factors a non-qual must know. For each requirement, the subject expert, the Leading petty-officers, Chiefs, and officers will verify the non-qual knows the material enough. The expert signatures show that the non-qual obtained the knowledge. The non-qual must get enough systems signed off at a selected rate to maintain satisfactory status; if not, he goes dink.
Rank or Rate	In the Navy, commissioned officers have rank, and enlisted personnel has a rate.
Red lead	Metal paint primer used as the first paint coat followed by a flat black paint finish coat on submarines hulls at the time
Reefer	Walk-in refrigerator.
Relative Bearing	Relative Bearing is the direction of a contact or object measured in degrees from own ship's bow in relation to the ship's bow to aft axis. The bow is 000 degrees. The stern is 180 degrees. Any contact or object on the Starboard side is reported as (zero degrees to one eight zero) Starboard. Also, Port contacts would report as (zero degrees to one eight zero) Port.
Report chit	A formal charge for not following regulations, slang for placing someone on report
Rocks and Shoals	An outdated military law that the UCMJ replaced.
Roll	The side-to-side motion of a ship or boat afloat underway
Sanitary tanks	The sanitary tanks receive and store the ship's sanitary drainage until conditions permit overboard discharge.

GLOSSARY	
TERM	**DEFINITION**
Screw wash	When a ship's screws or propellers are turning, they make water turbulence, a screw wash, seen as a wake, the track in the water behind a boat.
Scuttlebutt	The crew's primary drinking water dispensing equipment aboard the submarine, or the drinking fountain is called the **Scuttlebutt**. One scuttlebutt is located in the officers' pantry, and one in the crew's mess room. It is also a slang term for rumor generation.
Standard Submarine Phraseology	For submarine communications, standard phraseology combines precision, brevity, and audibility. Strict adherence to standard phraseology increases the speed of communications and reduces the chances of error and misunderstanding. See Appendix **F**
Shallow Water Club	Slang for the US Coast Guard
Shears	**Shears** is the term used for the lookout watch platforms located on the sail above the Bridge. Shears have metal handrails that surround the lookouts, like an open cage that does not protect from the sea's elements.
Ship's bubble	The term for the ship's pitch angle
Shit on the shingle	Slang for minced meat on toast
Skimmers	Slang for surface craft and shore duty sailors
Stern planes	The stern planes are horizontal diving planes, extending from each side of the submarine near the stern, used to control the ship's depth and pitch angle.
Striking for a rate	A non-designated seaman without a rate schooling is studying for a profession aboard ship, and learning the skills to become a designated rate is called a striker. While he is studying for the rate is considered as striking for a rate.

GLOSSARY	
TERM	**DEFINITION**
Stupid Study	**Stupid Study** is a slang term for the extra instruction time available for students to get help. Students volunteer for this help; some instructors will direct them to attend.
Sub-pay	Sub-pay is the hazardous duty pay extra pay for being attached to a submarine.
Submarines	Submariners refer to submarines as boats. This is a long tradition even though modern subs are more massive and heavier than some ships.
Submarine Qualification	A Qual Card lists all the systems, equipment, and practical factors a non-qual must know. The subject experts, the Leading petty-officers, Chiefs, and officers will verify the non-qual knows the material enough. For each requirement, an expert's signature shows that the non-qual obtained adequate knowledge. The non-qual must get enough systems signed off at a selected rate to maintain satisfactory status; if not, he goes dink. After a non-qual meets requirements, the ENG takes the non-qual through his final qualification walkthrough. Passing the ENG's walkthrough, the non-qual gets the ENG's signature showing he met all requirements for submarine qualification. Then, the CO presents the submariner with his Dolphins to display on his uniform, showing he's qualified in submarines.
Sub School	Slang for the Basic Submarine School for sailors
School boats	Submarines assigned to take Submarine School students to sea for submarine training
Split-tails	An old, rude slang term for attractive women, "babes."
TDU	Trash Disposal Unit

GLOSSARY	
TERM	**DEFINITION**
The Dive	Short for the Diving Officer. The Diving Officer station is in the control room below the CONN, a Chief or an Officer holds this watch with the responsibility of maintaining the ship's trim and depth
The Head	A ship's bathroom, the head holds the ship's toilet facilities
The Polaris Program	The Polaris Program was the Navy's Electronic, Missile, and Fire Control Technician training program to support the submarines carrying Polaris Missiles.
The Submarine Memorial	The Submarine Memorial located in Groton, CT, sits on a site where a visitor will have a partial view of the Thames River.
Submarine Sail	A submarine sail is above the main hull, holds the Bridge the OD's station where the Captain, Commanding Officer, Officer of the Deck, and Lookouts stay above decks while the boat is on the surface. The sail contains masts and antennas, the shears, stanchions above the Bridge, are the Lookouts stations, one port the other starboard.
Tin cans	Slang for destroyers
UCMJ	Acronym for the Uniform Code of Military Justice, composed of articles of law the military must follow
USS TIRANTE (SS420)	Another diesel boat in our squadron
Watch, Quarter, and Station Bill	Watch, Quarter, and Station Bill list all watch stations and assigned personnel to these stations.
Weapons handling	Weapons handling is loading and offloading of weapons mainly torpedoes

GLOSSARY	
TERM	**DEFINITION**
Waterslug	Shooting a **Waterslug** is firing a torpedo tube without a torpedo in it for maintenance and training.
WEPS	Acronym for the Ship's Weapons Officer
Westpac	Slang for a western Pacific deployment.
Westpac-Widows	**Westpac-Widows** is the slang term for married women who are faithful to their husbands when husbands are in port but become free spirits when the husband leaves on patrol for extended periods, like some widows who become available for courting after a husband's death.
Write up	Slang for placing someone on report for an infraction
XO	Acronym for the Executive Officer. LT G. L. Graveson, JR was Spikefish's exceptionally outstanding officer, our XO

APPENDIX B: AUTHORS NOTES

Because I lived life at sea, I experienced adventures with extraordinary experiences that triggered me to record my stories. I had encounters to share, with sea stories to tell to convey what I observed. In many places, I shared experiences and sea stories with shipmates—the spoken stories are worth preserving. After retiring from the Navy in 1981, I started writing sea stories, giving my accounts, and wanting to describe shipmates. I realized that the submariner characters' deeds and attributes added a visualization essence found on submarines. WWII experienced warriors men shaped my thinking, providing leadership guidance, forging me into the man I have become. But, the tragic events of September 11, 2001, made storytelling trivial, delaying the writing.

Later, knowing my family and those I love most understood little regarding my role in the Navy created issues resulting from my family's lack of knowledge concerning my naval service. For example, my daughter and I had an email discussion on political positions. An email my daughter forwarded attacked my values towards patriotism and responsibility. She upset me. With rushed anger, not considering the email had an extensive list of recipients, and without expecting my email's effect. I replied, expressing my irritation about political opinions that lack insight into issues that stir up emotions, are absent of problem solutions, and hold views that contribute nothing of worth for valid deductions. Without thinking, I replied, judging those holding political beliefs which offer disrespectful disagreement, question and attack the principles of anyone holding a different position, and, worse, defame those with different ideas. Within my judgment, I conveyed that the email's following offer nothing of value, making them counterproductive to any solution.

In response, my daughter expressed my lack of tact hurt her. I acted with and hostility towards the matter and to those who thought otherwise. Instead of challenging the issues, I belittled and abused those who believed differently than me, including her, mimicking those who disagreed with me, ridiculing their behavior considering their viewpoints wrong. Still, I was doing the same to them. Not intending to hurt my daughter, I regrettably did.

I did not understand my daughter's position, so different and insulting to mine. Did she want to upset me? Shouldn't she have known from my military history that her opinion will cause me to react the way I did?

After discussing this with my wife, her view expressed that no one in the family knows what I did in the Navy. When other Navy wives told her what we were doing, learning it from others made her angry. Enlightening me, "You always kept the simplest conditions from me. Lately, I'm finding out from you what you experienced in the Navy."

Right she was. The family was unaware of what I did during my naval career. I left my family lacking details regarding my time in the Navy. Family members were unfamiliar with naval traditions and did not understand how maritime traditions influenced my development and values. What the family realized regarding naval traditions was of minor importance. The family saw I was in the Navy, serving on both surface ships and submarines, and at sea on deployment—a lot.

The family grasped I was qualified in Submarines, functioned as a Chief Fire Control Technician, and served as a COB. But they didn't witness what I did at sea, my involvement in ship missions, facing dangers, shouldering responsibilities, and experiencing adventures. I never told them details concerning my participation in the Navy's role during conflicts like the Cold War. My family was unaware I played an essential part in that involvement role.

The family understood less about the leaders who shared my experiences, taught, inspired, guided, shaped my values and provided valuable insight they used in their dealings with others. My family lacked the leadership knowledge and values I gained and applied in my naval career and beyond.

To resolve this, I restarted writing stories with a well-defined purpose, telling my involvement, adding my naval experience account, providing missing information, delivering a better picture. Further, I portray the good times, the skillful day-to-day approach to responsibilities and duties, and the achievements that gave me great pride for carried out successes. For a full image, I account for the flaws, embarrassments, and mistakes I made along the way, so those I love best will understand me more.

The result is the book, *It's Your Duty,* a memoir, a period into a young sailor's development composed of those sea stories that summons up a window into an inexperienced submarine sailor's early career, describing my first experiences in the Navy. It reveals my impressions, and the emotions aroused when facing danger, accepting discipline, and experiencing adventure. The stories share a common theme—do your duty.

It's Your Duty will not account for submarine specific mission actions, but it revealed what had happened as I lived through adventurous events and other experiences. The prose embraces the enlisted sailor's view, a depiction deficient in most naval accounts. These early naval reflections happened over fifty years ago, making the recollection of details for these events blurred—specifics are not exact. My memory isn't as good as it should, perhaps a safety measure is in play, because specific memories are too painful to recall or too shameful to relive. Yet, one doesn't forget profound events, tattooed into one's mind. The stories happened, and convey a truthful foundation based on the actions of others I observed, the experiences I lived, and how I felt as I lived them. I can't guarantee an exact factual representation because the details are uncertain, making a story's exactness debatable.

For entertainment's sake like many a sailor, I overstated aspects, added inventions, and made exaggerations that turn my Sea Stories into enjoyable yarns, and might cause an incident to grow into a tall tale. Hence, the facts are suspect, making a story's accuracy questionable. Therefore, the reader must consider *It's Your Duty* as fiction.

In my stories with concern for privacy, I used pseudonyms for the sailors and leaders who taught, guided, worked, and had fun alongside me. Another reason for using false names, it would be unfair to name anyone who I placed in an unfavorable light. As I'm watching others' behavior in an event, making my perception of what I see. As a seaman, I lacked the knowledge about a senior's orders; he followed even though his foolishness seemed apparent. In my book, he has no way to defend himself. My critical perception could be a mistake degrading a competent outstanding individual. In a few places, for those whom I admire and wish to honor, I used their actual names accompanied by sadness as they have passed and are no longer with us.

Serving in the Navy, my course experiences, the great sailors I served with, the obstacles that shaped me, and the awesome adventures I lived through gave me much more to tell you. Future books will provide you with details about these events. I have more tales to tell you, more books I will write—I'm working on it—look for them they are coming.

APPENDIX C: MY COMMANDS

This list of my commands is for shipmates who wish to contact me, and it would be great to hear from you, please use the following e-mail: ggoeschel@comcast.net

The following are highpoints of my naval timeline.

On January 9, 1963, I qualified in submarines on my first submarine, the *USS Spikefish* *(AGSS 404)*, a Balao-class non-snorkel diesel submarine, a WWII fleet boat. Then my next sub, the USS *Sea Owl* (SS 405), [15] a WWII diesel submarine, converted to a Guppy Killer Class with advanced sonar and snorkeling ability. These boats were from a class of WWII Fleet Submarines so successful they were significant contributors in winning the Pacific battle in WWII. On the *Spikefish and Sea Owl*, several of my senior shipmates were WWII submarine veterans, making me feel honored—to know them was exceptional. On the *Sea Owl*, I learned more about taking on responsibility, leading a different life, being a qualified petty officer.

On surface ships, I experienced different adventures but similar duties. On surface ships, I was the Fire Control Division's leading petty officer with greater responsibilities. I trained my division's personnel,

---

[15] Guppy submarines are WWII Fleet boats with snorkel, hull, and sail modifications. Adding a bow sonar dome made them a Killer Class designed to hunt for other submarines.

maintaining equipment, applying submarine methods of doing one's duty to the surface craft, creating obstacles, but resulting in successes.

My first surface ship, was an Oilier of WWII vintage, the USS *Kaskaskia (AO 27),* Throughout her long existence, she was a workhorse providing at-sea fuel replenishment for the Navy's combat ships that allowed extending the missions of carriers, cruisers, and destroyers.

Next was the USS *Glacier (AGB 4),* an Icebreaker, during Deep Freeze – 65, I made one trip to Antarctica. That tour included a mutiny and plowing through a massive storm, creating a near-death experience. I must tell you about that adventure in a future book. Deep Freeze – 65 provided an Antarctic exploration adventure of a lifetime.

Completing my surface craft experience was serving on the USS *Arlington (AGMR 2),* a relay communications ship, with tall masts for antennas. The USS *Saipan (CVL 48)* started as a cruiser, then converted into a WWII jeep-aircraft-carrier, later she was converted to a communications ship with her name changed to the *Arlington.* The *Arlington,* with a Cruiser hull and power plant, also, a lightweight flight deck where masts replaced heavy guns and armament, was a fast ship. When he wanted to, the CO drove her like she was the largest speedboat in the Navy—exciting fun for crewmembers! My *Arlington* tour included going through a North Atlantic Storm where the severity of the storm seized the *Arlington's* forty-foot utility boat. The Storm's violent seas ripped two of my fire control radar antennas off their mountings attached above two of the forward 3-inch 50-caliber twin-gun mounts. The antennas sit over forty-five feet above the waterline, showing the severity of the storm. She also provided a more pleasurable experience; *Arlington's* North Atlantic deployment allowed visits to several Northern European ports that offered a more enjoyable experience.

After an adventurous time in the surface Navy, I made it back to submarines aboard the *USS Wahoo (SS 565),* a post-WWII diesel fast attack submarine. This boat gives me memorable events like embarrassing the Navy, just missing injury and possible death from an explosion, exceeding the ship's test depth—a hazardous situation—a perilous depth for a submarine. Other adventures included one West Pack deployment with a Viet Nam mission. While on the *Wahoo*, the Navy advanced me to Fire Control Technician Chief Petty Officer.

My first shore duty in Great Lakes, IL, was instructor duty teaching FT B-School[16] students.

My last sea duty was five years on the USS *Billfish (SSN 676)*, a nuclear-powered fast attack submarine engaged in the Cold War. The *Billfish* tour provided my most memorable and rewarding experiences, including looking at death's oncoming face that only Devine intervention prevented. I was the *Billfish's* weapons department leading chief when the Navy awarded the *Billfish* a Meritorious Unit Commendation.

In my last year aboard, Commander Volgenau, the Commanding Officer, appointed me as his Chief of the Boat—a high honor. With that appointment, I took ownership of the COB's responsibilities. With the COB's assignment, I found the COB's duty the most important, rewarding, demanding, enjoyable, and productive of my naval career. It gave me an influential position on events and others while allowing me to work with the best men on this planet. During this assignment, a competition between our Squadron's boats composed of outstanding officers and crews, where the *Billfish* received the "Battle E" an award for that year's best submarine performance in the Squadron. The Navy awarded the *Billfish* the Battle "E" makes me proud of being the COB. For submarines, winning the Battle "E" was like winning the super bowl but without the public hype and fanfare. It gives me enormous pride when I reflect on the boat's successful accomplishments while being the COB.

---

[16] FT B School is the Fire Control Technicians most advanced electronic technical school.

NAVAL TIMELINE

COMMAND	ADVANCEMENT and EVENTS	DATE
Federal Building, Detroit, Michigan	Enlisted in the Navy	June 30, 1961
USNTC Boot Camp GREAT LAKES, ILL	Started as a recruit left as a Seamen Apprentice, SA	JUNE 1961 TO OCTOBER 1961
FT "A" SCHOOL NTC BAINBRIDGE, MD	Advanced to FTGSN 27 April 1962	OCTOBER 30, 1961 TO APRIL 27, 1962
SUBASE SUB SCHOOL NEW LONDON, CT	Student, FTGSN Class started July 2, 1962,	MAY 1962 to AUGUST 22, 1962
USS SPIKEFISH (AGSS 404) Fleet Boat LANTFLT, SUNSHINE SQUADRON Home Port: KEY WEST, FL Executive Officer: LT CDR G. L. Graveson, JR	Qualified in Submarines on January 9, 1963, Rate FTGSN (SS)	SEPTEMBER 1962 TO JANUARY 1963

COMMAND	ADVANCEMENT and EVENTS	DATE
GMS Polaris School DAM NECK, VA	Student, advanced to FTG3 (SS) May 16, 1963	JANUARY 1963 TO AUGUST 1963
USS SEA OWL (SS 405) Submarine Hunter Killer LANTFLT Home Port: NEW LONDON, CT	I took and passed the FTG2 Test in the Philadelphia Naval Shipyard PA. I left the Sea Owl during her shipyard maintenance and battery change.	SEPTEMBER 1963 TO MARCH 1964
USS KASKASKIA (AO 27) Oiler of WWII vintage Home Port: MAY PORT, FL	Advanced to FTG2 (SS), 16 May 1964	APRIL 1964 TO OCTOBER 1964
USS GLACIER (AGB 4) Icebreaker LANTFLT, BSN Home Port: BOSTON, MA CDR V. J. Vaughan, CO	Leading FTG2 (SS) Antarctic Deep Freeze 1965 Glacier crossed the equator—I'm a Shellback	OCTOBER 1964 TO JUNE 1965 October 17, 1964
USN & MCRTC DETROIT, MI	FT Shore duty	JUL 1965 TO OCTOBER 1965
NAVSTA NORFOLK, VA	Leading FTG2 (SS) Pre-commissioning crew	OCT 1965 TO AUGUST 1966

COMMAND	ADVANCEMENT and EVENTS	DATE
USS ARLINGTON (AGMR 2) Relay Communication Ship Home Port: Norfolk, VA	Leading FTG2 (SS)	AUGUST 1966 TO JULY 1967
NAVSTA NORFOLK, VA	Advanced to FTG1 (SS), January 16, 1967	JULY 1967 TO SEPTEMBER 1967
SSC NTC UWFCS MK 101 School GREAT LAKES, ILL	Student	SEPTEMBER 1967 TO MARCH 1968
USS WAHOO (SS 565) Post-WWII Diesel Fast Attack Submarine Home Port: PEARL HARBOR, HW	Advanced to FTGC (SS) March 16, 1970	APR 1968 TO MARCH 1970
SSC NTC GREAT LAKES, ILL	Student	APRIL 1970 TO JUNE 1970
NAVADCOM NTC INSTRUCTOR DUTY FT "B" SCHOOL GREAT LAKES, ILL	Instructor	JUNE 1970 TO JANUARY 1973
NAVSUBSCHOOL MK 113 UWFCS School GROTON, CT	Student	JANUARY 1973 TO SEPTEMBER 1973

COMMAND	ADVANCEMENT and EVENTS	DATE
USS BILLFISH (SSN 676) Nuclear Powered Fast Attack Submarine Home Port: GROTON, CT COs: CMDR Butterworth Admiral Butterworth passed. CMDR Volgenau Admiral Douglas Volgenau passed March 25, 2014 XOs: LCDR Barns LCDR W. G. Ellis	Selected to COB 1977	SEPTEMBER 1973 TO JUNE 1978
NAVSUBSUPPFAC NLON, GROTON, CT LCDR, W. M Sherer, XO LT Brian Turley, Department Head W- 4 Chief Warrant Officer, Floyd Crisp, Division Officer	Retired July 31, 1981	JUNE 1978 TO JULY 1981

APPENDIX D: SUBMARINE SQUADRON 4

The US Navy's, Sunshine Squadron of Key West, Florida Submarines

Boat & Hull Number	Class	Note
USS Spikefish (AGSS 404)	Fleet Boat	Not modernized
USS Tirante (SS 420)	Fleet Boat	Not modernized
USS Sea Poacher (SS 406)	Fleet Boat	Not modernized
USS Atule (SS 403)	Fleet Boat	Not modernized
USS Grenadier (SS 525)	Submarine Hunter Killer	Modernized with Guppy Sail, Snorkeling ability, and special sonar
USS Balao (SS 285)	Submarine Hunter Killer	Modernized with Guppy Sail, Snorkeling ability, and special sonar
USS Chopper (SS 342)	Guppy	Modernized with Guppy Sail and Snorkeling ability

Boat & Hull Number	Class	Note
USS Quillback (SS 429)	Guppy	Modernized with Guppy Sail and Snorkeling ability
USS Sea Leopard (SS 483)	Guppy	Modernized with Guppy Sail and Snorkeling ability
USS Threadfin (SS 410)	Guppy	Modernized with Guppy Sail and Snorkeling ability
USS Barracuda (SST 3)	Experimental	
USS Marlin (SST 2)	Experimental	

APPENDIX E: SUBMARINE PHRASEOLOGY

The following is the Standard Submarine Phraseology for phone-talkers, lookouts, and helmsmen for expressing and reporting numerical data.

The numeral "0" is spoken as "Ze-ro" for all numerical data except ranges. In giving ranges, "0" is pronounced as "Oh." When "00" occurs at the end of a number, it is articulated as "Double-oh." The following are bearings and courses spoken examples:

- When giving Bearings, Bearing ze-ro zero thuh-ree
- Ordering a course change, Steer course wun niner six
- Speed and torpedo depths are spoken as two separate digits.
- Speed ze-ro six and wun half knots
- Set Depth wun too feet

Standard Number Phraseology

NUMERAL	SPOKEN AS	NUMERAL	SPOKEN AS
0	Ze-ro or Oh (stress on both syllables of Zero)	6	Six
1	Wun	7	Seven
2	Too	8	Ate

NUMERAL	SPOKEN AS	NUMERAL	SPOKEN AS
3	Thuh-REE (stress on the second syllable)	9	Niner
4	FO-wer (stress on the first syllable)	10	Wun Ze-ro
5	FI-yiv (stress on the first syllable)		

ABOUT THE AUTHOR

Gary A. Goeschel

After retiring from the Navy, Mr. Gary A. Goeschel supported the Navy for over 30 years on programs that provided advanced technology for Navy programs that include Trident, Seawolf, and Virginia Class submarines. As an Advanced Engineer/Scientist 1 - Systems, Mr. Goeschel provided engineering support for the Littoral Combat Ship and the Joint High-Speed Vehicle.

During his Navy career, Mr. Goeschel served on surface ships and submarines, experiencing the Cuban Crises, an Antarctic expedition, a Viet Nam submarine mission, and the Cold War. Chief Goeschel qualified in submarines on the *USS Spikefish AGSS (404)*. He proceeded to the *USS Sea Owl (SS 405)*. His surface ship tours were an oiler, the *USS Kaskaskia (AO 27)*, an Icebreaker, the *USS Glacier (AGB 4)*, and a relay communication ship, the USS *Arlington (AGMR 2)*. Mr. Goeschel found his way back to submarines to the *USS Wahoo (SS 565)*, when the Navy promoted him to Chief Petty Officer.

Chief Goeschel's last sea duty was the Weapons Department Leading Chief on the *USS Billfish (SSN 676)*, a nuclear-powered fast attack submarine. In that period, the Navy awarded the *Billfish* a Meritorious Unit Commendation. During his last year aboard, the Commanding Officer providing him the highest honor, appointed Chief Goeschel to serve as the Chief of the Boat, the COB. During this duty, the *Billfish* earned the Battle E award. For submarines, it was like winning the super-bowl without the public hype and fanfare. Chief Goeschel found the COB's duty the most satisfying and productive of his naval career—a job that's so important, demand more responsibility, where he had so much influence on events and others while working with the finest men in the U.S. Navy.

Mr. Goeschel lives with his wife of over 50 years in Connecticut.

ABOUT IT'S YOUR DUTY

While in the Navy, I enjoyed living the sailor's life with voyages full of adventure. So, I wrote sea stories about my early naval experience, which depicts an inexperienced sailor's development, describes events, and presents reflections on incidents while contributing to our country's defense. *It's Your Duty* as a memoir embraces the enlisted sailor's point of view, a depiction deficient in most naval histories. The stories within are about starting with awesome responsibilities, learning leadership skills, and developing into a valued sailor. These stories are also about my association with the men I served, many who fought in submarines during WWII—men that forged me into the man I have become. Embedded within these stories are the lessons—It's your duty.

The stories within also cover what the sailor would not disclose in letters home. The accounts exposed personal reflections when I encountered corrections for misconduct and uncertainty, but I'm inexperienced and didn't recognize the misbehavior or hazard until afterward. A sailor wouldn't describe his drunken conditions and mischief, nor boastfully explain joining the Brown Speckled Sparrow Club[17]. A club he wanted no membership. A sailor would not disclose the guidance his leaders gave, the mean talks, or how he enjoyed

---

[17] Brown Speckled Sparrow Club, when someone blows a sanitary tank's contents inboard all over himself, he unwillingly becomes a club member. I explained this nasty experience within.

cleaning a sanitary tank—the consequence received for not meeting requirements, or the other matters he experienced but kept to himself. Sailors don't tell family and loved ones that they could have died when confronting seas so violent; there would be no help possible or revealing more threatening dangers.

While enjoying reading, *It's Your Duty*, you will discover leadership guidance inflicted on me. You might adapt these leadership lessons to work and family without painfully experiencing what I went through getting those valuable lessons.

Printed in the United States
By Bookmasters